Rewriting the history of madness

Rewriting the history of madness

Studies in Foucault's *Histoire de la folie*

Edited by
Arthur Still and Irving Velody

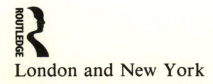
London and New York

First published in 1992
by Routledge
11 New Fetter Lane, London EC4P 4EE

Simultaneously published in the USA and Canada
by Routledge
a division of Routledge, Chapman and Hall Inc.
29 West 35th Street, New York, NY 10001

Typeset in English Times
by Pat and Anne Murphy, Highcliffe-on-Sea, Dorset
Printed and bound in Great Britain by
Mackays of Chatham PLC, Chatham, Kent

British Library Cataloguing in Publication Data
A catalogue record for this book is available from the
British Library.

Library of Congress Cataloging in Publication Data
Rewriting the history of madness: studies in Foucault's
  Histoire de la folie/edited by Arthur Still and Irving
  Velody.
          p.   cm.
  Includes bibliographical references and index.
  1. Foucault, Michel. Folie et déraison.
  2. Psychiatry – History.   3. Mentally ill – Care – History.
  I. Still, Arthur.   II. Velody, Irving.
  RC438.F63R49   1992   91–43296
  616.89′009–dc20   CIP

ISBN 0–415–06654–9

Contents

Contributors

Peter Barham is a psychologist and at present Visiting Senior Lecturer in Mental Health at Goldsmiths' College, University of London. His publications include *Schizophrenia and Human Value* (Blackwell 1986), *From the Mental Patient to the Person* (with Robert Hayward) (Routledge 1991) and *Closing the Asylum* (Penguin, in press).

Paul A. Bové is Professor of English and Cultural Studies at the University of Pittsburgh. He is the editor of *boundary z* and the author of *Intellectuals in Power* (1986) as well as of the forthcoming books, *The Wake of Theory* (Wesleyan) and *Mastering Discourse* (Duke University Press).

Robert Castel is Professor of Sociology at the University of Paris. Two of his publications include studies on the sociology of psychiatric institutions, practices and techniques, and have been translated: *The Psychiatric Society* (Columbia University Press 1982) and *The Regulation of Madness* (Polity Press 1988). He is presently working on current developments in social policy and political practice.

Mark Erickson wrote the contribution to this volume while working in a workers' co-operative in Durham. He has recently completed his MA thesis on postmodern social theory at Durham University.

Jan Goldstein is Professor of Modern European History at the University of Chicago and author of *Console and Classify: The French Psychiatric Profession in the Nineteenth Century* (Cambridge University Press 1987). She is currently working on a new book tentatively entitled 'The Post-Revolutionary Self: Competing Psychologies in Nineteenth-Century France'.

Colin Gordon edited and co-translated *Power/Knowledge* (1980), a collection of Michel Foucault's interviews and writings. He has published numerous articles in Britain and France on Foucault's work and related topics. He was an editor of the journals *Radical Philosophy* and *I & C*, and translated Michele Le Doeuff's *The Philosophical Imaginary* (Athlone Press 1989). He recently co-edited and contributed to *The Foucault Effect:*

Studies in Governmentality (G. Burchell *et al*. (Harvester 1991)). He works for the Imperial Cancer Research Fund.

Dominick LaCapra, at the Department of History, Cornell University, has contributed widely to the field of the history of ideas, including full-length studies of Durkheim and Sartre. His most recent publication, *Soundings in Critical Theory* (Cornell University Press 1989), is an assessment of the nature of historical thinking and includes discussion of Derrida, Foucault and Lyotard.

Allan Megill is Professor of History at the University of Virginia. He is author of *Prophets of Extremity* (1985), co-editor of *The Rhetoric of the Human Sciences* (1987), and most recently editor of an essay collection 'Rethinking Objectivity', to be published by the journal *Annals of Scholarship* in 1992.

H. C. Erik Midelfort (University of Virginia) has worked extensively on Renaissance psychiatry and the history of madness in sixteenth-century Germany. Among his publications are *Witch Hunting in Southwestern Germany, 1562–1684: The Social and Intellectual Foundations* (Stanford University Press 1972) and 'The Devil and the German People', in S. Ozment (ed.) *Religion and Culture in the Renaissance and Reformation* (1989).

Geoffrey Pearson is Wates Professor of Social Work in the University of London, Goldsmiths' College. His published work includes *The Deviant Imagination* (Macmillan 1975), *Hooligan: A History of Respectable Fears* (Macmillan 1983), *The New Heroin Users* (Blackwell 1987) and *Social Work and the Legacy of Freud* (Macmillan 1988).

Roy Porter is Senior Lecturer in the Social History of Medicine at the Wellcome Institute for the History of Medicine. He is currently working on the history of hysteria. His most recent books include *In Sickness and in Health. The British Experience, 1650–1850* (Fourth Estate 1988); *Patient's Progress* (Polity 1989) – these last two co-authored with Dorothy Porter; and *Health for Sale, Quackery in England 1660–1850* (Manchester University Press, 1989).

Anthony Pugh is a specialist in the area of contemporary French fiction and literary theory and has published numerous articles in these areas in British, French, Canadian and American periodicals. He has contributed chapters to several books about critical theory and published a monograph on the Nobel prize-winning novelist, Claude Simon. He is also a freelance translator, and Director of the Language Centre, University of Durham.

Nikolas Rose is Professor of Sociology and Head of the Department of Sociology at the University of London, Goldsmiths' College. Author of *The Psychological Complex* (Routledge 1985), *Governing the Soul: The Shaping* *of the Private Self* (Routledge 1990) and co-editor of *The Power of Psychiatry* (Polity, 1986), he is currently completing work on a social and intellectual history of the Tavistock Clinic and Tavistock Institute of Human Relations.

Andrew Scull is Professor of Sociology and Science Studies at the University of California, San Diego. His books include *Museums of Madness, Decarceration*, and *Madhouses, Mad Doctors, and Madmen: The Social History of Psychiatry in the Victorian Era*. He has written widely for leading journals in history, psychiatry, law and sociology.

Arthur Still is a part-time Lecturer in Psychology at the University of Durham. He is co-editor of *History of the Human Sciences* and *Against Cognitivism* (Harvester-Wheatsheaf 1991).

Irving Velody lectures in sociology at the University of Durham. He is co-editor of *History of the Human Sciences*. His most recent publication (with Peter Lassman) is *Max Weber's 'Science as a Vocation'* (Unwin Hyman 1989).

Preface

Retrieving the source not only of Foucault's *Madness and Civilization* but also of those who have contributed to this volume is an infinite task, but one contributor in particular must have special mention. This volume very much owes its existence to Colin Gordon's presentation to the Research Group for the History of the Human Sciences seminar at Durham University. In this sense the collection presented here is as much a tribute to Gordon's vigorous pursuit of the unread Foucault as to *Madness and Civilization* itself.

In addition to our colleagues at Durham University and to the contributors to *Rewriting the History of Madness*, we particularly wish to thank Donna Harris and Joan Trowbridge, our editorial assistants on the journal *History of the Human Sciences*, who have been of immense assistance in the production of the volume. We would also like to thank Harriet Bradley for her help in preparing the Introduction; and Gill Davies of Routledge for information on the publication history of *Madness and Civilization*. Our special thanks to Ann Moss for guiding us on the path to the black sun.

Apart from the papers by Paul Bové and Anthony Pugh, and the bibliography prepared by Mark Erickson, the source of the remaining papers is *History of the Human Sciences* (vol. 3, nos 1 and 3, 1990). Our thanks to Routledge for permission to reprint these materials.

AS
IV

Introduction

Arthur Still and Irving Velody

> *Books I have written and books I am writing reek of Foucault's effect upon me.*
>
> Ian Hacking

Behind the doors of well-bounded academic departments, activities in social science disciplines may seem to go on as they always have done. But more and more of the action takes place in the corridors between departments, and there what happens, whether classified as philosophy, sociology, history or just human sciences, reeks of Michel Foucault (it therefore, according to the *Shorter OED*, emits hot vapour, or it stinks, or it fumigates, a constellation of metaphors to capture the diverse and illuminating impact of Foucault's work in English-speaking countries). This book is about the beginning of this process, the reactions to Foucault's first major study, *Madness and Civilization*. These reactions concern most of the issues that have troubled the English philosophical mind since it became faced with the human sciences' refusal to acknowledge any allegiance to the methods of physics and chemistry. This collection is centred around a paper by Colin Gordon published in *History of the Human Sciences* in 1990. There he questioned the widely quoted scholarly criticisms that have been made of *Madness and Civilization*. Had the critics paid proper attention to the French text, they would have realized that some of the apparent flaws are mistranslations; as to the rest, *Madness and Civilization* is based on a considerable abridgement, and its shortcomings can be shown to vanish when gaps in the argument are filled in by reference to the original version.

This was a challenging thesis, vigorously presented, and as editors of *History of the Human Sciences* we felt, as did Gordon, that it raised much wider issues than the proper interpretation of *Madness and Civilization*. We invited a number of scholars, including some of those named by Gordon, to give their responses for publication in the journal. This created so much interest that we decided to use the material as a basis for a book. Most of the papers published in *History of the Human Sciences* are here, in many cases revised and extended. In addition there are chapters by Bové and

Pugh, and an annotated bibliography of Anglophone reactions to *Madness and Civilization* by Mark Erickson.

Until recently histories of medicine, including psychiatry, paralleled histories of science. Like science, medicine was seen to display a rising curve of development and shared with natural science its triumphalist character; and like science, too, medicine and psychiatry both dealt with objective, that is scientifically locatable, conditions and objects of investigation which, whatever the practical difficulties, could be considered open to rational investigation. Also like natural science the methodologies of psychiatric practice shared a conception of the objective and rational form of their methods of investigation and of the ultimately rationalistic accounting of the specific phenomena they were concerned with. Well into the twentieth century, madness has been considered a phenomenon assessable and resolvable within the terms of the nineteenth-century explanatory programmes of chemistry, physics and biology. Historiographic practice similarly implemented these assumptions concerning the structure of knowledge, its accumulation and its discovery. History mirrored the narrative of a research programme, with many false starts and wrong turnings, but overall progressing towards an increasingly clear-cut picture of the unchanging object of investigation. Triumphalism is as old as history and likely to last as long, since it serves an important rhetorical function, by sustaining the present at the expense of the past, by revealing the present as part of a progressive tradition, and by showing the excellence of character of past pioneers. Such histories are frequently selective. Often written by practitioners, they reflect, as Bynum points out, professional preoccupations. One example is Tuke's history, published in 1882, which celebrates the emergence of the well-ordered Victorian asylum (Bynum 1983: 11).

The simplest and clearest examples of this process are the potted histories at the beginning of textbooks or articles. Thus, one of the classic textbooks of psychiatry, Henderson and Gillespie's *A Textbook of Psychiatry*, starts with a historical introduction which finishes in the 'hospital period' of the early twentieth century. This account by two psychiatrists involved in both university teaching and hospital consultancies can be contrasted with an administrator's view. In 1962, Sir Geoffrey Vickers, the chairman of the Mental Health Research Fund, optimistically saw the passing of the Mental Health Act of 1959 as the end of the 'strange and terrible history' of mental illness (Vickers 1962). In similar vein, the medical historian Charles Singer established a long and progressive tradition of medicine in which psychiatry, however, provided a flattering contrast: 'Until the nineteenth century there was practically no scientific knowledge of the conditions classed as insanity' (Singer 1928: 286); then a new era began with Pinel in Paris and Tuke in York, 'where the antiquated, unnecessary and cruel restraints were abolished' (Singer: 288). In contrast, Zilboorg's monumental *History of Medical Psychology* makes much more of earlier developments, offering warm testimonials to the courage and good character of the great innovators. Similar points may be made about other of the major histories, such as Bromberg's *Man Above Humanity: A History of Psychotherapy* (1954) and Alexander and Selesnick's *The History of Psychiatry* (1966). In each case the course of history is seen to culminate in the author's present interests. While this makes for a kind of relativism (since there are many possible narratives), the assumption remains of an essential, unchanging madness – though new names (lunacy, insanity, mental illness) are invented to suit the times.

But even while such histories were being written, these assumptions about progress and the unchanging reality of the phenomena under investigation were facing an increasing challenge from continental philosophers of history. While this work was generally unavailable in English, the problems were certainly familiar to English historians. Butterfield's exposure of triumphalism in *The Whig Interpretation of History* appeared in 1931; and Mandelbaum's *The Anatomy of Historical Knowledge*, first published in 1938, includes a detailed discussion of the German debate on historical relativism. But it is only recently, from the 1960s when *Madness and Civilization* and Kuhn's *The Structure of Scientific Revolutions* were published, that an awareness of these issues has appeared routinely in the writings of professional historians of medicine and psychiatry. Triumphalism now seems largely absent, though this may be partly because the historian's main outlet is no longer the monumental history but the academic paper, focusing with all the apparatus of historical scholarship upon some limited period or series of events. When historical overviews do appear, the broad sweep of them, over several hundred years from past to present, still carries a flavour of triumph, however neutral the presentation of detail. Even W.F. Bynum, among the most sophisticated of medical historians, cannot avoid a story of purposeful progress when writing a historical chapter for the multi-volume *Handbook of Psychiatry* (Bynum 1983). If the history of a purposeful institution like psychiatry is conceived as a history of change, it is hard to present the change as neutral – if it is not an improvement and a matter for triumph, then it must be a deterioration, as in the historiography of antipsychiatry, which is Whiggishness in reverse. But the possibilities are different if the focus is not on the institutions constructed to deal with madness, but with the experience of madness, as in Foucault's *Madness and Civilization*.

Foucault published his doctoral dissertation as '*Folie et déraison: Histoire de la folie à l'âge classique*' in 1961. In 1964 an abridgement appeared as '*Histoire de la folie*', and it was from this that Richard Howard's English translation was made, though additional material was included from the original version. In 1972 *Folie et déraison* was reissued, with minor alterations and two new appendices, as '*Histoire de la folie à l'âge classique*, siuvi de *Mon corps, ce papier, ce feu* et *La folie, l'absence d'oeuvre*'. This is the work usually referred to as *Histoire de la folie*. In France the book was received very favourably as a brilliant if sometimes elusive essay on the history of ideas (see Chapter 2). It was clearly part of a tradition that allowed and expected an inseparable mixture of history and philosophy, a tradition that included Foucault's teachers and near contemporaries, Canguilhem and Althusser, and also Bachelard (Gutting 1989) – a tradition which also included those philosophical victims of English insouciance, Hegel, Marx, Nietzsche, Husserl and Heidegger. Foucault's study was a history of madness rather than psychiatry – a history of the significance of madness, of how madness was experienced, rather than a disciplinary history of how specially trained professionals dealt with it as a perennial problem. It was also about the evolution of the present concept, through the presuppositions that have coloured attitudes towards madness – unconscious presuppositions, we might say, thus making it sound familiar to readers of Bachelard's *La Psychanalyse du feu*.

However, in 1967, this French tradition of historical philosophy or philosophical history was unfamiliar in English-speaking countries. While most readers recognized that *Madness and Civilization* was the work of a serious thinker, beyond that there was little agreement about its significance. For some it was a revelation, notably those who seized upon it as scholarly support for their antipsychiatry movement. R.D. Laing's *The Divided Self* had appeared as a paperback two years earlier, and Laing's collaborator David Cooper provided an introduction to *Madness and Civilization* which began 'Madness has in our age become some sort of lost truth' (Cooper 1967: vii). He continues, 'Foucault makes it quite clear that the invention of madness as a disease is . . . a disease of our civilization . . . people are driven mad by others' (viii). While Cooper provides no textual evidence in support, the 'Introduction' swiftly appropriates Foucault to the fictive view of madness and its familial origins.

None of this radical glamour helped to recommend *Madness and Civilization* to academic historians of ideas or of psychiatry, to social historians or to philosophers, especially as Foucault seemed all or none of these at the same time. Philosophers generally were not interested, and probably had no reason to believe they should be. It seemed too speculative as history, and too empirical to be philosophy. Only sociologists welcomed it – which only confirmed the worst suspicions of the remainder.

There has been a gradual shift of attitude. The antipsychiatry movement has come to a halt, since the closing of asylums has failed to solve the problem of schizophrenia, and no hidden truth has been revealed. Its main protagonists are dead and discredited, and its early sympathizers have come to recognize that, even if psychiatry is an instrument of repression, madness is more than a form of deviant behaviour that happens to be offensive to the bourgeois establishment (see Chapters 2 and 12). The publication of later books by Foucault, especially *The Order of Things*, and the accelerating output of secondary literature made it easier to appreciate what Foucault was trying to do in his earlier work, and how he could have been both philosopher and historian even in his doctoral dissertation. Foucault's later concept of *episteme* had great appeal to historians of ideas, and it both supported and contributed to the move towards synchronic rather than diachronic histories. Trained historians became interested in madness, and made clear their debt to Foucault, if only because his empirical errors stimulated their scholarly motivation (Bynum *et al*. 1985a; 1985b; 1988; Digby 1985a; Donnelly 1983; MacDonald 1981; Porter 1990; Scull 1979; Skultans 1975; Weiner 1990). Often they emphasize their differences from Foucault, and '*pace* Foucault' begins to seem his natural place in life. Digby (1985b), for instance, in her exemplary studies of the treatment at the York Retreat, is able to correct some apparent exaggerations in Foucault's account of the same subject. She shows how Foucault makes too little of the genuine kindness in the regime, and the gratitude of cured patients speaks for itself. Yet Foucault's quotation from the founder, William Tuke, remains telling – removal to the Quaker environment served to protect the inmates from the bad example of non-Quakers and 'to encourage the influence of the religious principles over the mind of the insane' (Foucault 1967: 243). Was this liberating or was it segregation and religious indoctrination?

Historians and philosophers of ideas in other fields, less concerned with the details, and responding to Foucault's later work as well as *Madness and Civilization*, have generally been more unstinting in their acknowledgements (Alpers 1983; Bernstein 1983; Gillespie 1979; Hacking 1990b; Rose 1985; Slaughter 1982; Winkler 1990) and painstaking in their criticisms (Hoy 1986). In 1985 the editors of the three-volume *Anatomy of Madness* summed up this conflict between Foucault the intellectual mandarin and Foucault the unreliable spadeworker, when they wrote:

> The late Michel Foucault's *La Folie et la déraison* (translated and abridged as *Madness and Civilization*) is a truly magisterial work. But it would be a mistake to assume that on many topics its roots in historical evidence are very secure, as Eric Midelfort, Peter Sedgwick, and others have already pointed out.
>
> (Bynum *et al*. 1985a: 4)

But how, one may ask, could the book be magisterial, which implies, surely, that it is both reliable and authoritative, and yet shaky on evidence? Readers of Midelfort or Sedgwick were left in no doubt that these were not minor slips by Foucault, but gross errors that vitiated his whole argument. Perhaps the reputation that Foucault had by now acquired was sufficient to nullify the mistakes of a relatively juvenile work. Or perhaps the later work and the secondary literature had brought out the magnitude of Foucault's achievement as a philosopher/historian in *Madness and Civilization*. However, although *The Anatomy of Madness* owes much to Foucault, and this three-volume study would hardly have been possible without the impetus given by the interest in his ideas as well as the market for his books, this is not due to the assimilation of his philosophical concerns. Foucault may have hastened the end of the old Whiggish histories of psychiatry, but the *Anatomy of Madness*, with separate chapters each focusing on its own detailed story, is an energetic return to scholarly empiricism. Its traditional subtitle ('Essays in the history of psychiatry') makes a revealing contrast to that appended to *Madness and Civilization* – 'A history of insanity in the age of reason'.

A year or so after the publication of the third and final (as yet) volume of *Anatomy of Madness*, we invited Colin Gordon to talk to the Research Group for the History of the Human Sciences in Durham. There he made his challenge: that English criticisms of *Madness and Civilization* (including those by Midelfort and Sedgwick referred to in *Anatomy of Madness*) are based upon reading only the English translation. Even when writers are clearly familiar with the French original (as in the case of Midelfort, who quotes from it), they appear nevertheless to focus their thinking upon the English version. The criticisms therefore fail, partly because there are occasional but crucial inaccuracies in the generally excellent translation, and more importantly because it is so severely abridged (albeit by Foucault himself in the 1964 version of his work).

One inaccuracy of some consequence was the translation of *'Les fous alors avaient une existence facilement errante'* as 'Madmen then led an easy wandering existence' in Foucault's account of the *Narrenschiff*, the 'ship of fools' which, certainly in literature and also literally, according to Foucault, contained cargoes of madmen who had been expelled from cities by handing them over to boatmen. Perhaps this apparently trivial mis-wording was important in indicating, to members of the antipsychiatry movement, that the insane had a relatively comfortable time in those days (there is precious little else in Foucault's description of the *Narrenschiff* to warrant this conclusion). A corollary of this has been the dismissive labelling of Foucault by the pro-psychiatry backlash as 'romantic and impractical', 'a thoroughgoing romantic . . . whose eyes are fixed on ineffable spheres' (Wing 1978: 4, 196); or as an ideological axe-grinder of the scapegoat theory of mental illness (Maher and Maher 1982: 760). Moreover, those historians who take Foucault seriously (though scarcely uncritically) have been bracketed with him and dismissed by association; for a characteristic assault see Jones's assessment of Andrew Scull (Jones 1982). Martin Roth (1988) in his Manichean outrage most unjustly casts Roy Porter into the infernal circle reserved by the psychiatric establishment for Laing and David Cooper. Even such a respected historian as Midelfort had quoted this English mistranslation to make his point about Foucault's unscholarly nostalgia for the Middle Ages. Elsewhere, Wing argues that Foucault's romantic hankerings may be 'barbarous and inhumane' if it could be demonstrated that Kraepelin's psychiatric ordering (which Foucault is thought to undermine) leads to a 'decrease in suffering and dis-ability' (Wing 1978: 4). While such a demonstration is scarcely practical, there can be no doubt that Foucault continues to contribute to the sum of unhappiness among senior psychiatrists in Britain. Doubtless it is too much to hope that correcting a single mistranslation could put matters right.

Colin Gordon translates Foucault's sentence as 'The existence of the mad at that time could easily be a wandering one' (p. 33), and this changes one's reading of the crucial paragraph of the most famous part of *Madness and Civilization*. In the rest of the paragraph the madmen are described as being driven here and there, but not *explicitly* as being treated harshly — that possibility is left to an imagination which has already been set up, in Howard's translation, to think otherwise, so that the next sentence, for instance ('they were allowed to wander in the open countryside'), can carry a hint of freedom and rural pleasures. Gordon's suggested revision, on the other hand, allows full play to the possibility that the mad, like King Lear, were thrown out of doors and cruelly forced to fend for themselves in all weathers and without food:

> Poor naked wretches, wheresoe'er you are,
> That bide the pelting of this pitiless storm,
> How shall your houseless heads and unfed sides,
> Your loop'd and window'd raggedness, defend you
> From seasons such as these?
>
> (*King Lear*, III, iv, 28–32)

It is now almost a commonplace that writing is something of a blind gesture towards an unknown audience, and is therefore always open to the play of ambiguity and irony. If this is true even of the most rigidly structured experimental report, or the most painstaking phenomenological description, how much more so in the case of a writer who recognizes and revels in this openness. But this creates havoc with translation. Ambiguity and irony have always been a problem, but at least (it was once believed) most of the words in different languages more or less corresponded to the same more or less universal referents. But now that this seems so problematic in the best of cases, what can be done with Michel Foucault? Starting with Gordon's suggestion, Megill easily shows the difficulty by taking the reader through an illusory dialectical spiral of *offered translation – criticism – improved translation*; illusory, because the improvements are always cancelled by the loss of some crucial nuance from the earlier version. Happily, this does not make Foucault available only to the reader with French. For, with no single correct meaning, all readings, in translation or otherwise, must be more or less misreadings; if the English reader is handicapped, it is in a race that in any case nobody can win.

But, as Anthony Pugh points out, all this is (or should be) trivial in our reading of Foucault, presumably because the irony is indelibly *there* in *Madness and Civilization* and a translation can only be true to it by being a new and totally different text. (Nevertheless, Pugh throws off a brisk alternative.) All readings may be misreadings but some may be more so than others, especially when they are based on only part of the text. Less than half of *Histoire de la folie* is included in *Madness and Civilization*, and Colin Gordon's argument is that 'the absent 300 pages contain material which is not only crucial to some detailed English-language debates about Foucault's achievement, but also decisive for the way one views the overall shape and course of his career' (see Chapter 1, p. 20). The abridgement is responsible, Gordon argues, for the mistaken view that Foucault believed that the *medicalization* of madness is of recent origin and coincides with the beginnings of modern psychiatry. It is easy to find counter-examples to this, and Foucault himself provides several, but it is not what he believed – it is the concept of *mental illness*, not *mental medicine*, that is modern. Also, to take another misconception easily corrected by reading the original, Foucault did not think that the concept was slotted into a preformed category of deviancy – deviancy itself has a problematic history, as is made clear in one of the omitted chapters, 'Le monde correctionnaire'. Perhaps the simplest and most glaring effect of the abridgement is to obscure the historical continuity that was present in the original. Chapters tracing the transitions from one period to the next are omitted in the abridged version. Since these omissions were Foucault's own doing, and since the effect is to make the treatment closer to Foucault's later view, where there is discontinuity between successive *epistemes*, Midelfort (see Chap. 8) even suggests that he made these particular cuts in order to lend an appearance of consistency to his work as a whole. If so, judging from the evidence Gordon gives in reply (see Chap. 14), it was a concern for appearances confined only to English-speaking audiences.

Failure to take account of important sections of a text gives rise to real, old-fashioned, empirical misreadings, ordinary misreadings that can be rectified by closer attention to the relevant parts. Is, then, the answer the long-awaited translation in full of the 1972 edition of *Histoire de la folie*? English-speaking readers can get some idea of what they may have been missing by referring to Anthony Pugh's translation of Chapter 4 of *Histoire de la folie* (Foucault 1991). Even in that single chapter there is much to support Gordon's claims, enough certainly to make one wonder why commentators have not referred more to the missing parts. But will the full translation resolve all doubts? Certainly not, judging from the disagreements among our contributors, though all who consider the question would welcome an English version of the full text. Whatever the outcome, Foucault's *Histoire de la folie* will remain a fruitful source of essential contestability for many years yet.

Rather than rehearsing the debate here in full (impossible, anyway, to misread on behalf of another or to convey the scholarly passion that is evidenced by some of our contributors), we will conclude by examining some of the implications of both *Histoire de la folie* and the responses to it for current directions in the practice of the human sciences.

*

What are the scholars doing when they attempt to retrieve past thinking for the present? What are they reporting on and what characterizes the nature of these reports? These questions are at the heart of the present set of essays. For although they focus upon Foucault and *Madness and Civilization*, the task therein of identifying, situating and tracking madness is paralleled in other fields. The types of problems we have in mind are those which find expression at the conceptual level – as in clarifying our understanding of science, social class, gender and so on; and which require simultaneously their apprehension within the historical and social planes.

Madness raises in a poignantly ironic form the possibility of the rational, and of the rational explanation of both the phenomenon itself and the institutions created to deal with it. But it is not a peculiarity of Foucault's work to offer a major revision of our understanding of a syndrome and its correlative institutions. Such revisions have been recognizably a development since the beginnings of sociology and in the longer term of philosophy; and other specialisms have felt the effect of this, notably that broad range of writing we call history. What all such writings attempt is a revision that will make transparent that which was obscure; and in the case of madness, to clarify the everyday stories and 'myths' surrounding the mad, and to explain to us, the sane, not only how madness has come to be understood but how societies have exerted themselves in dealing with this problem. For like crime and child abuse, and other threats to the serenity of daily life, it is a problem and a preoccupation affecting many people. Thus, even to English readers unfamiliar with the French tradition discussed above, Foucault's explorations are neither unique nor totally unexpected. What seems more surprising is the response to his work and particularly to *Madness and Civilization*.

What is peculiar and in a sense old-fashioned about *Madness and Civilization* is the attempt to write the history of both concepts and institutions without much distinction between the two. It is peculiar because it distinguishes him from Kuhn and others who have made much of the connection between these two dimensions of history, but have retained the distinction. And it is old-fashioned because this refusal to keep them apart shows an affinity with the writings of three of the more equivocal 'father figures' of the social sciences – father figures whose most penetrating insights are precisely those that have failed to be seminal. The connection with Nietzsche is well known (Sheridan 1980; Dreyfus and Rabinow 1982), but more illuminating for our argument is the affinity with two writers with whom Foucault shows less familiarity, Max Weber and William James. At their deepest, we would argue, the insights of Weber and James have been diluted and rendered palatable for the same reasons that the implications of Foucault's project have been resisted.

William James's attempt to get the best of transcendentalism while remaining an empiricist culminated in his doctrine of pure experience or radical empiricism. Uncharitably viewed, this was a failure; pure experience

cannot itself be experienced by the social self, and is a manifestly transcendental realm. But in its transcendental aspect (that is, derived from experience
but not itself experienced) pure experience serves its pivotal purpose. By
appropriating all absolute status to itself, it leaves no room for pure
rationality, only rationalities, and this is the basis of James's refutation of
rationalism and the point of entry of pluralism and pragmatism.

> On the pragmatist side we have only one edition of the universe,
> unfinished, growing in all sorts of places where thinking beings are
> at work.
> On the rationalist side we have a universe in many editions, one real
> one, the infinite folio, or *edition de luxe*, eternally complete; and then the
> various finite editions, full of false readings, distorted and mutilated each
> in its own way.
>
> (James 1975: 124)

And now, by a characteristic piece of psychologism, he points fingers,
accusing and approving, at the political and institutional implications of
these two approaches to history.

> The rationalist mind, radically taken, is of a doctrinaire and authoritative
> complexion; the phrase '*must* be' is ever on its lips. The belly band of its
> universe must be tight. A radical pragmatist on the other hand is a happy-
> go-lucky anarchistic sort of creatures. If he had to live in a tub like
> Diogenes he wouldn't mind at all if the hoops were loose and the staves
> let in the sun.
>
> (ibid.)

These passages from James have been used by Lentricchia in *Ariel and the
Police*, where James, Foucault and Wallace Stevens are placed in parallel
for mutual illumination:

> Foucault's disciplinary society and James's systematic life are the
> outcomes of a historical process and are twin accounts insofar as they
> take the price of modernity to be the loss of self-determination in the
> normalizing actions of institutional life that James, long before Foucault,
> excoriated for 'branding, licensing and degree-giving, authorizing and
> appointing, and in general regulating and administering by system the
> lives of human beings'.
>
> (Lentricchia 1988: 25)

The world of the rationalist 'is a kind of marble temple shining on a hill'
(James 1975: 18) and Lentricchia helps us to see a connection between this
and James's prophetic horror at the military action against the Philippines
in 1989: 'We must sow our ideals, plant our order, impose our God' (quoted
in Lentricchia 1988: 21) – build our marble temples! It remains to emphasize what is only implicit in Lentricchia – that the administering systems (or
the bureaucratic institutions) are justified by, and themselves enforce,

principles of rationality. For James, what holds them together is the metaphysics of rationalism which reflects no absolute truth but is a mere construction upon pure experience. Foucault's 'experience of madness' serves a similar pivotal function in *Madness and Civilization*. It is prior to the institutions and conceptual rationalities based upon it and thereby keeps at bay their claims to a monopoly on truth. But once their teeth are drawn and their claims can be examined calmly, pure experience can be jettisoned, as it must be if experience is itself conditioned by the social and conceptual formations based upon it. We are left then with Jamesian pragmatism or Foucault's later discursive practices, which occur and can be investigated, but which are founded upon nothing. Pure experience is thus the illusory vehicle, or ladder to be thrown away, that conveys us from attachment to our local rationality (cleaved to as an absolute), through a modernist examination of the structure of founded rationalities, and on to (postmodernist) investigations of free-floating discursive practices, which are both constitutive of and constituted by experience.

> In 1913, in the midst of modernist revolution in poetry and philosophy, Josiah Royce replayed George Santayana's attack on Whitman as a poet of barbarism by characterizing this yearning for pure perception as a sign of the modernist times: perception as a moment of consciousness utterly final, with perceiver and perceived unified in an isolated fulfilment before all community and conversation.
>
> (Lentricchia, op. cit.: 13)

Foucault's affinity with Max Weber lies analogously in the latter's investigation of rationality and rationalization. This emerges most clearly in the contrast between Max Weber's work and the permeation of the social and historical sciences by variations of Durkheimian and Marxian proposals. For what these both propose and impose are varieties of what Kolakowski (1990) terms 'utopian epistemologies', clear-cut methodologies of a kind that both Foucault and Weber have been perceived as failing to offer. But if they are right this is no failure, since for both the clarity of social methodology, like the clarity of rationalism for William James, is a chimera which dissolves on close inspection.

The difficulty facing critics of Weber is the elusiveness of his strategy. As Talcott Parsons, the doyen of American sociology in the 1960s, put it, Weber creates a mosaic of ideal types with no particular way of organizing them (see Bershady 1973). Parsons, a confirmed triumphalist in his own work, who looked to sociology as a discipline retaining the same hopes and possibilities as natural science, was undoubtedly correct in this assessment of Weber. There is no fundamental unity of picture for Weber; and just as certainly there are no general laws of the social to be discovered. Rather, he explores themes such as the development of rational procedures in business enterprise; the formalization of law; the evolution of formal bureaucratic systems of management; and the same processes applying to the organization of knowledge and its practice. All these themes find a later echo in Foucault's undertaking. Even more emphatic is Weber's avoidance (some think evasion) of the technologial aims of western historical and social thinking. To expand Kolakowski's point, epistemological utopianism is not an event which effects merely political actions; it is an underlying assumption of the traditions which developed with such force and impetus in western societies of the nineteenth and twentieth centuries and marked so clearly their knowledge-creating and knowledge-safeguarding institutions: the universities and professions. This aspect of utopianism is usually referred to meekly as 'methodology' or 'the methodology of the social sciences', a verbal deflection which (unlike Weber's usage) takes the notion of rationality – and with it the rationality of natural science – as essentially unproblematic (for an extended discussion see Lassman and Velody 1989: 159–204).

It is this point, Foucault's attempt to take issue with the presumed rationality of the sane and their treatment of the mad, which has called forth the harshest comments. Perhaps these responses are close in origin to the sourness which greeted the publication of Kuhn's *The Structure of Scientific Revolutions*. As with Foucault, Kuhn's perceived carelessness was the order of the day. There was insufficient attention to detail and there was sloppy vagueness – as in the oft-quoted twenty-one different usages of 'paradigm' ('possibly more', according to Masterman 1970). No doubt all these comments were well placed; but they evade the main point, the vulnerable omission exposed by Kuhn. In spite of the extensive commentaries and histories of science which had hitherto been published, very little indeed was known about the practice of science. In a sense science in 1962 was *terra incognita* and the situation today is not greatly advanced. But what developments there have been much owe much to Kuhn, and very little either to the philosophy of science of the period, or to the dominant style of sociology of science of the 1950s and 1960s, that of Robert Merton; or indeed to the then existing histories of the subject.

That studies in science have begun to take a different direction is in part due to the recognition that the assumptions of rationality in the processing of scientific phenomena are no more than that: assumptions with little supporting evidence. Such challenges to the formerly sacrosanct status of rationality (more correctly, formalistic claims about rationality) might understandably produce some anxiety, not so much among practitioners but rather among their spokespersons – philosophers, methodologists and members of funding agenices. It is even more understandable that those deeply involved with the irrational may feel uneasy at having their own rationalities questioned. As we have seen, this is a consequence of reading or hearing about *Madness and Civilization*. There is no comfort there for those who identify professionally with redeeming therapies or social prophecies. For, very like Weber, and perhaps for similar reasons, Foucault offers no picture of a society steadily evolving humane and decent practices over a considerable period of time. More worryingly, he appears to imply that the greatest advance in the treatment of the insane can only be seen superficially as a positive development, and that perhaps a fuller understanding of 'humane' treatment in the nineteenth century would uncover aspects that we, its inheritors, would be shocked to accept.

In essence Foucault says: if you think you understand madness – just think again by looking at its history. Histories of institutions and treatments have now disclosed extreme varieties of engagement with this problem – each extreme being broadcast in its time with the same reassuring confidence. What evidence is there that our understanding of these phenomena has improved, that present-day certainties are more reliable than those of the past? They may be, but what evidence is there? Neither Foucault nor Weber are optimistic about the future in this respect. Neither believes that any utopian epistemology, with its associated methodology, will ever emerge to show the fundamental error in our thinking on the nature of madness (or any other social phenomenon). Salvation does not lie in the construction of a shining temple standing on a hill.

But why should this refusal to see an end to history be cause for alarm? Each new discovery creates new areas for investigation by scientists, and for secondary investigation by historians. The discovery or 'discovery' of child abuse (for example) has raised as many complexities and difficulties of comprehension and treatment as madness. As Hacking shows in his paper 'The making and molding of child abuse', it is apt to appear as though referring to a constant object of potential knowledge, but in fact the meaning of 'child abuse' is constantly changing. As in the case of madness, this does not mean there is no such thing or no problem, or that there can be no knowledge of it. 'We would like our interventions, our official agencies, our courts, our teachers, our doctors, our people on the street, and indeed ourselves to act caringly, helpfully, prudently, wisely, justly, *from knowledge*' (Hacking 1990c: 288; our emphasis). Such pragmatic knowledge is still gained through research, including historical and conceptual research like Foucault's and Hacking's. But it will not be furthered by forcing child abuse into a medical model that assumes a fixed object of knowledge, and is consequently threatened by a historical approach that refuses to acknowledge without question the rationality of such a 'scientific' approach. Research, including historical research, into madness and child abuse does not stand aloof, but itself contributes to the history of the problems, and to the constitution of the concepts.

One eventual consequence of *The Structure of Scientific Revolutions* was to encourage scholars to look more closely at the concrete practice of science and scientific workers – a practice which the highly utopian methodologies of Kuhn's sociological and philosophical contemporaries ignored. Similarly, the programmes which authors like Foucault encourage are those which require a broader understanding of their topic, by focusing on what goes on rather than on the rationally conceived object of knowledge: on 'existence in the concrete' rather than on the building history of a marble temple. With such an approach, writing a research report is no longer a neutral matter, or one that could ever be generated by the canons of a universal methodology. We should not therefore be surprised or disturbed if *Histoire de la folie* will prove to have changed our conception of madness, or if Michel Foucault has given us a far deeper appreciation of the empirical world as data previously excluded from research by dogma.

NOTE ON *MADNESS AND CIVILIZATION*

Foucault's thesis was published in book form as: *Folie et déraison: Histoire de la folie à l'âge classique* (Paris: Plon 1961). A truncated pocket edition was published as *Histoire de la folie à l'âge classique* in 1964 (Paris: UGE). The first edition was subsequently reissued in an expanded form by Gallimard in 1972, with a new preface by Foucault, and now included two essays as appendices; but the revised title *Histoire de la folie à l'âge classique* was retained. Meanwhile, Richard Howard's translation of the shortened version with some additional material appeared in 1965 under the title *Madness and Civilization* (New York: Pantheon).

The year 1967 was to see the British publication of this translation as a hardback by Tavistock in a series edited by R. D. Laing. It differed from the Pantheon edition in bearing an introduction by David Cooper. Tavistock's paperback version of *Madness and Civilization*, now in its fifth impression, apart from the deletion of the reference to Laing's series, follows the hardback edition – with the exception of the third impression of 1975. For although the third impression bears Tavistock's imprint it is otherwise in the same format as the Pantheon edition (it is in fact their Vintage paperback) and includes the introduction by José Barchillon, MD. Unlike Cooper, Barchillon lays claim to the widespread reality of the ship of fools with a confidence unwarranted by the succeeding text.

The current French edition, again with the title *Histoire de la folie à l'âge classique*, was brought out by Gallimard in 1972. This is effectively the earliest version published by Plon in 1961. Problems with the Foucault estate have up to now blocked any further attempts to publish the fuller version in English.

BIBLIOGRAPHY

Alexander, F. G. and S. T. Selesnick (1966) *The History of Psychiatry: An Evaluation of Psychiatric Thought and Practice from Prehistoric Times to the Present*, New York: Harper & Row.

Alpers, S. (1983) *The Art of Describing: Dutch Art in the Seventeenth Century*, London: John Murray.

Bachelard, G. (1938) *La Psychanalyse du feu*, Paris: NRF.

Bernstein, R. J. (1983) *Beyond Objectivism and Relativism*, Oxford: Blackwell.

Bershady, H. J. (1973) *Ideology and Social Knowledge*, Oxford: Blackwell.

Bromberg, W. (1954) *Man Above Humanity: A History of Psychotherapy*, Philadelphia: Lippincott.

Butterfield, H. (1973) *The Whig Interpretation of History*, Harmondsworth: Penguin Books.

Bynum, W. F. (1983) 'Psychiatry in its historical context', in M. Shepherd and O. L. Zangwill (eds) *Handbook of Psychiatry*, vol. 1. *General Psychopathology*, Cambridge: Cambridge University Press; 11–38.

Bynum, W. F., R. Porter and M. Shepherd (eds) (1985a) *The Anatomy of Madness*, vol. 1. *People and Ideas*, London: Tavistock.

Bynum, W. F., R. Porter and M. Shepherd (eds) (1985b) *The Anatomy of Madness*, vol. 2. *Institutions and Society*, London: Tavistock.

Bynum, W. F., R. Porter and M. Shepherd (eds) (1988) *The Anatomy of Madness*, vol. 3. *The Asylum and Psychiatry*, London: Routledge.

Cooper, D. (1967) 'Introduction', in M. Foucault *Madness and Civilization*, London: Tavistock; vii–ix.

Digby, A. (1985a) *Madness, Morality and Medicine: A Study of the York Retreat*, Cambridge: Cambridge University Press.

Digby, A. (1985b) 'Moral treatment at the Retreat, 1796–1846', in W. F. Bynum, R. Porter and M. Shepherd (eds) *The Anatomy of Madness, vol. 2: Institutions and Society*, London: Tavistock; 57–72.

Donnelly, M. (1983) *Managing the Mind: A study of medical psychology in early nineteenth-century Britain*, London: Tavistock.

Dreyfus, H. L. and P. Rabinow (1983) *Michel Foucault: Beyond Structuralism and Hermeneutics*, Chicago: University of Chicago Press.

Foucault, M. (1970) *The Order of Things: An Archaeology of the Human Sciences*, London: Tavistock.

Foucault, M. (1991) 'Experiences of madness', *History of the Human Sciences* 4: 1–25.

Gillespie, N. C. (1979) *Charles Darwin and the Problem of Creation*, Chicago: University of Chicago Press.

Gutting, G. (1989) *Michel Foucault's Archaeology of Scientific Reason*, Cambridge: Cambridge University Press.

Hacking, I. (1990a) 'Two kinds of new historicism for philosophers', *New Literary History* 21(2): 343–64.

Hacking, I. (1990b) *The Taming of Chance*, Cambridge: Cambridge University Press.

Hacking, I. (1990c) 'The making and molding of child abuse', *Critical Inquiry* 17: 253–88.

Henderson, D. and R. D. Gillespie (eds) (1956) *A Textbook of Psychiatry*, 8th edn, Oxford: Oxford University Press.

Hoy, D. C. (ed.) (1986) *Foucault: A Critical Reader*, Oxford: Blackwell.

James, W. (1975) *Pragmatism and the Meaning of Truth*, Cambridge, MA: Harvard University Press.

Jones, K. (1982) 'Scull's dilemma', *British Journal of Psychiatry* 141: 221–6.

Kolakowski, L. (1990) 'The death of Utopia reconsidered', in L. Kolakowski *Modernity on Endless Trial*, Chicago: University of Chicago Press; 131–45.

Kuhn, T. S. (1962) *The Structure of Scientific Revolutions*, Chicago: University of Chicago Press.

Laing, R. D. (1965) *The Divided Self*, Harmondsworth: Penguin Books.

Lassman, P. and I. Velody (eds) (1989) *Max Weber's 'Science as a Vocation'*, London: Unwin Hyman.

Lentricchia, F. (1988) *Ariel and the Police*, Madison, Wisconsin: University of Wisconsin Press.

MacDonald, M. (1981) *Mystical Bedlam: Madness, Anxiety, and Healing in Seventeenth-Century England*, Cambridge: Cambridge University Press.

Maher, B. W. and B. Maher (1982) 'The Ship of Fools: *Stultifera Navis* or *Ignis Fatus*', *American Psychologist* 37: 756–61.

Mandelbaum, M. (1967) *The Anatomy of Historical Knowledge*, Baltimore: Johns Hopkins University Press.

Masterman, M. (1970) 'The nature of a paradigm', in I. Lakatos and A. Musgrave (eds) *Criticism and the Growth of Knowledge*, Cambridge: Cambridge University Press; 59–89.

Porter, R. (1990) '*Barely Touching*: a social perspective on mind and body', in G. S. Rousseau (ed.) *The Languages of Psyche: Mind and Body in Enlightenment Thought*, Berkeley: University of California Press; 48–80.

Rose, N. (1985) *The Psychological Complex: Psychology, Politics and Society in England, 1869–1939*, London: Routledge & Kegan Paul.

Roth, M. (1988) 'Nobly wild, not mad?' *British Medical Journal* 296: 1165–8.

Scull, A. (1979) *Museums of Madness*, Harmondsworth: Allen Lane.

Sheridan, A. (1980) *Michel Foucault: The Will to Truth*, London: Tavistock.

Singer, C. (1928) *A Short History of Medicine*, Oxford: Oxford University Press.

Skultans, V. (1979) *English Madness: Ideas on Insanity, 1580–1890*, Routledge & Kegan Paul.

Slaughter, M. M. (1982) *Universal Languages and Scientific Taxonomy in the Seventeenth Century*, Cambridge: Cambridge University Press.

Tuke, D. H. (1882) *Chapters in the History of the Insane in the British Isles*, London: Kegan Paul.

Vickers, G. (1962) 'Mental disorder in British culture', in D. Richter *et al.* (eds) *Aspects of Psychiatric Research*, Oxford: Oxford University Press; 1–12.

Weiner, D. B. (1990) 'Mind and body in the clinic: Philippe Pinel, Alexander Crichton, Dominique Esquirol and the birth of psychiatry', in G. S. Rousseau (ed.) *The Languages of Psyche: Mind and Body in Enlightenment Thought*, Berkeley: University of California Press; 331–402.

Wing, J. K. (1978) *Reasoning about Madness*, Oxford: Oxford University Press.

Winkler, J. J. (1990) *The Constraints of Desire*, London: Routledge.

Zilboorg, G. (1941) *A History of Medical Psychology*, New York: Norton.

Part I
Reading Foucault

1 *Histoire de la folie*
An unknown book by Michel Foucault

Colin Gordon

Mais le malheur a voulu que les choses soient plus compliquées. (132)

So I have kept just one rule and method, the one contained in a passage by Réné Char which can be read as both the most exacting and the most restrained definition of truth: 'I will take from things the illusion they produce to save themselves from us, and let them keep the part of themselves which they offer us.' (x)

Michel Foucault's *Madness and Civilization* (1965) is a famous book. What is less well known is that it is a translation which omits well over half of its original, the book published in France in 1961 under the title *Folie et déraison: histoire de la folie à l'âge classique*. In the pagination of the almost unmodified main text of the second French edition (Foucault 1972[1]), the parts of *Histoire de la folie* included in *Madness and Civilization* amount to 236 pages, and the parts omitted (excluding the appendices) to 299. The abridgement of the book's scholarly apparatus is even more severe. Out of more than a thousand footnotes in the original, 149 are retained; a bibliography comprising over two hundred primary and secondary sources is omitted altogether. The untranslated part of *Folie et déraison* is roughly equivalent in length to (for example) the complete text of *Discipline and Punish*.

It is therefore not altogether surprising that a similar, and equally seldom noticed, disparity exists between the responses of French and English-speaking historians to these respective editions of Foucault's book. *Annales E.S.C.* published in 1962 a review by Robert Mandrou, to which was added a note by Fernand Braudel (Mandrou 1962).[2] Neither critic was stinting in his praise: '*Un très beau livre*' (Mandrou); '*ce livre magnifique*' (Braudel). Both express the perception that the book is original in the complexity of its method and that this complexity brings a certain elusiveness: Mandrou warns against seeking for a simple narrative unity, and Braudel remarks that close attention is sometimes needed to follow the work's expository thread. But neither leaves any doubt that they view the work as successful in conception and execution both as an intellectual construction and as a work of historical scholarship, whose author is, in Mandrou's words, '*à la pointe de recherches qui le passionnent et qui nous passionnent*'.

No English-speaking historian of comparable standing within the academic mainstream has subscribed to anything like so cordial an assessment of this book. Given the extent and duration of the Annales school's influence on historians in the English-speaking world, such a disparity might seem, prima facie, puzzling, and impossible to explain solely by the above-mentioned facts about the translation. A number of further factors suggest themselves.

For one thing, the Annales historians were of a somewhat more whole-heartedly interdisciplinary temper than their British and American colleagues: Lucien Febvre actually recognized a need, within the study of *mentalités*, for historians with a philosophical training (Febvre 1973: 248). Again, the climate of reception of Foucault's book was changed dramatically between the early and later 1960s by the coming of antipsychiatry. Historians reading *Madness and Civilization* after 1970 would be aware of its impact on a contemporary non-scholarly or non-specialist audience, a factor apt, especially in this case, to stimulate misgivings about its specialist and scholarly merits: the more so because of the very characteristics of the English version which made it accessible to a general readership unconcerned with, or actively indifferent to, the routine constraints of scholarship. Historians, of course, do not judge a work solely by the volume of its footnotes. But such factors undoubtedly have an effect.

Foucault himself made the abridgements in *Madness and Civilization* and the (now long out of print) 10/18 French pocket version which this was based on. The fact that his cuts were skilfully carried out is presumably evidenced by the fact that their extent is far from obvious or frequently remarked upon. The omissions do not make historical nonsense of what remains. Quite simply, the shorter version is considerably less rich than the longer one: my concern will be to show here that the absent 300 pages contain material which is not only crucial to some detailed English-language debates about Foucault's achievement, but also decisive for the way one views the overall shape and course of his career.

Why, in that case, has a complete translation never been produced? *Histoire de la folie* is Foucault's longest book; there is said to have been difficulty in finding a French publisher for it in 1961; publishers may well, especially in the case of a hitherto little-known author, have balked at the venture of a 600-page translation; later on, when these reservations might have ceased to operate, Foucault himself may well have preferred to leave the initiative to others. In any event, the deciding influence on publishers in such matters may be expected to come, and generally does come, not from the author of a work but from concerned members of its potential audience. The tenor of the secondary literature around *Madness and Civilization* does not lead one to imagine that over the past twenty years Random House or Tavistock Press can have come under much pressure from within the English-speaking academic community to undertake a completed translation. The great majority of published contributions to scholarly criticism of *Madness and Civilization*, along with the great majority of book-length expositions of Foucault's thought, provide little or no inkling of the drastic difference between its French and English versions. Moreover, it can easily be established, as I will show, that a series of critics whose declared object has been to measure Foucault's accomplishment as a historian against the standards of serious scholarship have dispensed with the preliminary task of reading the unabridged text of his book.

One of the reasons why the book is dealt with so cursorily even by sympathetic commentators on Foucault is the currency of various scenarios of intellectual biography, in terms of which *Histoire de la folie* predates several of Foucault's major conceptual and methodological advances. The main evidence adduced for this view is a series of brief self-critical remarks in Foucault's *The Archaeology of Knowledge*, published in 1969. But the scope and force of these self-criticisms turn out on close examination to be considerably less complete or damaging than an incautious reader might suppose: Gilles Deleuze (1986: 22) doubts whether Foucault's repentances are very seriously meant. Rather in the same way that the innovative achievement in each of Foucault's successive works is almost invariably supplemented by a set of proposals or announcements of further, subsequent investigations to be undertaken in related domains, many of which were never to be completed, his urge to sharpen a fresh perspective may have sometimes impelled him to overstate the shift which this departure signified relative to his previous thinking. Whether out of a polemical appetite for indications of unstable oscillation and damaging retreat, or through an inclination to apply the (often misunderstood) Foucauldian thematic of discontinuity to Foucault's own thought, or simply out of the need for a striking story-line, the evidences of a strong continuity from *Histoire de la folie* through to the end of Foucault's output have generally been paid too little critical attention.

A second and obvious hazard to understanding of this book is the involvement of its reception not only with the politics of psychiatric affairs but also with the roughly parallel emergence as a specialist academic sub-discipline of the historiography of insanity and its treatment. If one suggests to practitioners in the latter area that Foucault's contribution has received less than its due, one is often answered with emphatic personal testimony of his book's decisive and inspiring influence; words to this effect are indeed commonly to be read in prefaces. On the other hand, a settled community of expertise and inquiry may come to think that the achievement of heroic forerunners can be surpassed or made obsolete by subsequent advances. For at least one generation, it is hard to separate *Madness and Civilization* from the memory of a period where its ideas commingled with those of Laing and Cooper, Illich, Szasz, Fanon and Reich – a time which posterity now readily regards as half-crazed. However often Foucault expressed his surprise and vexation at the degree of animosity provoked in its present-day practitioners by his treatment of the historical beginning of the psychiatric discipline, and although his book was written some years in advance of the cultural movements within which it was taken up, he would have had no regret about the possibility of his work's influence contributing to a movement of practical criticism and reform which he undoubtedly supported; in later years he was quite prepared to say that improvements had been made in society's treatment of clients of mental medicine, and that the movements of critique were entitled to some credit for these changes. From the present point of view, however, it needs to be pointed out that in the course of all this the specific terms of Foucault's analyses became, in places, conflated with philosophical and sociological notions quite different from, and indeed strictly incompatible with, his own; and that some of these confusions persist in the conceptual framework of subsequent work in the field.[3] One reason, then, why Foucault's work may not have been altogether surpassed in this field is that its contribution has been often praised but seldom clearly grasped.

These points can conveniently be illustrated in terms of three key notions of the post-antipsychiatric lingua franca: deviancy, medicalization and Cartesian dualism.

In George Rosen's book *Madness in Society* (Rosen 1968) one can find elements both of a deviancy-theory view of psychiatry and of what reads in places like a deviancy-theoretical paraphrase of Foucault (though Rosen does not mention Foucault). After relating some biblical and classical anecdotes of insanity, Rosen comments that 'the behaviour of the people cited above was regarded as more than merely perplexing or perverse. They were regarded as deranged because their behaviour and, inferentially, their orientation to reality were considered excessively divergent from socially accepted norms'. He remarks that: 'At any given period certain criteria are employed to establish normal human nature, as well as any deviation from it'. Concerning the French decree of 1656 creating the *hôpitaux généraux*, a landmark, according to Rosen, in public policy for the treatment of the insane, Rosen writes that 'All individuals who were defined as asocial or socially deviant were segregated by internment. This procedure is analogous to the manner in which the leper was treated in the mediaeval period' (97, 163f).

One can divine here both the way in which Foucault was to be read by adherents of the theories of deviancy and social control current in the 1970s, and the intellectual vulnerability of such theories. To undertake a history of the treatment of the insane by recourse to the concept of deviancy is an effort at phenomenological subtlety which carries the cost of a peculiar ahistorical naïvety, in so far as it is certainly not the case that, as Rosen suggests, citizens in antiquity would have formed an opinion concerning (to take one of Rosen's instances) an individual who 'fancied himself a brick', by consideration of whether that person's 'behaviour' or 'orientation to reality' was 'excessively divergent from socially accepted norms'. And it is equally plainly the case that the French decree of 1656 did not and could not address itself to a category of individuals defined as 'asocial or socially

deviant', because the latter concepts, unlike those of madness or vaga-
bondage, were not available in 1656.

Foucault's dissent from this form of sociological relativism dates back to
his short first book published in 1954, *Maladie mentale et personnalité*:
here, after a consideration of the positions of Durkheim and Ruth Benedict,
Foucault proposes to treat the notion of deviancy as part of the problem,
rather than part of the answer, in the history of madness: one of the two key
historical questions which this book proposed for analysis was: 'How did
our culture come to give mental illness the meaning of deviancy, and to the
patient a status that excludes him?' (1954, trans. 1976: 63).

'Le monde correctionnaire', one of the chapters of *Histoire de la folie*
which is completely omitted from the English edition, deals with this
question of the genealogy of the category of deviancy. Foucault begins here
(pp. 92–4) by taking issue with an earlier generation of progressively
minded psychiatrist-historians writing in the early decades of this century
(Sérieux and Libert, Chatelain, Henry, Vié, Bonnafous-Sérieux and Tardif)
who in fact did much of the groundwork in the history of the internment
practices of the *ancien régime*. Their objective, Foucault writes, was 'to
"rehabilitate" the internment under the *ancien régime*, and to demolish the
myth of the Revolution liberating the mad, a myth constructed by Pinel and
Esquirol which was still alive at the end of the nineteenth century' (92n).
For these writers the decrees of 1656 corresponded to a 'spontaneous
elimination of the "asocial", the inarticulate perception of, and response to
a social malaise which the subsequent advances of science refined to the
articulateness of medical knowledge'.

Robert Castel's *The Psychiatric Order*, which can in many ways be read
as a historical sequel to *Histoire de la folie*, provides an account of these
author's own policy orientation. As successors of Morel and his theories of
degeneracy, they taxed the Pinelian school with laxity: 'classical alienism
had postulated too narrow a definition of the populations to be taken in
charge. The category of the "abnormal" must be distinguished from that of
the mentally ill' (Castel 1986: 188–90, 285). The combined resources of
psychiatry, justice and legal medicine remained, it was held, far from equal
to mastering the social plague of congenital deviancy.

Foucault remarks on these authors' special perspective that 'the fact that
we can find a resemblance between the internees of the Eighteenth century
and our own contemporary figure of the asocial individual is indeed a fact,
but probably one belonging only to the order of results: for that figure was
brought into being as an effect of the act of internment itself' (93–4). The
Sérieux school wanted a range of internment institutions more differentiated, if not more comprehensive in their catchment, than the *hôpitaux
généraux*; but Foucault's point is that it was the homogenizing influence of
the great internment that made possible the eventual formation of a single,
overarching concept of deviancy, through a process of what might be
called the reciprocal disenchantment of transgressions: the common

element of *déraison* neutralizes the distinct ethico-theological meanings attached to the different personages (the venereal, the sodomist, the alchemist, the suicide, the blasphemer, atheist, libertine and debauchee) who inhabit with the insane the spaces of eighteenth-century administrative detention. Unbelief, for instance, comes to be seen as no more than the sequel to a life of science. Foucault writes that internment produces 'a certain style of being which a person already possesses prior to being interned, and which makes internment finally necessary' (121f). He sees the ways in which the rationale of internment establishes a kind of promiscuous complicity between the different forms of unreasonable social existence as 'a subterranean network which marks out something like the secret foundations of our modern experience of madness' (119).

This is, then, a distinctly different analysis from the one, recognizable in some historical work influenced by Foucault and sometimes mistakenly attributed to Foucault himself, which considers the category of mental illness as itself correlated with a practice of relabelling as insane individuals whose conduct is perceived as deviant.

A further and related set of difficulties concerns the whole question in Foucault's study of the relationship between madness and medicine. It is well known that Foucault represents the concept of mental illness as being comparatively recent in historical origin, constituted and made possible by a set of changes in thought and practice dating from the end of the eighteenth century. What he has not uncommonly been mistaken as arguing is that the advent of modern psychiatry is synonymous with the medicalization of madness, madness being a phenomenon which previous epochs and cultures had regarded as falling outside the sphere of specifically medical concern.

This is a surprising reading, in so far as extensive sections even of the abridged edition are concerned with developments in seventeenth- and eighteenth-century medical doctrines concerning insanity, and with the shifts in medical thinking which are among the preconditions of the alienists' subsequent reforms. But Foucault's position on this point cannot be appreciated without some account being taken of its complexity.

The simplest and most essential point to be made here is that it is *mental illness*, not *mental medicine*, which Foucault takes to be a comparatively modern concept. As he concisely put it in the 1962 version of *Maladie mentale et psychologie*, 'It was at a comparatively recent date that the West accorded madness the status of mental illness' (Foucault 1962: 76), even though 'in the West, there had always been medical treatment of madness and most of the mediaeval hospitals had, like the Hôtel-Dieu in Paris, beds reserved for the mad' (ibid.: 78).[4] What he sees as one of the crucial epistemological contrasts between European mental medicine up to and including the early modern period on the one hand, and the schools of moral treatment and alienism which prefigure modern psychiatry on the other, is that in the former period the medicine of madness is far from being either a separate or a marginalized topic, and is indeed substantially integrated, in terms of aetiology and therapy, within the corpus of general medicine. Somatic and mental treatments, scalp frictions and sea voyages, baths and theatrical performances are, within this conceptual framework, capable of being envisaged as compatible and complementary medical remedies for insanity. Conversely, what according to Foucault is a constitutive feature of the forerunners of modern psychiatry is the formation of a specialist branch of medicine whose epistemological texture is, notwithstanding certain superficial appearances, quite distinct from that of contemporary general medicine; and in which older medical correlations between the mental and the somatic are either severed or radically reinterpreted.

In this connection it is desirable to notice Foucault's distinctive position on a topic which is arguably one of the most underexamined epistemological myths of the history of the human sciences, namely Cartesian dualism. The belief that Descartes's philosophy inspired or articulated what was to become a pervasive mind–body dichotomy in modern western culture has been a leading tenet in many currents of recent critical thought, including critiques of psychiatry: one of psychiatry's pernicious characteristics, along with its objectivizing, asocial, individualistic and scientist tendencies, being, according to this view, its share in our failure to achieve a medicine of the whole person.

Whatever the philosophical merits of this position, its applications as a perspective of intellectual history lead to highly questionable results; it has also inspired some drastic misunderstandings of Foucault.[5] His own divergence from this analysis is stated in *Madness and Civilization* (181–3):

> It is thus not possible to use as a valid or at least meaningful distinction for the classical period the difference – immediately apparent to us – between physical medications and psychological or moral medications . . . The heterogeneity of the physical and the moral in medical thought is not a result of Descartes' division of substances; a century and a half of post-Cartesian medicine did not succeed in assimilating that separation on the level of problems and methods, nor in understanding the distinction of substances as an opposition of organic to psychological. Cartesian or anti-Cartesian, classical medicine never introduced Descartes' metaphysical dualism into anthropology. And when the separation did occur, it was not by a renewed loyalty to the *Meditations* but by a new privilege accorded to transgression. Only the use of punishment distinguished, in treating the mad, the medications of the body from those of the soul. A purely psychological medicine was made possible only when madness was alienated in guilt.

There is, moreover, scope for a reappraisal of the real extent and meaning of 'Cartesian dualism', not only in the thought of the period as a whole, but within the Cartesian philosophy itself, especially in its applications to medicine and morality. Descartes says in the *Discourse on Method* that 'if it is possible to find a method that would make men wiser and cleverer than they have been, I believe that it is in medicine that it must be sought'. His reason for subsequently admitting to a 'partial failure' in this area was, as the eminent commentator Martial Guéroult has noted, 'the growing conviction that purely mechanistic notions could not suffice for explaining medicine, the human body being not solely pure extension, but also psychophysical substance' (Guéroult 1953: 247, 248, 252). The *Treatise on the Passions*, in which Descartes states that 'it is necessary to know that the soul is truly joined to the whole body', offers, as Guéroult remarks, 'a moral doctrine drawn from knowledge of essentially psychophysical facts: the passions', which 'thereby constitutes a veritable treatise on the substantial union' of the human body and soul. From this one might reasonably infer that the apparently un-Cartesian traits which Foucault notes in eighteenth-century medicine are in fact not particularly remote from or alien to the tendency of Descartes's own thought.[6]

In any event, Foucault's extended treatment of the mental medicine of the classical age makes it abundantly clear that he regards medical concern with madness neither as a historical novelty of modernity nor, in itself and in general, as a philosophically problematic activity. The point made by his commentaries on the reforms of Pinel and Tuke and their successors is that these represent not so much medicalizations of madness as medicalizations of interment. Foucault does not overlook the widespread existence in medieval and early modern Europe of institutions providing specific care and treatment for the insane. What he identifies as the crucial innovation effected by Pinel and Tuke is not the provision of a therapy for the insane within special institutions, but more precisely the invention of a type of institution where therapeutic efficacy is invested in the practice and personnel of internment themselves (455–7).[7]

Disobliging as Foucault's portrait of these early alienists may well seem, its point is immediately lost if it is blurred into that of a polemic against medical rationalism, or indeed western reason *per se*: an 'insufficiently dialectical critique of Enlightenment', in the words of Klaus Dörner, paraphrasing Habermas. Nothing becomes more increasingly apparent from a reading of Foucault's full text than the peculiar inappropriateness of this latter reproach. A recurring topic in Foucault's later writing is the perception that the posing by Kant and others of the question 'What is enlightenment?' marks the beginning of a new philosophical preoccupation with the decipherment of a present moment, a new style of time-related reflexivity (Foucault 1984, 1986; Gordon 1986a). In *Histoire de la folie* (383ff), Foucault illustrates a similar kind of reflexive consciousness at work in eighteenth-century notions on hysteria, hypochondria, nerves and vapours, where certain classes of mental ailment are seen specifically as ills of modernity and its vices. Foucault also notes here an early contemporary perception of a theme taken up by more recent historians, that the disenchantment of the world brings with it new hazards for the mental health of the devout (387–9). A new and more subtle sensibility to the problematic of unreason thus appears here as one of the fruits of critical culture. Also to be found in the French edition is an extended discussion (363–72) of Diderot's posthumously published fiction, *Rameau's Nephew*, which could serve as a sufficient refutation, if one were necessary, of the view that the Enlightenment is identical for Foucault with a self-complacent banishment of the possibility of an unreason internal to reasonableness itself.

In a more general way, and to borrow a term from Foucault's last writings, the classical age appears in *Histoire de la folie* as being, in its transactions with the question of madness, fundamentally an age of *problematization*. The manner in which the eighteenth century came to recognize the public treatment of the insane as a problem of morality and policy exemplifies, in his analysis, the interconnection of questions of governmental rationality and questions of the social organization of subjectivity: the linkage, to put it in the terms of his later investigations, between the macrophysics and the microphysics of power. The great internment which enfolded and juxtaposed in its confines destitute pauperism, insanity, and the multiple forms of unreasonable, scandalous and disorderly individuality embodied both an economic policy and a conception of the state's policing interest in public morality. Its practical workings, as Foucault was to show more fully in his essay on the Bastille archives, 'Lives of infamous men' (Foucault 1977) and (with Arlette Farge) in the documentary volume *Le désordre des familles* (Foucault and Farge 1982), created a curious tête-à-tête, peculiar to the *ancien régime*, between the majesty of royal authority and the humble protagonists of domestic and familial strife. This regime came in question both through the general discredit of monarchical power and the specific denunciation of the institutions of internment and the *lettres de cachet* as symbols of despotism. *Histoire de la folie* anticipates *Birth of the Clinic* and *Discipline and Punish* in its account of the medical and economic criticisms of internment, the fearful fascination exercised by the Bastilles and their occupants, and the simultaneous profusion of utopian proposals for new institutions of correction, 'the best of all possible worlds of evil' (448–51).

Foucault emphasizes here a point later developed in *The History of Sexuality*, Volume I, and his work on governmental rationalities, namely the profound transformation of thinking on government prompted by the idea that the object of governmental activity is a *population* (429, 430, 432). Thus, Turgot commends domiciliary assistance and *laissez-faire* as the most efficient form of state medical and social policy, on the basis of a Humean calculus of the forces of sympathy within a population serving to demonstrate that these operate most strongly over short ranges (435–7). 'Economists and liberals consider that a *social duty* means a *duty of man in society*, rather than a duty of society itself' (435). Foucault suggests that this new doctrine of 'liberty as assistance' (the proposal of deinstitutionalized policies of public health and public assistance) helps to make practicable and thinkable the idea of 'internment as medicine' which legitimates a new and public role for mental medicine (the invention of new forms of specialized institutional care, purged of the discredit attaching to the older, polyfunctional internment apparatus).[8]

Foucault's overall analysis both of the conditions of possibility of this new 'moral treatment' of the insane and of its meaning is arrived at by way of his consideration of the internal discrepancies and discontinuities within the classical age's practical experience of madness. One of the deepest of such discontinuities is the extensive decoupling of the practice of administrative internment from the domains of both medical and legal expertise. Administrative internment by reason of insanity was in general non-medical in purpose, but the procedures of admission involved a form of written categorization of the interned person's condition. Foucault's study of this documentation (409–14) concludes that it demonstrates a set of nosological categories different from those current in the medical literature of the same period, and characterized by its elaboration of a set of classifications of disorders in terms of the degree and form of their dangerousness to public order: notions which, according to Foucault, were to have a stronger formative influence on the alienists' moral treatment than the medical doctrines of the doctors. (This archaeological focus on a *'perception asilaire'* in *Histoire de la folie* marks the beginning within Foucault's work, continued in *Birth of the Clinic*, *Archaeology of Knowledge* and *Discipline and Punish*, of what may be called an institutional epistemology which correlates the possibility of particular developments in systems of thought to the means of observation and registration afforded by special institutional sites and mechanisms.)

Administrative internment is, like the other functions of police in the *ancien régime*, a non-judicial process (though there also exists a different, legal procedure known as interdiction which serves to determine mental competence to exercise property rights). Legal medicine, based in a long tradition of canon law, with its complex assessments of the degrees of personal responsibility and juridical competence, suffers a decline in scope and prestige; by the end of the eighteenth century, Kant questions the very idea of a medical expertise regarding the legal determination of insanity (139–43). Medico-legal knowledge of the 'fine structures of civil liberty' yields influence, in Foucault's words, to the more abrupt and summary expertise embodied in the police power of internment, the 'coarse structures of social liberty' (145). It was one of the crucial tasks addressed by eighteenth-century moral and political thought to effect a rearticulation of these disparate registers and their respective ways of defining the juridical and the socio-administrative subject. 'The positivist medicine of the Nineteenth century is the heir to this whole effort of the Enlightenment' (146); 'the psychopathology of the Nineteenth century (and even, still, that of our own, perhaps) believes that its standpoint and activity can be situated relative to a *homo natura*, a normal man given prior to all experience of illness. In fact, this normal man is a creation; and its context is, if anything, not the space of nature but that of a system which identifies the *socius* with the subject of law' (147). The nineteenth-century concept of psychological alienation is, Foucault argues, only a product of 'the anthropological confusion of these two (juridical and social) experiences of alienation'.

This strand of analysis which examines the history of problematizations of subjectivity in terms of stresses and clashes between conceptual formations operative in different regions of social practice (here, the legal and the administrative) is perhaps one of the most interesting as well as least-discussed hypotheses developed in this book. In his 1976 lectures on the theme of governmental rationality, Foucault was to propose a closely related reading of the problem-field of the Scottish Enlightenment, centring on the difficulty of reconciling economic conceptions of the individual as a subject of interest with juridically oriented conceptions of political subjectivity framed in terms of contract and obedience; here, Foucault characterized the newly emerging notion of civil society as the synthetic concept designed to reconcile these discrepant orderings (Gordon 1986b).

In *Histoire de la folie*, Foucault presents the new formulae for the public care of the insane as conjoining a new way of conceptualizing individual normality with a promotion of forms of judgement (and scandal) proper to civic consciousness, reinterpreting mental cure as social rehabilitation. The reconstituted *raison d'être* of the institutions of public treatment is arrived at along 'a line of compromise between sentiments and duties – between pity and horror, assistance and security' (453). It should be noted here that Foucault traces the parallel and partially similar psychiatric initiatives of Pinel and Tuke in some circumstantial detail to two quite different national windows of socio-political opportunity: in France, the Revolution; in England, the 1793 legislation dispensing friendly societies from the provisions of the Settlement Act, and the repeal of the Act in 1795 (484–91).

The alienist Pinel functions, in the French revolutionary and post-revolutionary context, as the deputee of sovereign, civic opinion, exercising the twin public-order roles which the Revolution vests in the citizen: 'at once "man of the law" and "man of government"' (465); the new expertise represents the harmonization of law and order, or rights, security and discipline. Foucault touches here on an enduring ambiguity of liberal polities which he was to re-emphasize in *Discipline and Punish* and *The History of Sexuality*. However, although he here indicates that the regimes of normalization subsequently elaborated in the nineteenth-century asylums and elsewhere can properly be understood as components in a political solution of problems formulated by the Enlightenment, he also signals at least one qualitative and morally significant discontinuity in this line of derivation. Nineteenth-century psychiatry does not, as some recent critiques have tended to argue, relapse into ignorance of, or indifference towards, the social dimension of its vocation. But its dominant image of the pathogenic social influences on mental health changes: where the eighteenth century incriminated urban luxury and idle affluence, the nineteenth denounces proletarian degeneracy and idle poverty. Foucault identifies in the medical thought of Morel an 'inversal of historical analysis into social critique' (398). The degenerate insane poor appear, not as casualties of progress, but as the detritus of evolution. Madness belongs now to the 'stigmata of a social class which has abandoned the forms of bourgeois ethics; and, at the very moment when the philosophical concept of alienation acquires a historical meaning through the economic analysis of labour, the medical and psychological concept of alienation frees itself totally from history, to become instead moral critique in the name of the compromised salvation of the species' (399).[9]

If the preceding rapid overview simply conveys the thought that, as Braudel and Mandrou judged in 1962, *Histoire de la folie* is a book which rewards careful study by historians, it will perform a more useful service than any commentary on the more polemical treatments which it has received in the intervening period. Nevertheless, I propose here to examine briefly one such critique whose theses have been copiously praised and repeated in the literature, namely H. C. Erik Midelfort's essay 'Madness and civilisation in early modern Europe: a reappraisal of Michel Foucault' (Midelfort 1980). Midelfort finds ground for extensive and damaging doubts as to the quality of Foucault's historical work. I shall summarize and comment on a few of his most important contentions, all of which have been repeated and elaborated by later critics.

Midelfort sees Foucault's arguments as being vitiated by a failure to consider some major epochs and episodes in the history of the European treatment of the insane ('recent research has shown the dangers of extrapol-ating from an idea, as Foucault does, without sufficient attention to chronological or regional differences' (256)). Thus 'Foucault is quite wrong in suggesting that [mental hospitals] were an invention of the early nineteenth-century reformers' (253): Europe's first hospital for the mad was founded by a Spanish friar at Valencia in 1409; 'such hospitals were a medieval Spanish invention, which probably explains their spread in fifteenth-century Spain and from there to all of Europe in the sixteenth and seventeenth centuries' (ibid.).

A second major European development which Foucault has 'completely overlooked' (257) is the extensive development in the eighteenth century of numerous purely private madhouses, especially in England: a fact which 'raises problems for his assumption that confinement of the mad by the state was uniform all over Europe' (ibid.).

Third, 'Foucault repeatedly implies that prior to the nineteenth century madness was not a medical problem but was regarded as either a condition having its own truth or as a reduction to brute animality' (257).

Fourth, in his treatment of an episode central to his narrative, Foucault 'clouds the perspective, first by accepting the story of Pinel's liberating the mad of Bicêtre from their chains and then by showing how hollow that liberation really was. Careful research has cast doubt on Pinel's famous gesture, showing that it may never have taken place at all and that far too many historians have remained content with the platitudes of psychiatric tradition' (258).

Midelfort is one of the few critics of *Madness and Civilization* who pay attention to the fact that it is an abridgement, and who cites from both its French and English editions. It is therefore doubly remarkable that Midelfort should repeatedly single out as major historical oversights committed by Foucault and fortunately rectified by subsequent research, events and episodes which receive explicit and detailed treatment in sections of *Histoire de la folie* missing from the English translation. There (133–9), Foucault enumerates and discusses at length the foundation of the Saragossa asylum, its numerous successor foundations in Spain, Germany, Sweden, Italy and England, its putative inspiration by medieval Islamic precursors and its acknowledged influence on Pinel (cf. also p. 358). As his footnotes indicate, all this information has already been assembled in histories of psychiatry compiled in the nineteenth century. Foucault also puts forward here (137–9) his reasons for considering that therapeutic institutions of this kind represent in the classical age the vestige of a declining tradition, rather than the model or precedent of subsequent innovations.

An almost identical comment can be made on Foucault's 'omission' concerning the new private and public madhouses created outside of France during the eighteenth century. At pp. 405–6 of the French edition Foucault enumerates and considers numerous foundations of this period in Germany, Austria and England (again citing nineteenth-century historians). He argues that these institutions cannot be regarded as precursors of the asylum for the reason that they make no more particular provision for medical treatment than the older public workhouses, *Zuchthäuser* and *hôpitaux généraux*, and moreover predate the currency of public demands for such provision. Foucault's arguments, both on this and the preceding issue, may be contestable. Before they are contested, however, they deserve to be read.

With regard to the existence in Foucault's eyes of a medical problem of madness prior to the nineteenth century, sufficient has perhaps already been said in the earlier part of this chapter. It is undoubtedly the case that Foucault adduces evidence that the status and treatment of the insane during these periods is not exclusively or even predominantly a medical one. It is also the case that the middle part of *Histoire de la folie* is given over to a treatise of nearly 200 pages in length on the mental medicine of the classical age.

Concerning Foucault's knowledge of and assumptions about the literal accuracy and reliability of the traditional stories of Pinel's liberation of the insane, one might, again, imagine that his words would speak unequivocally for themselves: 'images . . . familiar from all the histories of psychiatry'

(483), 'traditional tale' (496), 'myth' (497), 'legend' (497), 'chronicles of medical hagiography' (498), 'myth' (500), 'legends' (501). Foucault cites a refutation by a French historian, as early as 1889, of the historical authenticity of the received version of Pinel's exploit. One might think that Foucault could hardly have been more explicit and emphatic in signalling his intention neither to accept nor to debunk this material as putative fact, but to interpret its content and meaning precisely as a legend of foundation for the profession and institution which produced and used it. One may add that, prior to this commentary, Foucault also undertakes, on the basis of contemporary Revolutionary sources to clarify the terms of the ambiguous public and political mandate accompanying Pinel's appointment to Bicêtre.

One further set of objections raised by Midelfort may be mentioned in conclusion because of its vigorous subsequent popularity and its piquant illustration of the scholarly hazards of translation. *'Stultifera navis'* ('Ship of Fools') is the title of Foucault's opening chapter, alluding to a theme of literary compositions of around 1500 by Brant and other authors, illustrated by Bosch, Brueghel and Dürer. The chapter amounts to a short and wide-ranging prefatory fresco exploring the social and cultural meanings of madness in the late medieval and Renaissance epochs. There are substantial cuts in its translation. Midelfort's criticism is targeted on Foucault's claim that ships of fools really existed in late medieval Europe, in the sense that some German cities are recorded as having practised the forcible deportation by river transport of wandering madmen apprehended within their gates; that major pilgrimages of mad persons in search of their reason to shrines reputed for cures of this order were a common practice of the period; and, in a wider and more metaphoric sense, that the variable, erratic and ambiguous material condition and cultural-symbolic status of the medieval insane accommodated itself to an often nomadic form of existence.

Midelfort here launches with relish into a debunking commentary, depicting Foucault's chapter as a flight of rhapsodic fancy sharply at variance with the findings of serious researchers. There were no actual ships of fools. The substance of his difference with Foucault here appears to consist in the assertion that river-borne deportation is not documented as having been a systematic practice in the medieval treatment of the insane. This contention may well be correct, although the contrary is not asserted by Foucault. On the practice of pilgrimage Midelfort has nothing to say; other historians confirm them as having been current, widespread and prolonged over a number of centuries. Perhaps more telling is the evidence Midelfort marshals (249f) against the statement in *Madness and Civilization* that the medieval mad led an 'easy wandering life'. 'In the late Middle Ages and Renaissance, as recent work has shown, many of the mad were in fact confined to small cells or jails or even domestic cages, and not just to gate towers as Foucault suggests' (253): recorded instances abound from the period of physical restraint and harsh treatment of the insane.

Two points may be made about this criticism. First, Foucault himself cites, not indeed 'recent work', but historians writing in the nineteenth century on the existence of specific sites for the detention of the mad in 'most of the cities of Europe', and of the 'numberless Narrtürmer of Germany' (20; translation, 9); he also cites cases of mad persons being publicly whipped (21, 10). Second, Foucault did not in fact write the evocative and gleefully cited phrase, 'an easy wandering life', this being the product of a rare lapse by his translator. The French text is '*Les fous alors avaient une existence facilement errante*'[10] (19): 'the existence of the mad at that time could easily be a wandering one'. Whether it would be an easy life is, on Foucault's account of the matter, extremely dubious. Somewhat bizarrely, Midelfort uses the mistranslation in his main text and cites the original, without comment, in an accompanying footnote.

The extensive secondary documentation cited by Midelfort's essay, its seemingly comprehensive grasp of the specialist research literature, and its repeated invocations of 'careful' and 'recent' research, together (one may suspect) with the nature of its conclusions, have earned wide endorsement of Midelfort's essay and unrestrictedly credulous repetition of its claims by subsequent commentators on Foucault's book. Peter Sedgwick's *Psycho Politics* (1982) cites Midelfort as 'a brilliant analysis of Foucault's empirical deficiencies, using the full French edition and citing important Dutch and German sources', and proceeds to repeat the various criticisms discussed above. Sedgwick states, concerning the French and English versions of Foucault's book, that 'the full text has many important passages but these are not crucial to Foucault's argument'. His grounds for this latter assertion, other than an implicit reliance on Midelfort, are unclear, since his commentary proves that he could not have read the full text of Foucault's book.[11]

A review article by Lawrence Stone covering recent studies of the history of insanity and related topics (Stone 1982) opens with an extensive polemic against Foucault's work, which is described as providing 'a dark vision of modern society which accords with only some of the historical facts'. Stone states that many of his objections to *Madness and Civilization* are those raised by Midelfort. Foucault responded to these criticisms in some detail, his reply being accompanied by a further riposte from Stone (1983), belabouring Foucault's arrogant refusal to accept criticism of his work. One of Foucault's conclusions is that a number of Stone's historical reproaches 'consist in repeating what I said while pretending I never said it', while most of the others 'consist in turning round, word for word, what I said and ascribing to me the subsequent [*sic*] thesis which has become untenable' (Foucault 1983: 42). Foucault supports his rebuttal with numerous page references to the second French edition of 1972, many of which are to passages absent from the translation. Regrettably, perhaps, he does not consider the possibility that Stone may have read only the abridged edition.

Most recently, the discussion of *Madness and Civilization* in J. G. Merquior's volume on Foucault in the 'Modern Masters' series makes lavish use of Midelfort, Sedgwick and Stone, all of whom are endorsed and praised as reliable and independent scholarly witnesses (Merquior 1986). Foucault's response to Stone is not mentioned. The unabridged edition of this book is here described as 'a huge tome'; internal evidence confirms the impression that Merquior had not felt himself obliged to read this. His (very few) direct citations are all from the English edition, of which it may be said that he provides a résumé considerably briefer and more perfunctory than his accounts of the secondary literature on it.

In fairness, it should be added that Midelfort's essay has not only impressed critics such as Sedgwick, Stone and Merquior whose position is broadly hostile to Foucault's work. Ian Hacking, one of Foucault's most perceptive and generous English-language commentators and one of the very few English-speaking philosophers who has done work on the history of systems of thought comparable in perspective to Foucault's, remarks, *pace* Midelfort, that: 'Scholars remind us that the facts are vastly more complex than what Foucault describes. His predilection for French examples projected onto European history leads to mistakes' (Hacking 1986: 29). This is perhaps a good index of the extent to which the latter structure on Foucault has gained almost universal currency and credence. Foucault's short response to Stone on this specific point bears quotation.

> You argue that 'there are enormous differences in the degree and organisation of incarceration from country to country', England specialising in private institutions and France in state-supported ones. Now, on pages 67–74 and 483–496, I insist on the pronounced differences between a country like France and a country like England where religious organisation, legislation, institutions and attitudes provide much more scope for private initiative; I point out, in particular, the long tradition with which Tuke is in keeping and which evolved throughout the eighteenth century. Nevertheless, you are wrong in thinking that everything in France was state-controlled.
>
> (op. cit.: 42)

What lessons, if any, should be drawn from the history of the reception of *Histoire de la folie*, in terms either of the general standards of academic debate and commentary or of the specialist perspectives of work on the history of insanity, are questions on which interested readers may perhaps be left to drawn their own conclusions. But one response perhaps needs to be anticipated and examined. While the criticisms covered here may be disputed in significant areas, and while the scholarly practice of the critics cited may in places appear to fall demonstrably short of the rigorous canon of professional standards which they themselves are rather sententiously apt to invoke, it may be argued that they are at least justified in seeing *Histoire de la folie*, in its literary, aesthetic and philosophical aspects, as something other than a work of historiography in the conventional sense of the term; that Foucault's relation to his material is in places a palpably romantic one; and that his book's quixotic view of the relation between madness and reason marks it as both inescapably vulnerable to sober criticism and a product of youthful impetuosity which its author was subsequently obliged more or less candidly to repudiate.

The best that a brief review of these themes can do is to show that here, again, misfortune has decreed that things are more complicated, and the facts more elusive, than they might appear. To resolve some confusions it is necessary to turn not only to the French text, but to the text of a preface to the first French edition deleted by Foucault from the 1972 reprinting, a preface which in literary terms is certainly among the most remarkable things Foucault wrote, and of which certain fragments have had a problematical afterlife in the secondary literature. In his widely discussed critique of *Histoire de la folie*, Jacques Derrida cites and glosses a passage from this preface which has been afterwards repeatedly cited in turn by others (Derrida 1967). The passage deals, precisely, with the original, declared intention of Foucault's book. 'In writing a history of madness', Derrida writes, 'Foucault wanted – and this is the whole preciousness, but also the very impossibility of his book – to write a history of madness *itself*. *Itself*. Of madness itself . . . "A history, not of psychiatry", Foucault says, "but of madness itself, in its vivacity, before all capture by knowledge" ' (56). Directly after this passage cited by Derrida, however, Foucault's preface continues: *'But no doubt that is a doubly impossible task'* (vii: emphasis added): doubly impossible, he explains, because it would be an attempt to retrieve sufferings whose traces are now obliterated; and because 'the perception which seeks to seize them in their wild state necessarily belongs to a world which has already captured them'. (The immediately following sentences which develop this remark contain a passage which Derrida cites as illustrating the 'dense beauty' of Foucault's writing; in fact the passage is a quotation, set by Foucault between inverted commas, from the poet Réné Char's *Fureur et mystère*.[12]) Directly following, in turn, this recognition of double impossibility, Foucault continues: *'To do the history of madness will therefore mean:* to make a structural study of the historical ensemble – notions, institutions, juridical and police measures, scientific concepts – which hold captive a madness whose wild state can never in itself be restored; but, short of this inaccessible primitive purity, structural study must ascend back to the decision which at once joins and separates reason and madness; it must strive to discover the perpetual exchange, the obscure common root, the originary affrontment which gives meaning to the unity as much as to the opposition of sense and the senseless' (vii: emphasis added). Foucault qualifies the 'decision' which is thus to be investigated as 'heterogeneous to the time of history, but ungraspable outside of it'.

Derrida's account of this strategic passage in Foucault's preface with its reasonably straightforward tripartite structure (initial formulation of intent;

recognition of its possibility; second, different and actual project) is sufficiently tortuous as to have led more than one commentator to credit Foucault with the opposite of his real intention: John Frow writes, in *Marxism and Literary History* that 'What Foucault attempts to do in *Histoire de la folie* is "to write a history of madness *itself*" ' (Frow 1986: 215). J. G. Merquior and Peter Dews (24) cite these words as though they encapsulated Foucault's project in this book (Merquior 1986: 26; Benjamin 1989). Allan Megill writes that Foucault 'proposes to write a history "not of psychiatry, but of madness itself, in its vivacity, before any capture by knowledge" ' (Megill 1979: 478). Such slips might perhaps be explained simply by the critics' lack of access to the 1961 text, were it not that it is strictly impossible to find in Foucault's book anything remotely resembling a 'history of madness *itself*'. As a failure of basic critical understanding of what *Histoire de la folie* is actually about, this merits comparison with Peter Sedgwick's objection that 'Foucault never presents an intelligible account of any particular psychological syndrome'.

Another red herring generated by Derrida's commentary is the idea that what Foucault means by the 'originary affrontment' of reason and unreason is an initial historical event presumed to coincide with the starting-point of the historical narrative of *Histoire de la folie* – a reading which adds a potent contribution to the subsequent critical muddle, touched upon above in relation to Midelfort, about Foucault's treatment of the Middle Ages. Derrida here enters into a critique of Foucault's offhand treatment of the Greeks, and of what he perceives as Foucault's antiphilosophical solecism of positivistically historicizing the transcendental, a move which Derrida denounces somewhat heatedly as an a priori of violence and forced confinement in general (88). But the word 'originary' (*originaire; ursprunglich*) is not used, here or elsewhere, by Foucault in a chronological sense; his juxtaposed phrase, 'perpetual exchange', as well as the qualification 'heterogeneous to the time of history', would by itself tend to preclude such a reading; the 'obscure common root' of the duality of reason and unreason is not localized by the thesis of his book in any single historical epoch; and the Middle Ages are not – different though their cultural experiences of madness may indeed, according to Foucault, have been from those of subsequent periods – characterized in *Histoire de la folie* as such an epoch.

Foucault responded in his second (1972) edition to the section of Derrida's essay dealing with his interpretation of Descartes, but did not there address the matters mentioned here regarding the 1961 preface; instead, and for reasons apparently unrelated to Derrida's commentary, he removed that preface. *The Archaeology of Knowledge* (1969) contains a self-critical statement, which Foucault describes as 'written against an explicit theme of my book *Madness and Civilization*, and one that recurs particularly in the Preface', that 'We are not trying to reconstitute [historically] what madness itself might be' (47). This reads as though Foucault himself felt the force, or at least the ingenious plausibility, of Derrida's account and critique of his earlier intentions; a number of barbed allusions to Derrida's philosophy can be found in the *Archaeology* and the subsequent *L'Ordre du discours*. In fact, Foucault's shift of position between 1961 and 1969 is far less drastic than he here implies, or than others have inferred: it amounts to a change of accent, not one of metaphysical doctrine or investigative practice. In 1961, 'madness itself' is considered a meaningful and compelling, yet practically infeasible object of direct historical investigation; in 1969 it is still acknowledged as being, at least in principle, a possible object of inquiry ('Such a history of the referent is no doubt possible'), but set aside as a distraction from the specific programme of Foucault's archaeologies of discursive practices. (The term 'archaeology of knowledge' is, incidentally, already used in *Histoire de la folie* (265).)

Two other retrospective remarks by Foucault have influenced commentary on *Histoire de la folie* to a more than strictly justifiable degree. He writes elsewhere in *The Archaeology of Knowledge* that 'Generally speaking, *Madness and Civilization* accorded far too great a place, and a very enigmatic one too, to what I called an "experience", thus showing to what extent one was still close to positing an anonymous and general subject of history' (16, translation amended: Alan Sheridan here renders '*expérience*' as 'experiment'). In the later 1970s Foucault moved towards a form of analysis which emphasized the productive effects of relationships of power, as contrasted with what he criticized as having been his own earlier tendency, adequate to his task in *Madness and Civilization* but unsatisfactory as a perspective for, notably, a history of sexuality, to consider the operations of power as predominantly negative and repressive in form.

So far as the first point is concerned, one may notice the mild irony that it is precisely the perceived absence from Foucault's earlier analyses of experiences and subjects which made his work partially acceptable among some English Althusserians, and (in consequence) emphatically unacceptable to the English social historian E. P. Thompson (1978). In fact, the terms 'experience of madness' and 'experience of unreason' abound in *Histoire de la folie* (nearly always used in the sense of 'the existence of madness as experienced by the sane or reasonable subject'). But their use cuts almost perpendicularly across most recent battle-lines of vocabulary, in that the experiences in question are presented and analysed in terms of *structure*, or, rather, of structures (a point amply evident in the chapter 'Expériences de la folie'). These various experiences are indeed often formulated in terms of the anonymous and the general – as experiences of an epoch, the classical age; but 'general' here emphatically does not carry any connotation of homogeneity or unity: the only general and recurring structural trait in this account is dividedness (albeit that the thread of structural argument is here oriented towards explaining that trait, and not merely to describing it). Foucault's classical age is, in his own (Hegelian) words, an 'age of understanding' (189, 223) – and so an age of dialectics. Perhaps the term 'great internment' cannot but carry with it a certain image of massive and stony fixity; but the fact is that a historical object could scarcely be represented by a historian in less static or monolithic terms than is the experience in madness in the classical age by Foucault.

Two remarks may usefully be made about Foucault's uses here of the term 'experience'. The first is that they carry little connotation of any mantic intuition of essences. When Foucault talks here about depths, he is talking about deep structures, not accesses to hidden truths. To the (limited) extent that Foucault was ever a structuralist, he was one in 1969. The term 'experience' is used here largely in a sociological manner, almost indeed as a technical term of art; Foucault speaks, for example, of the juridical experience of madness and the medical experience of madness, to designate, in effect, the ways in which madness can be an object for different domains of social practice. The second point is that Foucault does not use a descriptive pluralism concerning the different experiences of madness as a means of access to a singular ontological substrate. There is no place within his analysis for such a notion as that of one particular and uniquely true experience of madness, and in Foucault's terms it is doubtful whether such an idea could have a meaning.[13] (It is true, however, that Foucault here takes a particular interest in one possible form of experience of madness which he calls the tragic, and which he represents as having been specifically excluded by the structures of experience in the classical age.)

With regard to Foucault's later thought about the analysis of power, it certainly cannot be denied that repression is a major and pervading topic in *Madness and Civilization*, and that the main historical mutation which it maps appears as a movement from one regime of repression of the insane to another (and that this has always been what has most antagonized its critics). But it should be added that not only is this, as Foucault remarks, an unobjectionable approach given the specific subject-matter of this work, but that it is very far from encapsulating the book's total approach. On the contrary, it might be said that *Histoire de la folie* illustrates rather convincingly that the repressive and the productive dimensions of certain forms of power cannot easily be disjoined. For, on Foucault's account, one of the central factors which make the modern psychiatric asylum possible is the revalorization of the practice of internment as an institutional form possessing an intrinsic and positive therapeutic capability: a milieu for the medical and moral government of the insane. Moreover, even in his discussion of the *ancien régime*'s carceral institutions there is an accent which seems directly to anticipate some of Foucault's ideas of fifteen years later, illustrating once again how a full reading of this book suffices to demolish every simple periodization of this thought: 'Internment played not only a negative role of exclusion, but also a positive role of organisation' (96).

Yet of course Foucault did change, and to overlook his extraordinary powers of inner perspective mobility is almost certainly to miss the heart of his philosophical legacy. I argue here only against the opposite error, the reduction of rich and singular achievement to the status of a preliminary or a stepping-stone. Perhaps there is not much of *Histoire de la folie* which can confidently be discarded as obsolete; but there is probably a good deal in it, little of which has been explored here, to which the present-day reader may prudently respond with hesitation, diffidence and perplexity. Perhaps some of the questions Foucault asks in 1961 are questions which we no longer ask – whether this is for better or worse being something we may be poorly placed to adjudicate. This seems most intuitively plausible with respect to the thread of ethical and ontological concern which runs intermittently through the text of *Histoire de la folie*, concerning our relations, past, present and future, with the fact of madness and the possibility of unreason. In the discarded 1961 preface, Foucault cited Nietzsche to the effect that the history of the West is founded in a refusal and forgetting of the tragic; his book intimates more than once that, since Nietzsche, our own time is being drawn towards a return of the tragic in the shape of a new dialogue or encounter with unreason. I do not know what the later Foucault would have made of this notion. Perhaps it could be shown that aspects of this set of concerns are not entirely absent from the framework of Foucault's later investigations of the ethical practices of antiquity. Perhaps literary critics will be able to trace a connecting path, by way of his citations from Char, between the style and temper of the younger and the older Michel Foucault.[14] Such themes need probably not disproportionately colour or preoccupy the reading of Foucault as a historian, by historians. But it is possible, and perhaps to be desired, that the historian and the philosopher may eventually find a common audience.

NOTES

1 Arabic numeral page references here are to this 1972 edition. Roman numeral page references are to the preface to the 1961 edition (Foucault 1961). The only difference I have been able to find between the main text of the first and second editions is the omission of a short footnote on Nietzsche's *Zarathustra* and the 'secret truths of man' (1961: 620; 1970: 537). In the original version of this essay, the 1961 title of Foucault's book was wrongly given as *Déraison et folie*. I am grateful to J. G. Merquior (1990: 40) for pointing out this error.

2 On the book's reception in France, see also Canguilhelm (1986) and Castel (1986).

3 See, for example, a number of the contributions to Ingleby (1981).

4 As Sheridan points out in his book *Michel Foucault: The Will to Truth*, the passages of this book which (in effect) summarize *Histoire de la folie* date from the 1962 revision only.

5 Notably by Peter Sedgwick (1982: 137–8). Sedgwick thinks Foucault's account of the mental medicine of the classical age is a critique of its Cartesian dualism.

6 A separate Cartesian issue in *Histoire de la folie* which can be only briefly noted here is the historical significance which Foucault attributes to Descartes's *Meditations* as a sign of the changing relation of reason to unreason in western thought, evidenced by the manner of Descartes's exclusion at the outset of the

philosophical venture, of the possibility of the philosopher's own insanity. What seems to emerge with greater clarity in the light of the appendix ('My body, this paper, this fire') which Foucault added to his second edition in response to a critique of this analysis by Derrida, is that his interest in Descartes is directed not towards a denunciation of Cartesian reason's self-absolutizing tendencies, but rather towards the cultural meaning of Descartes's investment of the activity of reason with the form of a regulated practice conducted by the reasoning self, a technique of meditation: a point which clearly prefigures the concerns of his last book. Cf. my discussion below of Derrida's essay.

7 This would seem to be the basis of a possible response by Foucault to a historical criticism by Klaus Dörner (1969). Dörner criticizes Foucault's neglect of the reforms undertaken at St Luke's Hospital in the mid-eighteenth century by William Battie, who introduced medical therapies into a public hospital for the insane. Battie's innovations do not represent a medicalization of the space of internment itself. Foucault notes (406) that by the 1790s, when Tenon visited St Luke's, its medical practices retained no notable progressive features. (Dörner's extremely stimulating and wide-ranging international survey has been contrasted in highly favourable terms with Foucault's work by several of the commentators discussed here.) The French sections of *Bürger und Irre* seem in places, if their replication of a number of Foucault's citations from Brissot de Warvill, Mirabeau and Récalde is anything to go by, to owe a considerable debt to *Histoire de la folie*.

8 Cf. the closely related discussions of technical critiques of hospitalization and custodial care in *Birth of the Clinic* and in 'The politics of health in the eighteenth century' (Foucault 1963; 1979).

9 On this theme see also Foucault (1978) and Pasquino (1980).

10 In the original version of this essay, this sentence was slightly mistranscribed, as '*Les fous avaient alors une existence facilement errante*'. I am grateful to Allan Megill for detecting this error (1990: 359, 347).

11 Sedgwick personally confirmed to me that this was the case.

12 '*La liberté de la folie ne s'entend que du haut de la forteresse qui la tient prisonnière. Or, elle "ne dispose là que du morose état civil de ses prisons, de son expérience muette de persecutée, et nous n'avons, nous, que son signalement d'évadée"*' (vii): 'Suzerain', in Char (1967: 19).

Foucault's attributed citation from Char in this preface (x: second epigraph to the present essay) precedes this passage by a few lines. The preface ends (xi) with a third citation from '*Partage formel*' (Char: ibid. 71): '*Compagnons pathétiques qui murmurez à peine, allez la lampe éteinte et rendez les bijoux. Un mystère nouvelle chante dans vos os. Développez votre étrangeté légitime.*'

13 Cf. Megill (1979: 477): for Foucault, 'a few great spirits . . . have had the true "experience of madness"'.

14 Foucault placed on the back cover of *L'Usage des plaisirs* and *Le souci de soi* this text from Char: '*L'histoire des hommes est la longue succession des synonymes d'un même vocable. Y contredire est un devoir.*'

BIBLIOGRAPHY

Benjamin, A. (ed.) (1989) *Problems of Modernity*, London: Routledge.

Canguilhem, G. (1986) 'Sur l'*Histoire de la folie* en tant qu'événement', *Le débat* 41: 37–40.

Castel, R. (1976) *L'Ordre psychiatrique*, Paris: Minuit; published in 1989 as *The Psychiatric Order*, Cambridge: Polity Press.

Castel, R. (1986) 'Les aventures de la pratique', *Le débat* 41: 41–50.

Char, R. (1967) *Fureur et mystère*, Paris: Gallimard/NRF.

Deleuze, G. (1986) *Foucault*, Paris: Minuit; published in 1988 as *Foucault*, London: Athlone Press.

Derrida, J. (1967) *L'écriture et la difference*, Paris: Seuil; published in 1978 as *Writing and Differernce*, trans. Gayatri Spivak, Chicago: Chicago University Press.

Dörner, K. (1969) *Bürger und Irre*; Frankfurt: Europäische Verlagsanstalt; published in 1981 as *Madmen and the Bourgeoisie*.

Febvre, L. (1973) *A New Kind of History*, ed. P. Burke, London: Routledge.

Foucault, M. (1961) *Folie et déraison: Histoire de la folie à l'âge classique*, Paris: Plon.

Foucault, M. (1962) *Maladie mentale et psychologie*, Paris: P.U.F.; a revised and retitled version of his *Maladie mentale et personnalité* (1954); published in 1976 as *Mental Illness and Psychology*, trans. Alan Sheridan, New York.

Foucault, M. (1963) *Naissance de la clinique*, Paris: P.U.F.; published in 1973 as *Birth of the Clinic*, London: Tavistock.

Foucault, M. (1972) *Histoire de la folie à l'âge classique*, Paris: Gallimard.

Foucault, M. (1977) 'La view des hommes infâmes', in *Les Cahiers du Chemin*, 29; published in 1979 in *Michel Foucault: Power, Truth, Strategy*, ed. M. Morris, P. Patton, P. Foss, trans. Meaghan Morris and Paul Foss, Sydney: Feral Press.

Foucault, M. (1978) 'The concept of the dangerous individual', *International Journal of Law and Psychiatry* 1: 1–18.

Foucault, M. (1979) 'The politics of health in the eighteenth century', in *Power/Knowledge*, Hassocks: Harvester.

Foucault, M. (1983) letter in *New York Review of Books*, 31 March 1983.

Foucault, M. (1984) 'What is enlightenment?', *The Foucault Reader*, ed. Paul Rabinow, New York: Random House.

Foucault, M. (1986) 'Kant on enlightenment and revolution', *Economy and Society* 15, 1.

Foucault, M. and A. Farge (1982) *Le désordre des familles*, Paris: Gallimard/Juillard.

Frow, J. (1986) *Marxism and Literary History*, Oxford: Blackwell.

Gordon, C. (1986a) 'Question, ethos, event: Foucault on Kant and enlightenment', *Economy and Society* 15,1.

Gordon, C. (1986b) 'The soul of the citizen; Max Weber and Michel Foucault on rationality and government', in Sam Whimster and S. Lash (eds) (1986) *Max Weber, Rationality and Modernity*, London: Allen & Unwin.

Guéroult, M. (1953) *Descartes selon l'ordre des raisons*, Volume II, *L'Ame et la corps*, Paris: Aubier Montaigne.

Hacking, I. (1986) 'The archaeology of Foucault', in David Couzens Hoy (ed.) *Foucault: A Critical Reader*, Oxford: Blackwell.

Ingleby, D. (ed.) (1981) *Critical Psychiatry*, Harmondsworth: Penguin.

Mandrou, R. (1962) (with a note by F. Braudel) 'Trois clefs pour comprendre la folie à l'époque classique', *Annales E.S.C.*: 761–72.

Megill, A. (1979) 'Foucault, structuralism and the end of history', *Journal of Modern History* 51 (September): 451–503.

Merquoir, J. G. (1986) *Foucault*, London: Fontana/Collins.

Midelfort, H. C. E. (1980) 'Madness and civilisation in early modern Europe: a reappraisal of Michel Foucault', in B. C. Malament (ed.) *After the Reformation, Essays in Honour of J.H. Hexter*, Philadelphia, Pa.: University of Pennsylvania Press, 247–65.

Pasquino, P. (1980) 'Criminology: the birth of a special savoir', *I&C7*, 'Technologies of the Human Sciences'.

Rosen, G. (1968) *Madness in Society*, Chicago: University of Chicago Press.

Sedgwick, P. (1982) *Psycho Politics*, London: Pluto Press.
Sheridan, A. (1980) *Michel Foucault: The Will to Truth*, London: Tavistock.
Stone, L. (1982) review article in *New York Review of Books*, 16 December 1982.
Stone, L. (1983) letter in *New York Review of Books*, 31 March 1983.
Thompson, E.P. (1978) *The Poverty of Theory*, London: Merlin.

Part II
Responses

2 Foucault and the psychiatric practitioner

Peter Barham

Histoire de la folie is, of course, much more than a contribution to this or that epoch in the history of psychiatry and not the least of its effects has been the threat it has provoked to the self-understanding and self-justification of the contemporary psychiatric practitioner. Foucault delivers a perspective on how the whole project of modern psychiatry is to be understood and assessed and, to judge from the history of critical reaction to his work, he did not appear to leave much space in which psychiatric practitioners could attempt to stake out a legitimate claim for themselves.

In large part, therefore, the debate around *Histoire de la folie* can be seen to focus a wider set of questions about the relationship between the history of madness and psychiatry and contemporary practices in relation to the mentally ill. How is the relationship between the history of psychiatry and the contemporary discipline of psychiatry to be conceived and understood? Is it a matter of the usurpation of the claims of one discipline by those of another, or is there a basis for cohabitation and mutual instruction? If, to borrow from Richard Rorty's jibe about philosophers (1980: 392), psychiatric practitioners of the modern era have claimed to know something about madness which nobody else can know so well, what forms of knowing can they now legitimately claim for themselves in the face of the deconstructions of the contemporary history of psychiatry?

Colin Gordon's moderate and differentiated account of *Histoire de la folie* is indeed helpful in embarking on a reappraisal of Foucault's contribution to the history of psychiatry, but he is perhaps guilty of wanting to load too much of the peculiarity of the work – and the reactions it has provoked – on the effects of selective translation and it is to be questioned, therefore, whether his effort at retrieval can altogether mitigate the perceived offence of the original work. Foucault may have chosen to suppress the original preface in the 1972 edition but its triumphalist spirit lives on in the body of the the text. The work concludes:

> Ruse and new triumph of madness: the world that thought to measure and justify madness through psychology must justify itself before madness, since in its struggles and agonies it measures itself by the excess

of works like those of Nietzsche, of Van Gogh, of Artaud. And nothing in itself, especially not what it can know of madness, assures the world that it is justified by such works of madness.

(Foucault 1967: 289; 1972: 557)

Those critics who recoiled against the impress of a seemingly timeless bourgeois rationality, the despotic effects of Reason on the vulnerable outpourings of Unreason, are unlikely to want to moderate their strictures in the face of Gordon's nuanced pleadings. As Foucault himself recognized, the reappraisal of *Histoire de la folie* must start from the circumstances of its original production – the time of its writing, the intellectual and emotional motivations that energize it – all of which are inseparable from the experience of the work. In a late interview Foucault was asked about the emotional undercurrent of outrage and sadness in the book:

Each of my works is a part of my own biography. For one or another reason I had the occasion to feel and live those things. To take a simple example, I used to work in a psychiatric hospital in the 1950s. After having studied philosophy, I wanted to see what madness was: I had been mad enough to study reason; I was reasonable enough to study madness. I was free to move from the patients to the attendants, for I had no precise role. It was the time of the blooming of neurosurgery, the beginning of psychopharmacology, the reign of the traditional institution. At first I accepted things as necessary, but then after three months (I am slow-minded!), I asked, 'What is the necessity of these things?' After three years I left the job and went to Sweden in great personal discomfort and started to write a history of these practices.

(Martin 1988: 11)

In his later writing Foucault came to recognize the need for a new set of bearings on the project in which he had been engaged in *Histoire de la folie*. He indicated a direction in an interview in 1983:

I would like to do the genealogy of problems, of *problematiques*. My point is not that everything is bad, but that everything is dangerous, which is not exactly the same as bad. If everything is dangerous, then we always have something to do. So my position leads not to apathy but to a hyper- and pessimistic activism . . . I think that the ethico-political choice we have to make every day is to determine which is the main danger.

He gives as example the critique by Robert Castel and others of the anti-psychiatry movement:

I agree completely with what Castel says, but that does not mean, as some people suppose, that the mental hospitals were better than anti-psychiatry; that does not mean that we were not right to criticize those mental hospitals. I think it was good to do that, because *they* were the danger. And now it's quite clear that the danger has changed. For instance, in

Italy they have closed all the mental hospitals, and there are more free clinics, and so on – and they have new problems.

(Rabinow 1986: 343–4)

Not bad, but dangerous. That marks a real shift in emphasis from the experience of *Histoire de la folie*, for the whole thrust of that book was to say that everything about the modern project of psychiatry was irretrievably bad. It did not leave any space for alternative forms of intervention, nor did it invite the differentiated judgements which might engender such a space. Foucault's perspective could hardly be said to have provided any grounds for social hope in our dealings with the mad. As Colin Gordon acknowledges, the operations of power in *Histoire de la folie* are predominantly negative and repressive, and the significant historical mutation which Foucault maps 'appears as a movement from one regime of repression to another' (Gordon 1990: 22). In mitigation, Gordon suggests that what we find conjoined in Foucault are not merely the repressive but also the productive dimensions of power. Yet power in its productive aspect signifies only an evaluation of the 'practice of internment as an institutional form possessing an intrinsic and positive therapeutic capability: a milieu for the medical and moral government of the insane' (ibid.).

In *Histoire de la folie* Foucault entertained a curiously innocent and untamed conception of madness. There is no sense of a residual reasonableness or sociability internal to the doings and beings of mad people, the struggles of the disturbed to secure recognition for themselves as intelligible agents not entirely dispossessed of their faculties. The re-entry of the lunatic into rationality is made to appear as a form of capture, a matter of what was put there or instilled, rather than the rediscovery of what was already there to be found. In the preface to the original edition of *Histoire de la folie*, Foucault eschewed the project of a history of 'madness itself, in its vivacity, before all capture by knowledge'. To attempt to retrieve the sufferings of the mad was, he declared, impossible because the 'perception which seeks to seize them in their wild state necessarily belongs to a world which has already captured them' (Foucault 1961: vii). For all the nuanced variations in Foucault's treatment of the modern experience of insanity, repression is nonetheless endemic to it and understanding is invariably represented as a form of capture or assault.

Foucault certainly attests to the reality of madness, but there was evidently nothing to be done here. All that could be hoped for was the resistance of Unreason – Unreason going its own way, and destroying itself, in the triumph of its refusal to be tamed. And it is then hardly surprising that *Histoire de la folie* should have lent itself to an appropriation in which, as Castel describes, 'madness became the paradigm for a subjectivity freed from the constraints of social adaptation, a kernel of authenticity that had to be preserved or rediscovered without making concessions to the established order' (Castel 1990: 29).

Madness is represented only in its 'otherness', as though in his theoretical discourse Foucault wanted to reproduce the abolition of dialogue for which the history of psychiatric rationalization was responsible. To attempt to show that it is feasible to engage with the mad, that the history of madness admits of alternative constructions of the mad as historical agents, what could this be but another form of capture? When he wrote *Histoire de la folie* Foucault seemed to want to retain the purity and integrity of madness, even at the expense of excluding the mad from our understanding, and thus of reproducing and confirming the exclusion that had already been inflicted on them.

Dominick LaCapra intriguingly suggests that Foucault 'at his most provocative writes neither from the side of the mad nor from that of the sane but from the problematic margin that divides the two' (LaCapra 1990: 36). Yet, as he goes on to acknowledge, the recurrent danger in Foucault's text is 'the tendency to sacrifice an attempt to regenerate a tense interaction between legitimate limits and hyperbolic transgression in deference to an unrestrained aesthetic of the transgressive sublime' (LaCapra 1990: 37). In Foucault's reconstruction of his project, there is 'always something to be done', but the aesthetic longings of *Histoire de la folie* were hardly an incentive to busyness. Foucault's integrity appeared to pride itself on the absence of role – 'for I had no precise role' – and the work delivers no conception of a feasible grounded project through which psychiatric practitioners and the mad could come to reconsider each other, no basis for the historical renewal of the broken dialogue between madness and reason.

Yet where does the alternative perspective of dangers lead us? The implication behind the appeal to dangers is that there is indeed something to protect. But what, from Foucault's perspective, could that be? To make the shift from bad to dangerous is necessarily, as Foucault recognized, to dispense with the sullen, obdurate conception of rationalization that permeates *Histoire de la folie* – 'the word rationalization', he came to judge, 'is dangerous' (Dreyfus and Rabinow 1982: 210) – in favour of the study of specific rationalities. Yet it is also, perhaps, to do something else besides. In Foucault's later writing there is a developing preoccupation not merely with the objectification of the subject in dividing practices but also with what he came to term 'technologies of the self', the ways in which a human being turns himself or herself into a subject. And it is here perhaps that, turned back on the history of madness, we can begin to detect an approach that yields more promise. If in much of Foucault the modern subject appears to be an artificial production of modernity, an agent of self-discipline and containment, his later writing accords more respect for the struggles of historically located subjectivities in their encounter with the 'government of individualization'.

Yet if we can detect the seeds of a more promising approach, they are poorly developed. In his intemperate attack on Foucault, first published in the *New York Review of Books*, Lawrence Stone held Foucault accountable for the discharge of patients from State hospitals onto the streets of New York (Stone 1987). Critics such as Andrew Scull have been right to accord this the dismissal it deserves (Scull 1988), but it must be admitted that Foucault has not been much help to us in the task of thinking through the issues that are raised by the contemporary project of closing the asylum. Foucault made much of the *'perception asilaire'* that excluded the mad from our understanding, but it is less apparent that there was for Foucault behind the authoritative pronouncements of the asylum regime an agent to be recovered or an individual to be understood.

Some of the most interesting approaches in the history of madness have been those that have attempted a view from below and helped us to see that, whatever may be wrong with the mad, they can nonetheless in important measure be understood as historical agents trying to make their way in a field of social and cultural forces (MacDonald 1981; Porter 1987).[1] But to do this kind of work, and to attempt to describe how real men and women thought and acted, requires, as Michael MacDonald has remarked, that we get beyond the confrontation between abstractions characteristic of Foucault (1981: xi). From this point of view, the challenge of the history of psychiatry to the practitioner is to show that the practitioner does not know his subjects as well as he thinks.

Contrary to the image of the grinding machinery of psychiatric naturalism, the modern experience of insanity has in reality given rise to a much more diverse and conflictual array of psychiatric traditions. To treat Foucault as a significant figure for the remembrance of a lost encounter between madness and reason that has been abolished by the history of rationalization is therefore quite misleading. In attempting to grasp the type of rationality through which the broken dialogue between madness and reason might be capable of renewal there is more to be gained from a close reading of the writings of, say, the Swiss psychiatrist Manfred Bleuler than from Foucault.[2] Foucault has certainly proved an inspiration to the demolition of established orthodoxies, but his animus against the achievements of modernity has meant that it has often been difficult to retain the important questions in sharp focus. A reassessment of *Histoire de la folie* is welcome but, in determining the dangers that confront us today, it is not obvious that Foucault is a particularly helpful guide.

NOTES

1 For a contemporary attempt to carry through this kind of project see Barham and Hayward (1991).
2 See Bleuler (1978) and for discussion Barham (1984).

BIBLIOGRAPHY

Barham, P. (1984) *Schizophrenia and Human Value*, Oxford: Basil Blackwell.
Barham, P. and R. Hayward (1991) *From the Mental Patient to the Person*, London: Routledge.
Bleuler, M. (1978) *The Schizophrenic Disorders: Long-Term Patient and Family Studies*, New Haven: Yale University Press.
Castel, R. (1990) 'The two readings of *Histoire de la folie* in France', *History of the Human Sciences* 3: 27–30.
Dreyfus, H. L. and P. Rabinow (eds) (1982) *Michel Foucault: Beyond Structuralism and Hermeneutics*, Brighton: Harvester Press.
Foucault, M. (1961) *Folie et déraison: Histoire de la folie à l'âge classique*, Paris: Plon.
Foucault, M. (1967) *Madness and Civilization*, London: Tavistock.
Foucault, M. (1972) *Histoire de la folie a l'âge classique*, Paris: Gallimard.
Gordon, C. (1990) '*Histoire de la folie*: an unknown book by Michel Foucault', *History of the Human Sciences* 3: 3–26.
LaCapra, D. (1990) 'Foucault, history and madness', *History of the Human Sciences* 3: 31–8.
MacDonald, M. (1981) *Mystical Bedlam*, Cambridge: Cambridge University Press.
Martin, R. (1988) 'Truth, power, self: an interview with Michel Foucault', in L. H. Martin, H. Gutman and P. H. Hutton (eds), *Technologies of the Self*, London: Tavistock.
Porter, R. (1987) *A Social History of Madness*, London: Weidenfeld & Nicolson.
Rabinow, P. (ed.) (1986) *The Foucault Reader*, Harmondsworth: Penguin.
Rorty, R. (1980) *Philosophy and the Mirror of Nature*, Oxford: Blackwell.
Scull, A. (1988) 'Keepers', *London Review of Books*, 29 September.
Stone, L. (1987) *The Past and the Present Revisited*, London: Routledge.

3 Madness, medicine and the state

Paul Bové

Not only is *Madness and Civilization* important for its being the first book of Michel Foucault's to deal explicitly with matters of power and institutional function in ways easily seen as continuous with his work in the 1970s, but it also stands out as a peculiar instance of the materiality of 'authorship' which, of course, was one of Foucault's central concerns. I am referring, of course, to the fact that *Madness and Civilization* has remained for more than twenty-five years the only available English version of *Folie et déraison: histoire de la folie à l'âge classique*, despite Foucault's presence among English-speaking academics.[1]

Dreyfus and Rabinow, in their defining study, *Michel Foucault: Beyond Structuralism and Hermeneutics*,[2] argue that in this book Foucault not only more explicitly discusses questions of causality and explanation than he does later – when he is more usually concerned to understand appearances and practices that produce the human sciences as we know them – but that he develops the book around a basic opposition between reason and what they call 'some fundamental form of Otherness' that grounds the possibility of reason and science (*SH*: 11). They also argue that 'Foucault associated himself with those rare and special thinkers who had a glimpse of the "sovereign enterprise of unreason" ' (*SH*: 11). In this reading they perhaps follow Michel Serres's comparison of Foucault's work to Nietzsche's *Birth of Tragedy*.[3]

Dreyfus and Rabinow develop an extended but conventional analysis of this text, yet, in so doing, they point an interesting direction for further study which they themselves do not develop. In the process of correctly insisting that Foucault grounds his later analyses in the body, they note how during this period he linked an understanding of ontology with the historicity of our human practices. They see this link as something better left behind for a more material method built around an understanding of the body as the object of discipline and ethics – 'giving publicly accessible concrete content to whatever remained of his temptation to find the ontological basis of our historical practices' (*SH*: 11). Without adopting their point that Foucault gave up his 'temptation' to ontological explanations, a discussion of which would lead us to Heidegger, we can take note of their perception that as early as 1961 Foucault hopes to study the basis of historical practices. This is important not because it is in any way an original perception, but because, in its very conventional correctness, it only partially illuminates Foucault's work of the time. Pursuing the question of ontology back to Heidegger's rethinking of 'history' would no doubt ground more rigorously what must be simply described as a feature of Foucault's interest in *Histoire de la folie* as well as *The Birth of the Clinic*.[4] In these two books from the early 1960s, Foucault takes up a profound concern with the relationship between history – as historical consciousness, as history writing, and as a form of knowledge – and the state, itself. Dreyfus and Rabinow note, apropos of *The Order of Things*, [5] that Foucault had an interest in the mid 1960s in matters of the state, specifically in the state's 'control over its inhabitants . . . as working, trading, living human beings' (*SH*: 139).

What is not so clear in Dreyfus and Rabinow's book, however, is that Foucault's interest in the state in relation to the problems of history exists from the early 1960s, although the topic seems not to have had much treatment in the Foucault scholarship. Following Dreyfus and Rabinow, most of Foucault's sympathetic readers have until now treated the problem of the state primarily in terms of his later work on governmentality or bio-power.[6]

Foucault has had, however, usually from the disciplines of History and Philosophy, a number of hostile readers.[7] Some of this hostility comes from fairly overt ideological objections as, for example, when Gadamer decries Foucault as some sort of proto-fascist for being an antimodernist. More of it, certainly in the United States, results from disciplinary formations, from Foucault's challenge to given orders of disciplinary knowledge.[8] For this reason, it should not be unexpected that insight into Foucault's difficult relation to the problems of history might appear in the work of those who have the most severe reservations about his writings. Often these antagonistic readers cannot get beyond their ideological and disciplinary predispositions to attempt, sympathetically, a careful reading of Foucault's work, as it is said in English, 'in its own terms'. But the issue here is not the disciplines as such, not yet. The issue rather is Foucault's early investigations into the formation of history in the age of enlightenment, at the time of the emergence of the state with its doctrine of *raison d'état*.

Although it is an uninteresting book, J. G. Merquior's *Foucault* conveniently instantiates the troubled insight that marks most of Foucault's Anglo-American trained enemies.[9] Interestingly, Merquior carries out his critique of Foucault's *Madness and Civilization* with reference to his essay, 'Nietzsche, Genealogy, History'. He heaps scorn on Foucault's praise for Nietzsche's contempt for 'the history of historians', with its pursuit of a transcendental point of observation. Foucault, like Nietzsche, adopts a genealogical model that blatantly accepts its perspectivism and its 'injustice'. Merquior's scorn arises from deep within his own enlightenment commitment to questions of determinate truth, to empiricism, and to conventional forms of historical judgement. Tired of being told that one misunderstands Foucault when one asks 'Does Foucault get his history right?', Merquior, like other historians – and he quotes Allan Megill on this point[10] – makes a conventional move against Foucault, one similar to that made on occasion by philosophers. This ploy involves asserting that, despite Foucault's 'intent' or 'plan', his work 'actually is' history or philosophy or whatever and so liable to indictment for being a failed or bad version of what it claims not to be.[11]

Merquior's version of this gambit is noteworthy only because it makes central to the discussion of *Madness and Civilization* the problem of Foucault's writing's relation to 'history'. Merquior typifies the common view that Foucault's work is 'anti-historical' but that *Madness and Civilization* is a failed and immature effort that does not get beyond 'counter-history' (*M*: 26). Foucault's project, Merquior would have it, was purely historical, an attempt to get at madness before it fell victim to psychiatry.[12] 'It is true', says Merquior, 'that later Foucault came to deny he was aiming at a reconstitution of madness as an independent historical referent – but there is no gainsaying that, *at the time*, he had a "normal" historiographic purpose in mind when he wrote *Madness and Civilization*' (*M*: 26).

Approaching Foucault's problematic indirectly, that is, by looking at some of the combined ideological, disciplinary and rhetorical moves that characterize a 'normal' or 'disinterested' professional's response to the writings of the early 1960s – approaching Foucault's problematic indirectly reveals fairly clearly – albeit only as a sketch – a set of issues at stake in those texts, without attempting to judge, for better or worse, their 'success' or 'efficacy'. Merquior, for example, is at haste to establish, like professional historians and those of a liberal ideological bent, that Foucault is writing history so that his work can be dismissed and so his critique of enlightenment discredited, *tout court*, by an appeal to what is already known and to the mechanisms for legitimating what is already known as it spreads itself to include 'new knowledge'. Merquior has rushed to deny the charge that one should not ask of his texts, 'Does Foucault get his history right?', by asserting that, in *Madness and Civilization* at least, Foucault's efforts were those of a standard historian: to set the record straight about madness. Merquior, however, also covers himself against a charge from some who might not find his assertion convincing by 'arguing' that, even if Foucault, like Nietzsche, is writing a "presentist" history', he is not released 'from his empirical duties to the data. On the contrary: in order to prove their point, present-centered *histoires à thèse* must try and persuade us of the accuracy of their reading of the past' (*M*: 26).

Having made these gestures to reinscribe Foucault's work into the disciplines of history where it can be judged and, of course, dismissed – along with its author – as uninformed and prejudiced, Merquior feels free to appeal to precisely the standards of historical knowledge and judgement which, by his own actions, he admits that Foucault's work puts in jeopardy. What is it that is put to risk? What does Merquior typically rush to defend? The short answer is the enlightenment – whatever we take that to mean. For Merquior, it seems to mean a commitment to rational enquiry, tested by empirical research, embodied, preserved and deployed in and from bibliographies, footnotes and the rest of the material apparatus that marks the existence of history as a discipline and established form and depository of knowledge and its reproduction.

Merquior goes on to show that Foucault gets his facts wrong, especially in comparison with a series of 'splendid' books by historians such as Sedgwick, Midelfort and Dörner: 'Sedgwick pulled the carpet from under several key assumptions in Foucault's historical picture . . . Midelfort has assembled a number of historical points which further undermine much of the ground of *Madness and Civilization* . . . he also evinces a formidable command of an impressive literature on the history of both madness and psychiatry [Midelfort's book is not 'splendid' but 'brilliant']. . . . Indeed, since 1969, we have the natural corrective to Foucault's Manichaean [sic] picture in Klaus Dörner's well-researched "social history of insanity and psychiatry" ' (*M*: 28–30).

There is something interesting in all this far beyond Merquior's personal inability to read Foucault carefully. What is at work is a defensive response to Foucault's strong challenge to the stories told of the histories of madness by those employing techniques which the 'enlightenment' legitimates. Merquior cannot simply ignore Foucault: not only because of Foucault's 'influence' – no doubt unjustified to someone of Merquior's predispositions – but also because that influence casts a critical eye on both the 'content' of histories and also on the very embedded legitimation processes within the practices of 'history' itself. Indeed, in both *Madness and Civilization* and *The Birth of the Clinic*, Foucault extends Canguilhem's critical ideas about the normal and pathological[13] to discuss some of the ways in which the production of historical knowledge can be seen as linked to the production of certain sorts of state formations, certain 'regimes of truth', as Foucault would later teach us to call them, and, of course, certain procedures of subject and truth formation. Dörner's book 'naturally' corrects Foucault's, for Merquior, because it shows that Foucault is not only wrong, having failed to consider such substantive and specific phenomena as 'the spread of preromantic sensibility', but that he 'offers "too one-sided" an account – one where the dialectics of Enlightenment is "unilaterally resolved in terms of its destructive aspect" ' (*M*: 31). The interest in this passage is obvious: putting Foucault into a sort of 'Frankfurt School' context, it becomes possible to condemn him, as Habermas does on occasion, for being an 'irrationalist', to deal with him, in other words, as an already known quantity, and thereby to extend the reach of a legitimated way of judging 'knowledge' to disarm one of its most severe critics. Curiously, Merquior, claiming to be an heir and defender of enlightenment and reason, would have the workings of thought stand still, would have the activity of critique suspended for the sake of the status quo within knowledge procedures – suspended within, to put it bluntly, stories that history tells about how important and beneficial certain forms of knowledge production are, especially as they have come to be called 'enlightened'.

Merquior represents, in other words, a betrayal of enlightenment as a critique of and engagement with the present – a turning away from Kant's efforts to answer the question, 'What is Enlightenment?', an effort replicated by Foucault; and as such a betrayal it calls to mind, most ironically in the context of Foucault's critique of dialectical thinking, a certain passage from Hegel's 'Preface' to *The Phenomenology of Spirit* which perfectly represents the kind of static knowledge and knowledge-producing apparatus one finds defending itself in Merquior's typically thoughtless work. It is 'typical' just in that it instantiates the characteristically repetitive and formalist nature of 'historical' inquiry:

> Regarding the contents, the others certainly sometimes make it easy enough for themselves to have *great spread*. They *drag a lot of material into their field, material that is already familiar and well ordered*. And when they deal preferably with the queer and curious, they only seem that much more to have firm possession of the rest which knowledge has long taken care of in its way, as if their mastery of the unruly came in addition to all this. . . . But when . . . it becomes manifest that [this comprehensiveness] was not attained insofar as one and the same principle differentiated itself into different forms, but it is rather the formless repetition of one and the same principle which is merely applied externally to different material and thus receives a *dull semblance of differentiation*. The idea, true enough by itself, remains in fact just where it was in the beginning as long as the development consists merely in such repetition of the same formula. When the knowing subject applies the one unmoved form to whatever is presented, and the material is *externally dipped into this resting element*, this is not, any more than arbitrary notions about the contents, the fulfilment of that which is in fact required – to wit, the wealth that wells forth out of itself and the self-differentiation of the forms. *Rather it is a drab monochromatic formalism that gets to the differentiation of the material solely because this is long prepared and familiar.*[14]

In 1821, Hegel was worried about the various tendencies, in Schelling and others, to construct disciplines of knowledge which defined knowledge by the already known, by a repetition formalistic in its embrace of the 'queer and curious' within orders of knowledge guaranteed as knowledge precisely by the fact that thought no longer moved within them. And, despite the anti-Kantian moments in the 'Preface', Hegel, in these critiques, can be seen to maintain the Kantian ideal of thought's engagement with the present as the essential characteristic of modern philosophy, of modernity itself.[15]

Hegel writes against precisely the 'thought-lessness' girding the work of Merquior and other defenders of the knowledge/power apparatus Foucault calls the 'regime of truth'. And in their wide-spreading stasis, they point towards important movements of thought in the early Foucault which, as Dreyfus and Rabinow's work indicates, sometimes even his favourable commentators have not pursued.

Madness and Civilization rests upon not only an often noted opposition between reason and unreason, but also a linkage of reason with state authority and so an opposition between the state and unreason. This implies as well an opposition between unreason and a certain set of notions of subjectivity and a certain set of notions of subjectivity as well as a certain linkage between that set and the state. Unpacking such a complex of issues thoroughly is beyond the ambition of this essay. Reading *Madness and Civilization* does, however, reveal some of these connections and complex binaries and so reminds us of the centrality of language to Foucault and, in so doing, points out why 'readers' such as Merquior cannot deal with his works: in the most literal sense, they pay no attention either to his writing or to the problem of language as such in his writing.

For example, writing of the 'imaginary landscape' which 'reappears' during the Great Fear and its confinements, Foucault carefully links his emphasis on the workings of power in the construction of 'fortresses' for the mad with the renewal of the problem of language; and he does this as preparatory to raising the problem of modernity itself: 'Sadism appears at the very moment that unreason, confined for over a century and reduced to silence, reappears, no longer as an image of the world, no longer as a *figura*, but as language and desire' (*MC*: 210). While this moment represents an important step in what has been described as Foucault's effort to bring madness back from silence, to 'free' or 'recover' its voice – and as such it has been objected to by Derrida who sees in it a certain transcendence[16] – it should also be read in context. When it is placed over and against the powerful 'historicizing' remarks that follow, we see that it is primarily an instance of Foucault's concern with the understanding of modernity:

> This awareness, however, has a very special style. The obsession with unreason is a very affective one, involved in the movement of icono-graphic resurrections. The fear of madness is much freer with regard to this heritage; and while the return of unreason has the aspect of a massive repetition, connecting with itself outside of time, the awareness of madness is, on the contrary, accompanied by a certain analysis of modernity, which situates it from the start in a temporal, historical, and social context.
>
> (*MC*: 212)

The Merquioran misprision depends, in one sense, upon not being able to read this passage. Foucault seems to be saying that 'madness' returns and

that he himself follows on a movement of the rediscovery of madness –
only, his work, against the medicalization that forecloses a listening to
unreason as an essential part of its work. It is not the case, however, that
this departure from a 'modernizing' tradition exemplified by medicine
commits Foucault to either an essentialist or transcendent position regarding such a thing as 'madness in itself'. There are more complex positions,
one of which he takes here.

It is clear, for example, that Foucault denies that the return of madness
he is discussing is a 'repetition'. He will not accept the essentialist ideal that
there is an identity of 'madness' across time nor an identity of cultural
productions for the representation of 'madness'. Furthermore, Foucault
has already completely denied that the return he means here is 'figural'.[17]
Language and desire replace *figura* as the modes of cultural production and
embodiment: in modernity, language displaces figuration.[18]

These taken together link Foucault's work to the problem of history
within modernity, or, to put it another way, indicate that in modernity
history is a problem in a new way, in a way inseparable from the problems
of language. *Figura* had maintained itself upon a religious basis, specifically
the Catholic notion of the Incarnation which, interestingly, provides a basis
for a certain notion of repetition, especially as imagined by Kierkegaard.
The problem of language within modernity is a movement away from the
Christian cultural structures – or perhaps a displacement – and towards a
modern schema of time that involves the simulacrum of repetition within
modernity's endless iteration of the new – which, of course, involves as well
the endless political, cultural production of 'discrete subjects' or 'individuals' as agents and authors.

Foucault finds in the awareness of madness not merely a sign or element
of modernity – although that is certainly there – but also that which characterizes modernity as a form of historical knowledge production, as a
cultural, political project determining to produce secular and so finite
knowledge as its legitimization.[19] Indeed, it is relatively clear that in this
passage Foucault's concern is not with 'madness', or even with the
'representations of madness', but rather, most importantly, with
modernity: attend to the awareness of madness because that awareness is
'accompanied by a certain analysis of modernity'. And, further, if we recall
the striking originality of Kant's insistence that enlightenment is marked by
philosophy's becoming a critical concern with the present – the very point
Foucault reiterates in his own comments on Kant's essay – then the force of
Foucault's comment appears more fully: it is the fact that an analysis of
modernity accompanies the awareness of madness 'which situates it from
the start in a temporal, historical, and social context'. *Figura*'s historical
force always requires that the present – for example, Christ's incarnation –
be seen as both a fulfilment and an anticipation of another event at some
other time; this commits history to its meaning outside time. The rejection
of figural interpretations or structures of history newly involves history

within temporality and so language as discourse; language as the embodying figuration of figural history's timeless patterns had nothing problematic about it. Strangely, language had no inherence in time; its temporality was a stasis fulfilled outside time in spatial repetition.

Foucault's work here marks the demise of that sort of spatial repetition and, we might say, the emergence of the problematics of modernity as the philosophical, literary problem of temporality which, at least potentially, subverts, from the start, the postulated englightenment discrete subject:

> In the disparity between the awareness of unreason and the awareness of madness, we have, at the end of the eighteenth century, the point of departure for a decisive movement: that by which the experience of unreason will continue, with Hölderlin, Nerval, and Nietzsche, to proceed ever deeper towards the roots of time – unreason thus becoming, *par excellence*, the world's *contratempo* – and the knowledge of madness seeking on the contrary ever to situate it ever more precisely within the development of nature and history. It is after this period that the time of unreason and the time of madness receive two opposing vectors: one being unconditioned return and absolute submersion; the other, on the contrary, developing according to the chronicle of a history.
>
> (*MC*: 212)

In a footnote to this passage, Foucault makes clear that the problem he discusses exists in the different forms time takes in the literary as opposed to scientific writings of madness/unreason. The awareness of unreason abrogates scientific time – the time which aims to contain it within the histories of madness and the sciences of nature – but it does not empty out time altogether. On the contrary, it 'deepens' time: 'it is not the absolute collapse of time. . . . It is a question of time turned back' (*MC*: 297).

Modernity, we might say, effects two forms of time but as science takes only one as its paradigm. That is, Foucault's work does not merely, as critics have often argued, prefer the time of poets to that of scientists, but it marks the profound emergence of the fact of time's agonistic being as a template for cultural existence as a fact of modernity itself. And, in so doing, it forms a fundamental challenge to the basic knowledge-regimes whose beginnings are roughly corollary to the awareness of unreason in the enlightenment. It forms a special challenge to the history writing of those disciplines which, it becomes clear, are constitutive products and producers of that modernity. At the beginning of the disciplines' efforts to produce scientific knowledge, to intervene in the world, to form subjects – in this case by medical means – and to write the record of the 'attempt to do these things', that is, to write the history of disciplines themselves as they are being established as legitimate – at the beginning, there is a necessary analysis of modernity itself. These disciplines are, as it were, aware of the traditionally ungrounded nature of their being; of their part in the revolution against traditional cultures; and, as well, of their being written into time and history in newly problematic ways not grounded on a secure figural foundation.

The disciplines' awareness of their own problematic stature, of the confusion of their origins, has often been forgotten by those disciplines themselves – as the Merquioran misunderstanding exemplifies. A symptom of that confusion is history writing. Finding themselves in 'a temporal, historical, and social context', the disciplines in general – no matter whether they study time or nature – develop, as Foucault says, 'according to the chronicle of a history'. That is, they write the story of their existence as a development understood as 'history'; or, to put the matter in a way that reverses apparent priorities, they invent history writing as a way of grounding their being in a context that has as given neither linguistic nor traditional societal legitimacy. Within a finite world, modernity demands its disciplines produce history, not merely to avoid the corollary temporality of unreason, but as part of the political, cultural struggle – embodied on the level of general material epistemology – to produce authoritative knowledge, institutions and political order within the society and within the new individual subjects they also help create.

In his rewriting of those analyses of modernity science carries out in studying its objects, Foucault does more than debunk the liberal or Whiggish myth generated as the story by modernity's secularizing, but progressive finitude; he also notes how the disciplines cannot legitimate themselves without producing histories of themselves which, as it were, always link the stories they tell to the central project of the state:

> Increasingly, a political and economic explanation was sought, in which wealth, progress, institutions appear as the determining element of madness. At the beginning of the nineteenth century, Spurzheim made a synthesis of all these analyses in one of the last texts devoted to them. Madness, 'more frequent in England than anywhere else', is merely the penalty of the liberty that reigns there, and of the wealth universally enjoyed. Freedom of conscience entails more difficulty than authority and despotism.
>
> 'Religious sentiments . . . [Foucault's elision] exist without restriction; every individual is entitled to preach to anyone who will listen to him' and, by listening to such different opinions, 'minds are disturbed in the search for truth'. Dangers of indecision, of an irresolute attention, of a vacillating soul! The danger, too, of disputes, of passions, of obstinacy: 'Everything meets with opposition, and opposition excites the feelings; in religion, in politics, in science, as in everything, each man is permitted to form an opinion; but he must expect to meet with opposition.' Nor does so much liberty permit a man to master time; every man is left to his own uncertainty, and the State abandons all to their fluctuations.
>
> (*MC*: 213–14)

*

Foucault concedes that when Spurzheim was writing, reactionaries found it easy to blame liberalism for all the world's ills. He prefers to draw our attention to the fact that Spurzheim's critique of liberty is less important than 'its very employment of the notion that designates for Spurzheim the non-natural milieu in which the psychological and physiological mechanisms of madness are favored, amplified, and multiplied' (*MC*: 214–15). This 'non-natural milieu' clearly includes the state – even if, for Spurzheim, it is a state which abandons its charge to preserve order. More important is Spurzheim putting madness in relation to state politics at all. His formulations – despite their ideological antiliberalism – emerge from and exist within a set of discourses in which a conjunction between regulation, structures of knowledge, the 'free agency' of the bourgeois subject, the need to prevent and treat madness, and so on gather at the intersection of the state and time.

In 1961, Foucault's work intersects that of Lefort which rigorously draws attention to the global cultural and political changes achieved by 'democracy'. Indeed, Spurzheim's antiliberalism sounds at moments like de Toqueville when the latter tries to formulate his sense of the power's new regime emerging in so-called 'American democracy'. The momentary intersection of Lefort and Foucault suggests some of the importance of Foucault's statement that Spurzheim's antiliberalism is not his primary concern. Given that Foucault is himself a staunch radical critic of liberalism, conservative antiliberal appeals to regulating state authority could seem neither new nor important. Yet Spurzheim's critique of democratic liberalism is also, as Lefort helps us specifically to understand, a critique of modernity, or, better, it is itself a mark of modernity as precisely part of the societal turn from traditional towards democratic political organizations, with all that this portends for cultural institutions, languages and subjects in modern societies.[20] When Lefort discusses the relation between modernity and democracy in terms of overt political philosophy, he notices that, for the most part, conservative thinkers – such as Heidegger – who call democracy into question also call into question modernity. The point for Lefort is that 'From a political point of view, the questioning of modernity means the questioning of democracy' (Lefort 1988: 55).

Since, for Foucault, there can be no writing about madness without an analysis of modernity, there cannot, in turn, be writing about either which does not exemplify and/or analyse the antitraditional nature of democratic societies. Unreason clearly cannot be merely a return or simple repetition (to the traditional or 'premodern', as it were), but it is a deepening of time as modernity is an opening into temporality which enlightenment – as we may now call it – deals with by means of history. Throughout the early 1960s Foucault is concerned to show that the nexus of relations within modernity reveal history to be not a natural form of knowledge, even though it is a necessary mode of political and cultural legitimation and identity formation for secular modernity itself – and perhaps never more often than when it is appealed to as that which has been lost in whatever the newest movement of modernity might be.

The Birth of the Clinic is often more explicit on these points than is *Madness and Civilization*, perhaps because modern medicine, as we call it, writes its histories compulsively from its beginnings. There is one moment in *The Birth of the Clinic* in which Foucault gathers together all these strands of modernity in terms of the state, the subject – especially as the 'gaze' – and history itself:

> What now constituted the unity of the medical gaze was not the circle of knowledge in which it was achieved but that open, infinite, moving totality, ceaselessly displaced and enriched by time, whose course it began but would never be able to stop – by this time a clinical recording of the infinite, variable series of events. But its support was not the perception of the patient in his singularity, but a collective consciousness, with all the information that intersects in it, growing in a complex, ever-proliferating way until it finally achieves the dimensions of a history, a geography, a state.

> (Foucault 1963: 29)

The fact of totality, of a regulating socius, of an order of already known knowledge – and here Foucault intersects doubly with the Hegel who criticizes such modernist 'spread' and who embodies a version of it in his dialectical 'system', of the state itself, all this makes up the story of the regime of truth that is modernity. Above all, it should make uneasy all historical thinkers, writers and scholars. It should make uneasy all those uncritically committed to their training within the disciplines whose reproductions – racist, sexist, orientalist, and so on – both produce and make known the total consciousness of humanity, the study of which, we recall, is the task of humanism itself. This last idea we find not only in Nietzsche, but also in *The Order of Things*. How foolish then the naïve return to the given in the work of someone like Merquior! How utterly inane a form of repetition! How completely failed a piece of criticism to hurl the charge that the critic violates the rules of the game! And by implication, of course, how foolish to attempt to make Foucault 'available', to have him 'make sense' to the philosophers, to the historians! They know him too well when they criticize and reject him. Foucault should not be 'explained' and 'justified' by being brought into the folds of normal secular enlightenment thought – for how little that effort has thought about the way in which its own enterprise had its beginnings in a world fleeing into madness from unreason.

Critics, one hopes, will not easily work the word 'history' like a mantra, take up the chage 'against theory', or naïvely press the case for 'progressive politics'. If there is hope that marginal crops might, in their life-forms and life-experiences, produce new cultures and politics, the critics and scholars who putatively hope to join, to assist, or to work in parallel to those efforts – they cannot simply take up the enlightenment tools that 'progressive politics' seem to offer. For they are tools which, as we have seen over and again, are themselves the machines to maintain dominance, to keep the marginal down (Edward Said (1978) on the great literatures and scholars of Europe – all shown within the rubrics of Orientalism; Cornel West (1982: 47–68) on the racism of European enlightenment aesthetic philosophy). To paraphrase a great contemporary critic, one can't tear down the master's house with the master's tools!

Madness and Civilization is part of that once immensely powerful work of serious critics to join the efforts of emergent subjects to strike against the massive authority of a western project of modernity that, despite its internal cultural complexities, often operated on the colonized world as a univocal force – just as it had operated to destroy the traditional western societies upon which it follows or the emergent subcultures which it absorbed. In a recent essay on Bakhtin and Kant, Wlad Godzich (1991) indicates that the Bakhtin circle understood modernization to be the issue of the Russian revolution. Godzich's complex essay makes inescapable the truth of Foucault's claims that history, modernity, modernization and political democracy are inseparable areas of thought circulating always around the nexus of state and subject. A fuller reading of Foucault's work along these lines would show, I suspect, that it has not yet received the *political* reading it deserves. It would show that the critique of disciplines, of representation, of the state and of the subject are fragments of a complex effort to rewrite the tools of intellectual political work made possible by the enlightenment. It would prove, ironically, the truth of what Habermas took to be his worst charge against Foucault, namely, that he was an antimodernist. It would also show Habermas insisting on the obvious – like Merquior – as if the 'normal' had some bite on an intellectual project that extends its own critique to the very beginnings of the rules of knowledge that underlie modernity itself.

NOTES

1 Foucault (1961) and Foucault (1965; cited hereafter as *MC*).
2 Dreyfus and Rabinow (1983). Second edition, with an afterword and an interview with Michel Foucault. Cited hereafter as *SH*.
3 See Serres (1968: 178f).
4 Foucault (1963), published in French as *Naissance de la clinique* (Paris: Presses Universitaires de France).
5 Foucault (1973).
6 I include myself in that list. See Bové (1990).
7 I capitalize these terms in the way that Richard Rorty capitalizes the latter to specify their existence as organized institutional disciplines of knowledge with, as such, their own interests, discourses and prejudices. See Rorty (1979).
8 I have argued this case before in relation to both Philosophers and Historians. For the former, see my discussion of Charles Taylor in the 'Preface' to Gilles Deleuze (1988: vii–xix); for the latter see Bové (1986: passim).

9 Merquior (1987), first published by Fontana Press, London, 1985. According to the publication notes, Merquior, a Brazilian, did his Ph.D. in sociology with Ernest Gellner at the London School of Economics. Hereafter cited as *M*.
10 Megill (1979).
11 For an interesting example of this from a friendly philosophical reader, see Nancy Fraser (1989: 18–23, 35–8). See also my reading of Taylor in the 'Preface' to Deleuze (1988) for a closer demonstration of the tactics I mention here.
12 Here Merquior relies on Foucault's famous essay responding to George Steiner, although he confuses the reference in his own notes. See Foucault's (1971a) first response to Steiner. Also Steiner's (1971) reply to Foucault's response and Foucault's (1971b) final remarks.
13 Canguilhem (1978), originally published as *Le normal et la pathologique* (Paris: Presses Universitaires, 1966), and earlier in part as the author's thesis, Strasbourg, 1943. See also my essay 'The rationality of disciplines: the abstract understanding of Stephen Toulmin' in Arac (1988: 42–70).
14 From Kaufman (1966: 24, 26). Emphases in this quotation are mine.
15 I realize I am withholding serious discussion of an entire range of problems here. Not only the relations between Kant and Hegel, and Hegel and Foucault, but also the problem of modernity and of Hegel's system's role in constructing modern disciplines and the state. For some sense of the complexities at hand, see Wlad Godzich's as yet unpublished paper, 'Thirty years' struggle for theory'.
16 See 'Cogito and the history of madness' in Derrida (1978), originally published in France as *L'écriture et la différance* (Paris: Editions du Seuil, 1967).
17 Of course, Erich Auerbach has authored the major study on the 'figural' tradition and so it need not be resdescribed in this context. See 'Figura' in Auerbach (1984: 11–78), first published in *Neue Dantestudien* (Istanbul, 1944).
18 One might say in passing that 'theory' should be seen as the recuperation of figure, but within the problematic of language.
19 Foucault's Kantian obsession with 'finite' in the early 1960s can be traced in part in Bové (1986).
20 See Lefort (1988), especially pp. 183–210.

BIBLIOGRAPHY

Arac, J. (ed.) (1988) *After Foucault*, New Brunswick: Rutgers University Press.
Auerbach, E. (1984) *Scenes from the Drama of European Literature*, trans. Ralph Mannheim, Minneapolis: University of Minnesota Press.
Bové, P. (1986) *Intellectuals in Power*, New York: Columbia University Press.
Bové P. (1980) 'Power and freedom', October 53: 78–92.
Canguilhem, G. (1978) *On the Normal and Pathological*, trans. Carolyn R. Fawcett, Dordrecht: Reidel.
Deleuze, G. (1988) *Foucault*, trans. Sean Hand, Minneapolis: University of Minnesota Press.
Derrida, J. (1978) *Writing and Difference*, trans. Alan Bass, Chicago: University of Chicago Press.
Dreyfus, H. L. and P. Rabinow (1983) *Michel Foucault: Beyond Structuralism and Hermeneutics*, 2nd edn, Chicago: University of Chicago Press.
Foucault, M. (1961) *Folie et déraison: histoire de la folie à l'âge classique*, Paris: Librarie Plon.
Foucault, M. (1963) *The Birth of the Clinic: An Archaeology of Medical Perception*, trans. A. M. Sheridan Smith, New York: Random House.

Foucault, M. (1965) *Madness and Civilization*, trans. anon., New York: Random House.
Foucault, M. (1971a) 'Monstrosities in criticism', *Diacritics* 1, 1: 57–60.
Foucault, M. (1971b) 'Foucault responds, 2', *Diacritics* 1, 2: 60.
Foucault, M. (1973) *The Order of Things*, New York: Random House.
Fraser, N. (1989) *Unruly Practices*, Minneapolis: University of Minnesota Press.
Godzich, W. (1991) 'Correcting Kant: Bakhtin and intercultural interactions', *Boundary 2* 18: 16.
Kaufman, W. (ed.) (1966) *Hegel: Texts and Commentaries*, Garden City, New York: Doubleday Anchor.
Lefort, C. (1988) *Democracy and Political Theory*, trans. David Macey, Minneappolis: University of Minnesota Press.
Megill, A. (1979) 'Foucault, structuralism and the end of history', *Journal of Modern History* 51: 451–503.
Merquior, J. G. (1987) *Foucault*, Berkeley: University of California Press.
Rorty, R. (1979) *Philosophy and the Mirror of Nature*, Princeton: Princeton University Press.
Said, E. W. (1978) *Orientalism*, New York: Pantheon Press.
Serres, M. (1968) *La communication*, Paris: Les Editions de Minuit.
Steiner, G. (1971) 'Steiner responds to Foucault', *Diacritics* 1, 2: 59.
West, C. (1982) 'A genealogy of modern racism', in *Prophesy Delivered: An Afro-American Revolutionary Christianity*, Philadelphia: The Westminster Press.

4   The two readings of *Histoire de la folie* in France

Robert Castel

The thesis that the truncated version of *Histoire de la folie* represented by *Madness and Civilization* imposed a simplified version of Michel Foucault's thought upon English-language readers appears to me to be very much to the point. Colin Gordon's remarkable article demonstrates this quite clearly, and I am in total agreement with him. This interpretation does not, however, rule out the possibility that another reason may also account for the different ways Foucault's work was read: *the historical gap* between the intellectual context of the beginning of the 1960s, at the time when *Histoire de la folie* was published, and that of the end of the 1960s and the beginning of the 1970s, when Foucault's book began to reach another audience and to assume a political/practical meaning rather than a theoretical one. Colin Gordon himself raises this possibility at the beginning of his article. But I would like to insist upon its importance and show how, even in France – where the *same* text has circulated since the beginning of the 1960s – the book has been the subject of *two very contrasted readings*. My contribution will not therefore be a direct commentary on Colin Gordon's article (with which I am in overall agreement). Instead, by illuminating the French side of things, it may help English-language readers to understand some of the elements of a situation, in France, in which *Histoire de la folie* was the catalyst.

In the first period, *Histoire de la folie* was read in what could be called an academic way. In spite of the originality of the thought and the flamboyant style, the book actually fits very directly into the solid French tradition of the epistemology of the sciences, a tradition featuring, among others, the names of Maurice Brunschwicz, Jean Cavaillès, Gaston Bachelard and Georges Canguilhem. It involves enquiring into the claims to truth of a field of knowledge, and laying bare its implicit conditions of possibility. Michel Foucault himself made this fundamental intellectual motivation explicit in 1977:

For me, it was a matter of saying this: if one sets a science like theoretical physics or organic chemistry the problem of defining its relationship with the economic and political structures of society, isn't one posing a too complicated question? Doesn't this place the threshold of possible

explanations too high? If, on the other hand, one takes a field of knowledge [*un savoir*] such as psychiatry, won't the question be easier to
resolve, given the low epistemological profile of psychiatry and the fact
that psychiatric practice is linked to a range of institutions, immediate
economic requirements, urgent political issues, and social rules? In the
case of a science as 'dubious' as psychiatry, wouldn't one see more clearly
the intertwining of certain effects of power and knowledge?

(Fontana 1977: 16)

The *epistemological* intentions of the work could not be more clearly
expressed. And it was indeed within the framework of a debate about the
status of knowledge and ways of putting the idea of scientificity to the test
that the book was first received by a limited readership of philosophers and
intellectuals, one that we can also describe as 'academic'. If I may be
permitted to evoke my own experience here, such was my own 'first
reading' of *Histoire de la folie* in the mid 1960s. I already had in mind a
project which would consist of an attempt to provide a sociological interpretation of the whole set of functions assumed by psychiatry, and I saw in
Michel Foucault's book the presentation of a *method* which allowed one to
put brackets round medical rationalizations. It was a way of carrying out
the 'epistemological break' required in order to construct a theory of
psychiatry detached from professionals' interpretations. In sum, this
reading of *Histoire de la folie* was exactly congruent with my reading, at
about the same period, of Irving Goffman's *Asylums*: the position Foucault
and Goffman were advocating represented a break with medical discourse,
and they provided tools for talking otherwise about a given professional
practice.

Even without taking into account the specificity of this project, I do not
think I was alone in seeing in *Histoire de la folie* a kind of historical inquiry
into the non-scientific nature of psychiatric knowledge. Not that this
excluded the other, more philosophical dimension of the work, its evocation, in the manner of Nietzsche, Lautréamont, and Antonin Artaud, of
'extremes of experience' and the obscure powers of the unsayable. But in
the one case as in the other, there was no direct connection with practice or
politics. *Histoire de la folie* seemed a great book, a splendid achievement,
but one whose bisecting lines of interpretation and magisterial recourse to
history made it loom large in the present.

An unforeseeable event led to a re-examination of the context of this first
reading: the sudden emergence, after May 1968, of a social movement
characterized by political activism and a generalized antirepressive sensibility. In such a set of circumstances, the thematics of *Histoire de la folie*
appeared doubly overexposed. The practice of segregating people by
locking them up, whose historical metamorphoses Foucault had described,
seemed to provide a model for challenging all the types of exclusion which,
from asylums to prisons and factories to schools, set limits to desire;

correlatively, madness became the paradigm for a subjectivity freed from the constraints of social adaptation, a kernel of authenticity that had to be preserved or rediscovered without making concessions to the established order. Praise of folly and criticism of systems of constraint thus appeared as the major thrusts of a work whose utilization in the political struggle became, from that moment on, a matter of course. We might add that in the framework of the 'sectional struggles', as they were called at the time, at the heart of which, representing a priority target, was the struggle against psychiatric hospitals, militant activism did not burden itself with theoretical subtleties. Hence an impressive but rather stereotyped quantity of references to Foucault in order to denounce repression, institutional violence, the arbitrary character of power, imprisonment, systematic surveillance, segregation and exclusion. These preoccupations were far from the philosophical or epistemological concerns of the readers of the first period. To sum up, at the price of often outrageous simplifications, Michel Foucault's work would appear to have served as a cover for institutional struggles inspired by an ideology of spontaneity, and this slide into activism may well have skewed the rigour of the theoretical analyses.

It is certainly true that *Histoire de la folie* was taken up and reinterpreted by a current of thought and action far removed from the system of preoccupations at the origin of the work. But it also appears to me to be important to underline the fact that, for Michel Foucault himself, this dual reading did not represent an opposition between truth and error or good and evil. Indeed, Michel Foucault never disowned militant reuse of his work. He even collaborated in it, to the extent that he committed himself to a number of ventures inspired by such trends by participating in the 'antipsychiatry' movement, in the broad sense of the term.

This poses a difficult problem. It is certainly necessary to distinguish between two very different readings of *Histoire de la folie*, and, *at the same time*, to understand that they do not stand in absolute opposition to each other, being linked, rather, by a relationship between the theory and practice proper to Michel Foucault which he tried to formalize by means of his concept of the 'specific intellectual'. A specific intellectual remains an intellectual, with all that the term entails in the way of a deontology proper to it, a requirement of rigour and a refusal of opportunism and demagogy. But he abandons the traditional position of theoretical sovereignty which made the intellectual a representative of the universal in history. Thenceforth, he can – he must – create *alliances* with social groups by putting his 'specific capital' at the service of a practical objective.

Now, there is a relation of congruence between the most specifically theoretical dimension of *Histoire de la folie* and the practical stakes involved in the struggles against confinement which make such an alliance possible, almost 'natural' even. On the theoretical register, Michel Foucault's work reveals the arbitrariness of the cultural postulates on which the psychiatric system is built and provides a way of measuring its costs, with particular reference to the positivist banalization of madness and the social segregation of the mad. It is thus tightly connected to the attempts to obtain practical changes aiming at doing away with, or at least greatly attenuating, such violence.

I hope I have not subjected my English-lanuage readers to an over-exotic excursion into the French cultural and political landscape. I also hope my contribution will not appear too distant in relation to Colin Gordon's article. In fact, while accepting totally its pertinence, as I said, I wish to suggest that it deserves to be crossed with another more diachronic approach. One can and must read *Histoire de la folie* as a rigorous and demanding intellectual construction and, as Colin Gordon does, restore it to its original dimensions. But that does not prevent one from paying attention to the question of the *reception* of the work, even a truncated, distorted version of it.

BIBLIOGRAPHY

Fontana, M. (1977) 'Vérité et pouvoir', *L'Arc* 70: 16.

TRANSLATOR'S NOTE

For a full translation of the Fontana interview, see Michel Foucault, *Power/Knowledge*, ed. C. Gordon, Brighton: Harvester, 1979: 109–33.

5 'The lively sensibility of the Frenchman'

Some reflections on the place of France in Foucault's *Histoire de la folie*

Jan Goldstein

It would perhaps be to fall into intellectual vagueness to treat in a manner that is general and uniform for all peoples the question of the institution of corporal punishment for lunatics. For how can we be sure that Negroes who live in servitude on Jamaica, or Russian slaves, shaped by an oppressive system for the whole of their lives, ought not, in the case of insanity, to be subjected to the same harsh and despotic yoke. But . . . does not the lively sensibility of the Frenchman and his violent reaction – as long as he conserves a glimmer of his reason – against every shocking abuse of power determine on his behalf the forms of repression that are gentlest and most in conformity with his character?

(Pinel 1801: 63–4)

Thus mused Philippe Pinel, one of the pivotal figures in Foucault's *Histoire de la folie*, about the so-called moral treatment of the insane. This new practice, which Pinel championed, has been viewed by most historians as the ground zero of modern psychiatry; Foucault was no exception in this regard, calling his chapter devoted to the moral treatment 'The birth of the asylum' and going on to trace a direct line from the moral treatment to the 'doctor–patient couple' of Freudian psychoanalysis (Foucault 1972: 529). What is interesting about this passage in the context of Colin Gordon's welcome reassessment of *Histoire de la folie* is Pinel's rumination on the cultural specificity of appropriate modes of managing the insane. It is, Pinel ventures, the political consciousness produced by the French Revolution which qualifies Frenchmen beyond a doubt for the humane and respectful practices of the moral treatment.[1] On the other hand, it is entirely possible that madmen in less enlightened cultures may not require, or even benefit from, such niceties. The unenlightened cultures Pinel has chosen as examples are non-European: a Caribbean island and tsarist Russia, both places so obviously barbarous that slavery remains legal at the end of the eighteenth century. What, then, is the significance of 'France' in this passage? Does it stand merely for itself, or is it meant as a synecdoche for all of the civilized, enlightened west?

Either reading is, of course, possible. Cast in the language of universality, the Enlightenment had been a self-consciously pan-European intellectual movement. Supporters of the French Revolution (of whom Pinel was one) saw the political changes in their country as a thoroughgoing operationalization of Enlightenment philosophy and hence as a phenomenon that was similarly European in its circle of reference. Advocacy of the moral treatment, everywhere identified as 'enlightened', was likewise pan-European in scope rather than being confined to France. Yet alongside this undifferentiated European consciousness, enlightened Europeans could experience keen and not always charitable awareness of national difference. Thus, Pinel, cognizant of English pioneering efforts in the moral treatment, referred to his English predecessors as 'rivals' and berated them for keeping the details of their therapeutic practice 'impenetrably veiled' in violation of the norms of an open scientific community (Pinel 1789: 13; Pinel 1801: 47–8). The English reciprocated this rivalry: a contemporary notice of Pinel's *Traité* in the *Edinburgh Review* adopted a superior, jaded tone. 'To medical readers in this country, many of [Pinel's] remarks will appear neither new nor profound, and to none will his work appear complete' (Anon. 1803: 161). Given the instability of European enlightened identity, Pinel's 'France' could only vacillate uneasily between a literal and a synecdochic signification, between the denotation for a specific country and a figurative name for the universal Republic of Letters. Or perhaps, better put, 'France' was an iridescent term occupying both positions simultaneously.

Without further exploring this ambiguity in Pinel's text, I want to use it to point to the similar ambiguity that runs through Foucault's own *Histoire de la folie* and has provoked a good deal of unfriendly criticism. The reader of that book is never quite certain whether it is about France, or whether the France in its pages is supposed to represent the west. Certainly Foucault has sprinkled the book with citations from English and German sources, but the overwhelming bulk of his documentation comes from French materials. Take, for example, the discussion of the seventeenth-century 'Great Confinement', one of the critical moments in Foucault's story. While Foucault refers in passing to English workhouses and German *Zuchthäuser*, his detailed argument in fact revolves around the French *hôpital général*, which is presented as the archetype of the new incarcerative institution and of the new taxonomical sensibility that it embodied: madness, idleness, debauchery, venereal disease and old age lumped together and perceived as fully comparable species of unreason. Conveniently for Foucault-the-narrator, the French institution has a fixed point of origin – a royal decree of Louis XIV. There were even two such decrees, one in 1656 calling for an *hôpital général* in Paris, another some twenty years later generalizing the scheme to all the cities of provincial France. Foucault reprints the first of these decrees in the book's appendix, where the Great Confinement is represented exclusively by documents of French provenance.

Is the ambiguity of 'France' in *Histoire de la folie* an authorial oversight?

Is it, as critics allege, a form of historiographical sloppiness bred of some combination of Foucault's Gallocentrism, his ignorance of the variation of national developmental patterns, and his self-promotional desire to write a 'big' book without doing the necessary work?[2] Or might this ambiguity be more accurately regarded as a deliberate rhetorical strategy on Foucault's part? Might it be a historicist play on the iridescence that the term 'France' had during the classical age (as Foucault calls the period from the mid-seventeenth century to 1800) and, at the same time, provide a way for Foucault to articulate a thesis that is more tentative with respect to 'the west' than with respect to France but is none the less intended to embrace both?

It is fairly easy to dispose of the first set of interpretations. While Foucault may be guilty of a certain amount of Gallocentrism – one can imagine him acquiescing in Pinel's formulation about the 'lively sensibility of the Frenchman' – he can hardly be considered a serious offender. Instead, his whole intellectual career testifies to his receptivity to non-French perspectives. His doctoral dissertation on madness was, a recent biography reminds us, accompanied by a secondary dissertation on Kant's *Anthropology* (Eribon 1989: 134–5). The *Histoire de la folie* already reveals the fascination with Nietzsche that would colour much of his subsequent work. In the 1970s, he would use Bentham's Panopticon as the epitome of the concept of the disciplinary gaze. (With respect to Bentham, Foucault may even be seen as bringing belated word of British utilitarian philosophy to the Left Bank student population. At his 1973–4 lecture course at the Collège de France, which I attended, Foucault's mention of 'Jeremy Bentham' produced such palpable bewilderment in the audience that the professor felt obliged to spell the last name.) Nor can Foucault be seriously accused of ignorance of the different developmental patterns of European nations. While *Histoire de la folie* is hardly the work of a systematic comparativist, Foucault does emphasize, as Colin Gordon has pointed out, the different national cultures in which the Englishman Tuke and the Frenchman Pinel articulated the moral treatment. And he expounds at length upon the divergent contextual circumstances – the role of religion, the relative centrality of the public and private spheres in matters of welfare – that variously shaped the therapeutic prescriptions of each, 'the oeuvre of Tuke and that of Pinel, whose spirit and values are so different' (Foucault 1972: 484–523, esp. 523). Finally, the complete version of *Histoire de la folie* makes clear, as the abridgement does not, the breadth and depth of Foucault's labours as a researcher which, even by the most stringent academic standards, earn him the right to make large claims. I have at times been amazed at just how much learning is packed unobtrusively into the book – for example, a single paragraph-length sentence in the final chapter sets forth in stunningly compressed form the main theoretical options and debates of early nineteenth-century psychiatry, aptly characterizing the positions of some ten doctors whose importance in their era is matched by their obscurity in our own (Foucault 1972: 540–1).

If the ambiguity of 'France' does not fall under the heading of oversight or error, what kind of case can be made for Foucault's deliberate manipulation of that ambiguity? First, it should be stressed that, much like *Discipline and Punish* (a Foucauldian work which similarly focuses on French data but claims to be describing the west), *Histoire de la folie* offers a global reinterpretation – and defamiliarization – of the Enlightenment. This is an aspect of the book inevitably ignored by readers of the abridged version, which omits the chapter on 'Experiences of madness'. In *Discipline and Punish*, the Enlightenment appears as an ingenious conflation of knowledge/power. Foucault redefines it as the creation of 'sciences of man' based on empirical observation whose knowledge-generating 'gazes' serve at the same time to render docile and productive the human bodies on which they are fixed and thus function as the 'micro-powers' undergirding the modern liberal state. The reinterpretation of the Enlightenment in *Histoire de la folie* is far less thoroughly worked out and certainly not as dazzling, but it is dazzling and original enough to warrant more attention than it has hitherto received. Foucault derives it from the two discrepant conceptualizations of madness that, he argues, coexisted during the classical age, each rooted in a set of distinctive institutional practices: the older juridical analysis of mental capacity, with its myriad of finely shaded gradations; and the newer administrative analysis of social conduct, which operated with the coarse, binary categories of dangerous/undangerous, needs confinement/does not need confinement. Not only, according to Foucault, did modern psychiatry in the mode of Pinel and Tuke emerge from the combination of these two conceptualizations, but that act of combination formed the problematic which produced the Enlightenment more generally. In Foucault's words, 'The eighteenth century saw constant efforts to adapt the contemporary experience of social man to the old juridical notion of the "subject in law". Political thought in the Enlightenment postulated a fundamental unity between these two notions and always suggested that a reconciliation was possible . . .' (Foucault 1991: 17–18; Foucault 1972: 145–6).[3]

That Foucault sets about to illuminate the Enlightenment in *Histoire de la folie* underscores the European scope of his project in that book. His subject-matter is the genealogy of a 'Europe radiant with humanity', as (in another context) he quotes Vico's depiction of the early eighteenth-century intellectual environment (Foucault 1984: 34). The Enlightenment focus also underscores the philosophical-cum-historical nature of the book's project and hence, once again, the level of transnational generality at which it is pitched. For as Foucault characterizes the question 'What is Enlightenment?' that Kant attempted to answer in a short essay for a Berlin periodical in 1784, it is 'a question that *modern philosophy* has not been capable of answering, but that it has never managed to get rid of, either. And one that has been repeated in various forms for two centuries now' (Foucault 1984: 32; emphases added).

Given this level of generality, France (and indeed the other nations which appear in *Histoire de la folie*) must function at least intermittently as synecdoche, as microcosmic renditions of the Enlightenment macrocosm. After all, Foucault is presuming the Enlightenment to be, though not without internal differentiation, still at a certain level of analysis, a 'something' discernible as a whole. This alternation between the literal France (or England) and its synecdochic counterpart can be observed in a close reading of Foucault's discussion of Tuke and Pinel in the chapter 'The birth of the asylum'. More important, this reading can also show us that what appear as 'errors' to historians expecting a more straightforward, prosaic prose are notoriously hard to pin down as such. Instead, these apparent 'errors' seem to function as deliberate ambiguities in a text seeking to occupy a middle ground between the literal and synecdochic registers.

Take the issue of William Tuke's professional identity. The sources indicate that he was a layman, 'a respectable tea-dealer, living in York', when he established the Retreat for insane Quakers (Anon. 1814: 189).[4] Now Foucault never reports that fact, and he has thereby brought some harsh criticism upon himself. According to the historical sociologist Andrew Scull, who refers to Foucault's 'cavalier way with the evidence', the author of *Histoire de la folie* overlooked both Tuke's lay status and his damning attack on the medical profession's ability to deal with mental illness; instead, says Scull, Foucault mistakenly depicted Tuke as having 'opened the asylum to medical knowledge' (Scull 1989: 14, 19). Relying on Scull's earlier work, H. C. Erik Midelfort made a similar accusation: in England the moral treatment was, contrary to Foucault's depiction, a lay innovation, perceived by physicians 'quite correctly as a lay threat', and was certainly no agency of 'medicalization' (Midelfort 1980: 258).[5] What is at stake here is Foucault's apparent factual error and his presumed tendentious hurry to blur national differences, to assimilate the English case to the French case.

If we look at Foucault's text carefully, however, we see that while he never identifies Tuke as a tea-merchant or other layman, he never identifies him as a physician either. If anything, he clearly implies the reverse. He tells us that William Tuke *appointed* a physician to the Retreat (and hence, by implication, was not one himself). Furthermore, Foucault continues, this physician's qualifications for the job were much more in the area of human traits than of Physick: a man of 'indefatigable perseverance' and anxiety about the well-being of his 'fellow-creatures', he utterly lacked any 'particular knowledge of mental illnesses' (Foucault 1972: 524). Since Foucault discovered these bits of information in the standard primary source on the subject, Samuel Tuke's 1813 *Description of the Retreat*, and since he mined that source extensively, quoting it on some dozen occasions (Foucault 1972: 492–4, 502–8, 524–5), it seems hard to imagine that he was simply and carelessly ignorant of the fact that William Tuke was a layman. Why, then, would he have failed to mention this seemingly important fact?

After specifying the national cultural differences that separated Tuke from Pinel, Foucault was eager to delineate an area of commonality that joined them; he says this explicitly.[6] And he observed, quite rightly, that these two psychiatric founding fathers shared a peculiar relationship to 'medicine'. True, Pinel was an accredited physician and Tuke was a tea-merchant, but they were none the less in fundamental agreement on the apparently contradictory propositions that (1) there ought to be a physician in the asylum; and (2) the moral treatment did not require the kinds of expertise or skill ordinarily described as 'medical'. Starting in fact from different cultural premises (which Foucault tells us) and from opposite professional poles (which he does not), Tuke and Pinel thus begin to merge at Foucault's hand. The English merchant hires for his new-style asylum a physician who is not really a physician; the French physician acknowledges that when it comes to administering the moral treatment in his new-style asylum 'a man of great probity . . . who has had long experience with the insane could just as well be substituted for [the physician]' (Foucault 1972: 524, 524 n2): In his rendering of the situation, Foucault may have slighted certain details, but he has not made errors or falsified fact. Rather, remaining within the bounds of factual accuracy, he has subtly reworked the English and French experiences so that they more nearly approximate one another and stand for what is, in Foucault's view, the common European experience.

The ambiguity of who is and is not a physician, then, serves the European dimension of Foucault's narrative. But it also serves to direct our attention to another critical ambiguity on which that narrative turns: the very meaning of 'medicine'. Foucault exploits this ambiguity, revels in it. He never stops to analyse it or to provide us with a sober definition of terms that would clarify it. Thus, for example:

> The essential plunge is taken: confinement has acquired its medical pedigree [*lettres de noblesse médicale*]. . . .
> The important point is that this transformation of house of confinement into asylum is not accomplished by the progressive introduction of medicine – a sort of invasion coming from outside – but by an internal restructuring of that space to which the classical age had given no other functions but those of exclusion and correction.
>
> (Foucault 1972: 457)

A curious formulation – a medical pedigree acquired without adding medicine to the equation. Later Foucault will regale us with more of the same:

> It is the apotheosis of the medical personage. . . . [T]he doctor takes a preponderant place within the asylum insofar as he converts it into a medical space. However, and this is the essential point, the doctor's intervention is not made by virtue of a medical skill or power that he possesses

and that would be justified by a body of objective knowledge. It is not as a scientist [*savant*] that *homo medicus* has authority in the asylum, but as a sage.

(Foucault 1972: 523–4)

An equally curious formulation – the doctor converting the asylum into a medical space without using medical skill – and one that is signalled by the same insistent verbal marker ('the important point is', 'this is the essential point'). The reader, feeling a bit dizzy, can regain balance by realizing that Foucault is cultivating the ambiguity, using 'medicine' in two senses without distinguishing them: medicine as that which, generically, relieves suffering; and medicine in the narrower meaning of the classical age, as those practices belonging to the traditional domain of the accredited *médecin*, or physician, and consisting of the application of physical remedies.[7] The asylum, then, is medicalized – that is, made a scene of healing – by the agency of the *médecin* but not by means of his (traditionally defined) medical art. With respect to a nascent psychiatry, medicine has become non-medical.

One might upbraid Foucault for failing to straighten out a central terminological ambiguity and thus befuddling the reader; one might view this failure as a product of his own intellectual confusion or, as Andrew Scull does, of his neglect of the sociological problem of 'provid[ing] us with [a] coherent [and] persuasive account of how professional control over madness was secured by physicians' (Scull 1989: 19). But if one assumes that Foucault was generally in control of his audacious intellectual project, such supposed failings reverse their valence and take on the quality of strategies. The ambiguity of Tuke's professional identity, the ambiguity of 'medicine', the ambiguity of 'France', are all strategies for breaking down conventional categories of analysis and thereby defamiliarizing the past. Foucault uses the ambiguity of 'medicine' to rewrite the emergence of psychiatry, pointing to the strange fact that at the moment that the medicine of insanity first declared its status as a positive science, it was far more immersed in 'thaumaturgy' than it had been a century before (Foucault 1972: 526–7). As Paul Veyne has vividly described Foucault's defamiliarization of history, it relies on a Cézanne-like unsettling of the boundary lines around objects:

> This [archaeological] method produces strange pictures, where relationships replace objects. Certainly these are very much pictures of the world we are familiar with: Foucault is no more an abstract painter than is Cézanne. As in a Cézanne canvas, so in a Foucault history, the countryside around Aix is recognizable, only it has been provided with a violent affectivity: it seems to issue from an earthquake.

(Veyne 1979: 241)

Colin Gordon's masterful paper argues that a variety of circumstantial factors – especially an exclusive concentration on the abridged English translation – have led to a substantive misreading of Foucault's *Histoire de la folie* and a correspondingly low evaluation of it. I agree with Gordon but would go a step further. Once Foucault's full textual canvas is restored, we cannot only give a correct rendition of its main propositions. Appreciating its degree of historical sophistication and, hence, less inclined to find Foucault guilty of obvious errors of fact, we are also in a position to understand his project more deeply, to construe its 'errors' as strategies.

NOTES

1 Pinel first published this section of the *Traité* during the Revolution; it appeared in 1798 as an article in the *Mémoires de la société médicale d'émulation de Paris*.
2 As Colin Gordon notes, this line of criticism, which 'has gained almost universal currency and credence', has been articulated by H.C. Erik Midelfort, Lawrence Stone and Ian Hacking (Gordon 1990: 18). Other scholars who fall into the same camp include Andrew Scull, who will be discussed below; and Roy Porter, who depicts Foucault's method in *Histoire de la folie* as an unwarranted 'project[ion] of French ideology onto the rest of the Continent' and on to Britain (Porter 1987: 9).
3 I am here building on Colin Gordon's excellent point (Gordon 1990: 13) that Foucault's discussion of the history of various forms of subjectivity 'in terms of stresses and clashes between conceptual formations operative in different sectors (here, the legal and the administrative) of social practice, is perhaps one of the most interesting as well as least-discussed hypotheses developed in [*Histoire de la folie*]'. But I am going beyond Gordon in suggesting that Foucault has already, in *Histoire de la folie*, used this form of analysis to sketch the rudiments of a full-scale reinterpretation of the Enlightenment.
4 The same pattern of combining a mercantile occupation with active involvement in the Retreat was followed by his son and grandson; see the entries on the members of the Tuke family in the *Dictionary of National Biography*.
5 I should make clear that it is not Scull's factual point that I am disputing here; I have myself cited his work to show the difference between the early view of the moral treatment by the representatives of 'official medicine' in France and England (Goldstein 1987: 201). What I am disputing is whether marshalling this factual evidence really does reveal Foucault's text to have inadequacies and inaccuracies.
6 'The oeuvre of Tuke and that of Pinel, whose spirit and values are so different, meet [*vient se rejoindre*] in this [fourth structure peculiar to the world of the asylum], the transformation of the medical personage' (Foucault 1972: 523).
7 See my discussion of this eighteenth-century notion of 'medicine properly so-called' (Goldstein 1987: 51).

BIBLIOGRAPHY

Anon. (1803) review of Pinel, *Traité médico-philosophique sur l'aliénation mentale, ou la manie*, in *Edinburgh Review* 2: 160–72.
Anon. (1814) review of Samuel Tuke, *Description of the Retreat*, in *Edinburgh Review* 23: 189–98.
Eribon, D. (1989) *Michel Foucault (1926–1984)*, Paris: Flammarion.
Foucault, M. (1972) *Histoire de la folie à l'âge classique* [History of Madness in the Classical Age], Paris: Gallimard.

Foucault, M. (1984) 'What is Enlightenment?', in P. Rabinow (ed.) *The Foucault Reader*, New York: Pantheon, 35–50.

Foucault, M. (1991) 'Experiences of madness', Chapter 4 of *Histoire de la folie à l'âge classique*, trans. A. Pugh, in *History of the Human Sciences* 4: 1–25.

Goldstein, J. (1987) *Console and Classify: The French Psychiatric Profession in the Nineteenth Century*, New York: Cambridge University Press.

Gordon, C. (1990) '*Histoire de la folie*: an unknown book by Michel Foucault', in *History of the Human Sciences* 3: 3–26.

Midelfort, H. C. E. (1980) 'Madness and civilization in early modern Europe: a reappraisal of Michel Foucault', in B. Malament (ed.) *After the Reformation: Essays in Honor of J. H. Hexter*, Philadelphia, Pa.: University of Pennsylvania Press, 247–65.

Pinel, P. (1789) 'Observations sur le régime moral qui est le plus propre à rétablir dans certains cas la raison égarée des maniaques' ['Observations on the moral regimen most suitable for curing certain cases of the distracted reason of maniacs'], in *Gazette de santé* no. 4: 13–15.

Pinel, P. (1801) *Traité médico-philosophique sur l'aliénation mentale, ou la manie* ['Medico-Philosophical Treatise on Mental Alienation, or Mania'], Paris: Richard Caille & Ravier.

Porter, R. (1987) *Mind-Forg'd Manacles: A History of Madness in England from the Restoration to the Regency*, Cambridge, Mass.: Harvard University Press.

Scull, A. (1989) 'Reflections on the historical sociology of psychiatry', in *Social Order/Mental Disorder: Anglo-American Psychiatry in Historical Perspective*, Berkeley and Los Angeles, Calif.: University of California Press, 1–30.

Veyne, P. (1979) 'Foucault révolutionne l'histoire' ['Foucault revolutionizes history'], in *Comment on écrit l'histoire* ['How History Is Written'], Paris: Seuil, 203–42.

6 Foucault, history and madness

Dominick LaCapra

Colin Gordon is entirely convincing in arguing that Michel Foucault's *Histoire de la folie* deserves to be translated in its entirety and that it is a book that is largely unread even if the reader's eyes have in fact passed over the 600 + pages of the French edition of either 1961 or 1972. In fact, I would be tempted to argue that *Histoire de la folie* is in important ways Foucault's most impressive book – perhaps his most ambitious venture in writing.

Gordon is also to the point in maintaining that many of Foucault's later concerns are intimated or even elaborated in striking form in this book. One may even wonder whether the cuts in the abridged edition were to some extent motivated by a desire to heighten the 'originality' of the later works by curtailing drastically the scope and impetus of the earlier one. In any case, Gordon is again cogent in pointing to the role of interpreters, at times following Foucault's lead, in spinning out a *Bildungsroman* in which stress is on decisive development or even epistemological break between stages in Foucault's intellectual career. In addition, the tendency of neo-Foucauldians and so-called new historicists to look to the later Foucault also serves to underestimate the significance of the study of madness. Indeed, there may even be a marked loss in subtlety and nuance when the sinuous complexity of *Histoire de la folie* is left behind for the seemingly more programmatic and 'positive' if not positivistic emphasis upon power and the symptomatic role of high-cultural artefacts in reinforcing the system of power-knowledge.

What is perhaps more open to question in Gordon's own approach is his dominant reliance upon conventional historiographic assumptions in attempting to effect a rectification in the reception of *Histoire de la folie*. Here he may be too close to many commentators he criticizes. In any event, it may be too simple to focus attention on portions of the longer version of Foucault's book omitted in the shorter versions. Such an emphasis tends to make differences in reception of both the longer and the shorter versions of the book too straightforward a matter – one in which there appear to be only losses that can be recuperated rather than more crucial theoretical and ideological issues at stake. Gordon himself emphasizes the need to get Foucault's theses straight and to see how they are validated empirically, and he objects to critics who fail on one or both scores. These concerns are certainly important and legitimate. They may also be strategically necessary given the audience of historians that seems to constitute Gordon's own primary reference group. But Gordon does not sufficiently elucidate the more basic challenge Foucault poses to historiography and to the human sciences in general – a challenge to which Gordon turns at the conclusion of his article. His brief but pointed discussion ends with the statement: 'But it is possible, and perhaps to be desired, that the historian and the philosopher . . . find a common audience' (p. 39). Foucault's venture in *Histoire de la folie* can, I think, only be appreciated in terms of that possibility and desideratum.

Certain of the issues I would like to emphasize are adumbrated in two of the most forceful critiques that Gordon discusses: those of Midelfort and Derrida. I think that both the challenges they pose to Foucault and the opportunities they offer even to sympathetic readers of *Histoire de la folie* are greater than Gordon indicates.

Midelfort, like Gordon himself, proceeds largely on the level of conventional historiography, but where Gordon gives Foucault high grades, Midelfort tends to give him low ones. Gordon criticizes Midelfort in terms of four rather local points supplemented by a fifth. The fifth and supplementary point is perhaps the most significant, and it concerns what Gordon recognizes as Midelfort's striking criticism concerning Foucault's mistaken belief that the ship of fools actually existed as a prevalent institution in dealing with the mad in early modern Europe. Midelfort asserts: 'There is only one known instance of a madman's having been set adrift on a boat, and it is quite possible that the intention was to drown him' (p. 254) – a phenomenon that is difficult to interpret as an embarkation of the mad in search of their reason. Midelfort's argument with respect to the ship of fools is telling given the metaphoric and argumentative role of Foucault's correlation of the Renaissance with embarkation in contrast to the linkage of the classical age with confinement and the house of confinement.[1]

The more general point, however, is that Midelfort's argument is more forceful than Gordon allows and countering it poses difficulties Gordon does not sufficiently confront. I think the types of criticism Midelfort makes may have a beneficially sobering effect, but they do not adequately address important dimensions of Foucault's text that Midelfort, however negatively, at times touches upon. With reference to the question of Foucault's 'style', Midelfort asserts: 'Although Anglo-Saxon readers have often objected to his obscure, arrogant, sensationalist, and opaque form of discourse, which by his own admission is a "labyrinth into which I can venture . . . in which I can lose myself", his philosophy may become a major force among self-consciously avant-garde intellectuals' (p. 249). Although he clearly sympathizes with the 'Anglo-Saxon' audience he invokes, Midelfort adds that Foucault's 'philosophy' – his understanding of 'language and the human condition' – may be right but his history – or idea of 'the route by which we have arrived where we are' – may be wrong. In assessing Foucault's history, Midelfort implicitly identifies history with accurate empirical and analytic reconstruction of the past, and the terms of his argument indicate that history is clearly separated from philosophy, thereby obviating the problem of the interaction between reconstruction of the past and dialogic exchange with it.

Yet it is none the less important that Midelfort does not restrict himself to local points in criticizing Foucault. His major arguments take the form of maintaining that while Foucault may note certain facts or factors, he does not weight them accurately or properly in arriving at significant conclusions or reconstructions of complex phenomena. In other words, Midelfort does recognize the importance of interpretation on empirical and analytic levels of enquiry. The very effect of his article depends upon his own remarkable lucidity and succinctness in addressing complicated issues in historical interpretation. One of his important general points is that 'there is too much diversity in any one period, and too much continuity between periods, for the relentless quest for the elusive *episteme* to prove ultimately useful' (p. 259). Gordon would like to counter Midelfort by showing that Foucault does in fact bring out elements of continuity and diversity, but the argument here must be somewhat more nuanced in terms of the interaction of continuities and discontinuities both at the same time and over time.

Midelfort also complicates Foucault's account by stressing the importance of the monastery as a model for the hospital and the madhouse – 'a feature Foucault notices but does not fully assimilate' (p. 256). Whether the monastery should be seen as having a more important role than the leprosarium, as Midelfort maintains, is moot, and Midelfort is wrong in believing that Foucault sees the treatment of lepers in terms of a 'monolithic image of rejection' (p. 253). (Foucault presents lepers as ambivalent objects of 'social exclusion but spiritual integration' (p. 16)). Still, Midelfort does indicate how Foucault's argument may be complemented on one crucial level by the exploration of more intricate, overdetermined displacements of highly charged and at times ambivalent phenomena over time – displacements such as those linking the monastery or leprosarium and the madhouse.[2] A similar point may be made concerning Midelfort's contention that Foucault underestimates 'the force of sin as a source of horror and madness' in the Renaissance because of Foucault's 'general conclusion that madness was seen as cosmic tragedy by medieval and Renaissance artists' (p. 255). The very connection of sin and madness might well strengthen Foucault's contention that madness in the Renaissance was a source of temptation and ambivalent fascination/repulsion rather than a narrowly circumscribed object of disciplinary control.

Rather than rehearse other aspects of Midelfort's argument (such as the view that Foucault oversimplifies the response of Renaissance humanists to madness), I would observe that Midelfort converges with Derrida in one respect but diverges from him drastically in another. He is close to Derrida in the view that Foucault's construction of preclassical phenomena is situated somewhere between the actual historical stage or even origin, on the one hand, and the idealized, stylized type or at best critical fiction, on the other. Gordon may be correct in asserting that in Foucault the ' "obscure common root" of the duality of reason and unreason is not localized' (p. 20) in the Middle Ages, but it may at times seem to be localized somewhere else, to wit, in pre-Socratic Greece.

Midelfort diverges drastically from Derrida in his understanding of the relation between history and philosophy. Midelfort is content with a clear and distinct separation of the two. By contrast, the relation is highly problematic and unstable for Derrida. In fact Derrida's extremely difficult 'critique' of Foucault seems to move on the transcendental level in the Kantian sense, that is, in terms of the conditions of possibility of Foucault's argument.

Gordon somewhat plausibly sees Derrida as presenting Foucault as 'positivistically historicizing the transcendental', but he may misconstrue certain important factors of Derrida's approach. Derrida's essay is, I think, best seen as a radical yet sympathetic rereading that destabilizes and repositions certain crucial elements of Foucault's argument. Gordon makes two specific charges against Derrida. First, Derrida falsely accuses Foucault of attempting to write a history of madness itself by ignoring Foucault's own explicit indication of the impossibility of this alluring venture. Derrida also misses the play of citations in Foucault's preface of 1961 with respect to a text by René Char (Gordon pp. 19–20). (The nicety of Gordon's argument need not be sacrificed if one were to observe that Derrida seems to deconstruct a project that Foucault already elaborates in an explicitly deconstructed manner.) Second, Derrida falsely sees Foucault as localizing the ' "originating affrontment" of reason and unreason' (p. 20) in the Middle Ages. Yet here I would reiterate that Derrida points to the fleeting, obscure allusion to Greece in Foucault's original preface. Foucault writes: 'The Greeks had a relation to something that they called hubris. This relation was not merely one of condemnation; the existence of Thrasymachus and Callicles suffices to prove it, even if their language [in Plato's *Republic*] has reached us already enveloped in the reassuring dialectic of Socrates. But the Greek logos had no contrary.'

In this elusive passage, pre-Socratic Greece does seem to be invoked as the scene of an authentic dialogue between reason and unreason with hubris in the role of unreason. The notion that the Greek logos had no contrary would seem to indicate that, at least prior to the figure of Socrates, the Greek world was a cosmos in which reason and unreason were not disjoined but viably and tensely related in a manner we can at best approach in obscurely invocatory gestures. With Socrates the putative older interaction is lost, and one has the domination of a tyrranical, one-dimensional logic.

This brief passage indicates Foucault's obvious indebtedness to Nietzsche's *Birth of Tragedy from the Spirit of Music*, which he in a sense rewrites in *Histoire de la folie*. The fact that this important intertextual relation remains largely implicit perhaps facilitates the tendency to repeat the equivocations of Nietzsche's account – its unstable weave of (1) a linear narration of discontinuous structures, (2) a complex, uneven narrative of repetition with more or less traumatic change, and (3) periodic lyrical interludes. In Nietzsche, the reason/unreason pair is discussed in terms of the Apollonian and the Dionysian. And in Nietzsche, as in Foucault, one line of the narrative presents a rather traditional story. Once upon a time in pre-Socratic Greece there was a creative dialogue or agon between reason and unreason. Then Socrates came along and this 'tragic' dialogue was lost or repressed. Reason became a one-dimensional tyrant, and unreason was reduced to mere subjectivity and emotional expressiveness. The apparent goal is to get back the lost dialogue.

But in Nietzsche as in Foucault (and others, for example, Lukács and Heidegger) a more complex story-line complicates the tale and situates the pre-Socratic scene as an enabling critical fiction or rhetorical motivation for an argument. It offers an account of time itself as marked by a struggle between more or less dominant and submerged forces. And the very interaction between continuity and discontinuity both at a given time and over time becomes a variable question in which breaks, while possibly traumatic, are never pure. In the modern period, a one-sided reason *tends* to be relatively dominant, and it both provokes irrational outbursts and functions to repress a different kind of interaction with unreason or the Dionysian that discourse – including Nietzsche's own discourse – may none the less re-enact or reinvent in however broken and partial a form.

Foucault's evanescent reference to Greece may be read as a figure for the promise and the problems of the book. Foucault accounts for long-term transformation in a somewhat divided manner. In the most thought-provoking dimension of his argument, he construes historicity as displacement, that is, as repetition with more or less traumatic change. The cosmic and tragic frame of reference evoked by the reference to pre-Socratic Greece receives different articulations in medieval and Renaissance Europe. It recurs in more problematic form in the classical age itself despite the major move towards division, dissociation and confinement. *Rameau's Nephew* to which Gordon refers is one sign of 'dialogue' on the level of high culture, but there are also the prevalent images of the fall and the beast. And the very image of embarkation through which Foucault interprets the Renaissance was a favourite of Pascal in the classical age. As Gordon intimates, the very figure of Descartes is more ambivalent for Foucault than a hasty reading of his book – or his polemic with Derrida – might indicate. Here a passage from an untranslated section of Foucault's book could have been written by Derrida himself:

If contemporary man, since Nietzsche and Freud, finds deep within himself the point of contestation with respect to all truth, and is able to read in what he now knows of himself the indices of fragility where unreason threatens, on the contrary the man of the seventeenth century discovers, in the immediate presence of his thought to itself, the certitude in which reason announces itself in its first form. But that does not mean that classical man was, in his experience of truth, more distant from unreason than we ourselves can be. It is true that the Cogito is absolute beginning; but one must not forget that the evil demon [*le malin génie*] is anterior to it. And the evil demon is not the symbol in which are resumed and systematized all the dangers of the psychological events which are the images of dreams and the errors of the senses. Between God and man, the evil demon has an absolute meaning; it designates the peril which, well beyond man [*bien au-delà de l'homme*], could prevent him in a definitive manner from reaching truth: a major obstacle, not of such a spirit but of such a reason. And it is not because truth which takes its illumination from the Cogito finally masks the shadow of the evil demon that one should forget its perpetually menacing power: up to and including the existence of the external world, this danger will hang over Descartes's advance [*ce danger surplombera le cheminement de Descartes*]. How in these conditions can unreason in the classical age be reduced to the scale of a psychological event or even to the scale of human pathos? By contrast it forms the element in which the world is born to its own truth, the domain within which reason will have to answer for itself.

(pp. 195–6; my translation)

The age of positivism beginning in the nineteenth century is the apex of dissociation and the breaking of the dialogue between reason and unreason, but even here the underground voices of Sade, Hölderlin, Nietzsche and others serve as anguished or elated reminders and partial enactments of a broken dialogue. An undeveloped comment in Derrida's essay indicates how Foucault in the very writing of *Histoire de la folie* joins his voice to that of other 'underground' figures in a provocative attempt to renew a broken dialogue. Derrida comments that silence, which cannot be said, seems to be 'indirectly, metaphorically made present [*rendu présent indirectement, métaphoriquement, si je puis dire*] by the pathos of Foucault's book'.[3] Silence for Derrida is not mere muteness but essential for the articulation and rhythm of language. In this respect, one may go on to argue that Foucault at his most provocative writes neither from the side of the mad nor that of the sane but from the problematic margin that divides the two. Yet a liminal status on this margin, which allows or constrains a hybridized, internally divided voice, is particularly tenuous in the modern world as Foucault himself understands modernity, for modernity has been largely successful in reducing unreason to pathological madness if not at times to mere muteness. In some obscure fashion, Foucault would apparently like that torn and ragged margin to expand or even to explode in affirmatively changing society and culture.

It is the latter possibility and its problematic assumptions that help account for many critics' distance from — and their very resistance to — recognizing the more basic challenge Foucault poses to historiography and the human sciences. (It would be the height of disavowal — in Freud's sense of *Verleugnung* — to relegate that traumatic challenge to 1960s 'craziness' or even to the circumscribed 'antipsychiatry' movement.) Foucault in his own fashion links history and critical theory in a manner that does not simply pour new wine into old bottles of periodization by way of an 'epistemological' structuralism. Through his distinctive manner of articulating empirical–analytic reconstruction with critical dialogic exchange, he destabilizes the most sophisticated positivistic rendition and hermeneutic interpretation of the past. A more extensive investigation of the manner in which he does so in a book like *Histoire de la folie* would require a closer look at the division and at times the internal dialogue in his own narrative voices (or subject-positions) — division and internal dialogue between chiaroscuro lyrical interludes (often seemingly mad and maddening), scientific or even postivistic structuralism (which may have endeared him to an earlier generation of Annalistes who recognized their own official self-image here), and more problematic and self-questioning liminal overtures. I think that Foucault's more forceful challenges to conventional historiography as well as his most ambitious forms of writing occur with respect to the third, liminal or hybridized voice.

More generally, one important question that arises from a reading of *Histoire de la folie* is whether one can recognize the appeal of Foucault's evocation of a mutually tempting and contestatory relation between discursive forces even if one takes a critical distance from certain of its features. Aside from the very free, indeed rather uncontrolled, use of free indirect style in rendering voices of the past, perhaps the primary mode in which the temptation and threat of 'madness' arise in Foucault's own writing is in terms of the abyss or void of hyperbolic self-referentiality — the inversion of the speculatively dialectical quest for identity and totalization. In *Histoire de la folie* one can see Foucault lyrically acting out, positivistically situating, and ambivalently relating to that temptation and threat as well as pointing towards a transforming, tragic cosmos in an untimely gesture made at times with a cataclysmically violent sense of urgency. Both in this text and elsewhere in Foucault, the recurrent danger is the tendency to sacrifice an attempt to regenerate a tense interaction between legitimate limits and hyperbolic transgression in deference to an unrestrained aesthetic of the transgressive sublime. The dubious political analogue of this aesthetic combines seeming nostalgia for a lost 'tragic' past, total condemnation of the present except for scarcely audible echoes or evanescent lightning flashes of that past, and blind, apocalyptic hope for a radically transformed future — a combination of traits that lends itself too easily to a politics of cultural despair. The admittedly problematic yet more promising possibility Foucault leaves one with is that of work exploring the interaction between contending forces in language and life. My own view here is that – at least on a discursive level – one has to be open to certain risks of transgressive hyperbole that test limits, but one should not become compulsively fixated on these risks or surreptitiously constitute them as the *telos* or the hidden agenda of language. Instead one should investigate and explore their tense relation to other forces, including those attendant upon normative limits, in a larger discursive and practical field.

NOTES

1 Gordon hedges in asserting that 'the contary [to Midelfort's denial that riverborne deportation was a systematic practice in the medieval treatment of the insane] is not asserted by Foucault' (p. 16). Foucault quite explicitly states: 'But of all these romantic or satiric vessels, the *Narrenschiff* is the only one that had a real existence – for they did exist, these boats that conveyed their insane cargo from town to town' (Michel Foucault (1972) *Histoire de la folie à l'âge classique*, Paris: Gallimard, p. 19). One may also note that Midelfort does recognize the role of pilgrimages. Gordon states that 'on the practice of pilgrimage Midelfort has nothing to say' (p. 16). Midelfort writes: 'Pilgrimage was a thoroughly common remedy for madness (and other afflictions), and other spiritual aids, including exorcism, were widely used as well' ('Madness and civilization in early modern Europe: a reappraisal of Michel Foucault', in Barbara Malament (ed.) (1980) *After the Reformation: Essays in Honour of J. H. Hexter*, Philadelphia, Pa.: University of Pennsylvania Press, p. 254). Further references are to these editions and will be included in the text.
2 My own attempt to relate certain psychoanalytic notions to a reconceptualization of historiography would indicate that I think one of the limitations of *Histoire de la folie* is its very restricted understanding of Freud's significance.
3 'Cogito and history of madness', in (1978) *Writing and Difference*, trans. Alan Bass, Chicago: Chicago University Press, p. 37.

7 Foucault, ambiguity and the rhetoric of historiography

Allan Megill

Colin Gordon's essay on Foucault's *Histoire de la folie* reminds us once again how enigmatic and seductive a writer Foucault was (Gordon 1990). One has the impression that at any given moment Foucault knew precisely what he wanted. Yet his directness often found manifestation in prose of a quite astonishing ambiguity. The combination has much to do with the appeal that Foucault's writings had, and continue to have. To be sure, some readers cannot abide the style (Weightman 1989). But others take to it with passion, for the directness suggests that important insights are being conveyed, while the ambiguity allows the text to be received, and used, in a variety of ways.

Foucault's mode of writing deserves our attention. I shall here focus on several textual fragments that figure in Gordon's essay. I aim to show how the texts work, and in particular how ambiguity is central to them. I hope thereby to cast light on an issue with which Gordon is much concerned, namely, the relation of Foucault's historiography to the more conventional historiography practised by professional historians. Much of the difference between the two boils down to matters of rhetoric – to matters, that is, of language and argument. The tension that Gordon rightly finds between Foucault and 'the historians' is largely a matter of adherence to different rhetorical conventions. Gordon takes Foucault's side in the conflict, criticizing some of Foucault's historian critics. Ironically, like many of the historians, Gordon is himself not sufficiently attentive to Foucault's rhetoric. But his essay raises an important issue, and provides a good entry point into the tension between Foucauldian rhetoric and the kind of rhetoric favoured by academic disciplines.

I

Consider the following sentence from *Histoire de la folie*:

> *Les fous alors avaient une existence facilement errante.*
> (Foucault 1961: 10; Foucault 1972b: 19)

Richard Howard, the translator of the (much abridged) English version of *Histoire de la folie*, renders the sentence as follows:

Madmen then led an easy wandering existence.

(Foucault 1973a: 8)[1]

Gordon contends that Howard's translation is faulty and that the sentence is correctly rendered as follows:

The existence of the mad at that time could easily be a wandering one.

(Gordon 1990: 17)

The difference between the two versions is important, because if Gordon's translation is correct, Foucault is at least partly rescued from criticisms offered by the historian of early modern Europe, Erik Midelfort. As Gordon points out, in a critical article on *Histoire de la folie*, Midelfort contended that Foucault was wrong to think that in the Middle Ages there existed 'ships of fools' (*Narrenschiffe*) carrying cargoes of madmen from town to town. Midelfort also contended that Foucault was wrong to think that the medieval man led an 'easy wandering life' (Gordon 1990: 16; Midelfort 1980: 249–50). It turns out, on Gordon's rendering, that Foucault did not say that the life of the mad was 'easy'. It also turns out that the mad did not necessarily wander. One would thus infer that Foucault did not believe that ships of fools were as important in the life of the medieval mad as Midelfort and some other readers have thought him to have believed. Thus Midelfort's criticism of Foucault on this score would involve a misunderstanding of what Foucault's position actually was.

When one looks at the disputed sentence in isolation, one has to agree that Richard Howard slipped up in translating '*une existence facilement errante*' as 'an easy wandering existence'. But Gordon's version is also problematic, although I am persuaded that it captures more of what lies behind the original than does Howard's version (how odd, one is tempted to observe, that a seemingly simple sentence should prove so difficult to translate). When I tried out '*les fous alors avaient une existence facilement errante*' on two well-educated native speakers of French, both puzzled over it a bit before offering translations into English – a language, incidentally, that they knew well. The first informant, a mathematician, thought that '*facilement*' had the force of '*souvent*' ('often'). The second, a graduate student in film studies, thought that it meant '*le plus souvent*' ('most often'). When the first informant learned of the second informant's preference, he opted for 'most often' as well. In their view, then, '*Les fous alors avaient une existence facilement errante*' ought to be translated as:

Most often, the mad at that time led a wandering existence.

The third version differs significantly from Gordon's preferring rendering. To write, as in Gordon's version, that the mad 'could easily' lead a wandering existence is to sound a note of dubiety that is not present in the assertion that 'most often' the mad led a wandering existence. 'Do you think I'll win the lottery?' 'You easily could.' Here 'You easily could' is equivalent to 'You probably won't'. By implication, 'could easily' makes the mad more sedentary than 'most often' does.

But the translation, 'Most often, the mad at that time led a wandering existence', is itself problematic. If, as Gordon seems to hold, Foucault's intention in writing the sentence was to convey the idea that it was merely *possible* that the mad led a wandering existence, why did he not write '*Il se peut que les fous . . .*' or '*Il est [bien] possible que les fous . . .*' ('It is [indeed] possible that the mad . . .')? Similarly, if Foucault's intention was to convey the idea that *most often* the mad led a wandering existence, why did he not write '*Le plus souvent, les fous . . .*' ('Most often, the mad . . .')? He could easily have written one or another unambiguous version of the sentence. But he chose not to. Instead, he opted for the ambiguous '*Les fous alors avaient une existence facilement errante*'. Note, moreover, that the difficulty is not only with '*facilement*', for the word '*alors*' also conveys an ambiguity, if somewhat less insistently. Like 'then' in English, its primary dictionary meaning (that is, its primary meaning for normal speakers of the language) is 'at that time'. But '*alors*' also has a secondary meaning – 'therefore' or 'so'. As we shall see when we look at the sentence in relation to those around it, there is reason to think that Foucault wished to activate the secondary meaning as well.

The trouble with Gordon's suggested translation is not that it is wrong, but rather that it is only partly right. For it is reductive. It betrays the original by eliminating the ambiguity. To be sure, *all* translations are betrayals: *traduttore traditore*. No version can escape accusation. In fear and trembling, then, I offer a fourth version:

The mad, then, had easily a wandering existence.

Like '*Les fous alors avaient une existence facilement errante*', this last version forces the attentive reader into puzzlement. In the spirit of 'blame the translator', it is likely to be condemned as a bad translation; yet it may well be the least traitorous of the lot.

Let us now widen our gaze, to take in the surroundings of the disputed sentence. The sentence occurs in the first chapter of *Histoire de la folie*, which not so incidentally is entitled '*Stultifera navis*' ('ship of fools'). It appears several pages into the chapter, in a passage where Foucault first introduces the 'figure' of the ship of fools. It connects directly with the questions, encountered above, of whether ships of fools actually existed and of whether Foucault thought that they existed. As Midelfort and other researchers have emphasized, there seems to be no evidence that they did. Scholarly consensus holds rather that the *Narrenschiff* is an instance of late medieval allegory or symbolism. The symbolism found expression in some Shrovetide processions and was developed in literary works, most notably Sebastian Brant's didactic-satirical poem *Das Narrenschiff* (1494). But we do not seem to have justification for holding that real ships filled with real mad people navigated real rivers and canals (Maher and Maher 1982).

What is Foucault's position on the matter? Did he hold that ships of fools really existed? Or did he hold that they did not really exist? Or did he hold that, like the supposedly wandering mad, ships of fools 'could easily' have existed? Or did he he hold some other view entirely? Read carefully the following passage (which I have slightly abridged), and try to decide what Foucault's position on the matter really was (here, as in subsequent quotations where Howard has translated all or part of the text, I have relied on, but also diverged from, his rendering):

Let us begin with the simplest of these figures, which is also the most symbolic.

A new object has just appeared in the imaginary landscape of the Renaissance; soon it will occupy a privileged place: it is the *Ship of Fools*, a strange 'drunken boat' that glides the length of the calm rivers of the Rhineland and of the Flemish canals.

The *Narrenschiff*, obviously [*évidemment*], is a literary composition, probably [*sans doute*] borrowed from the old Argonaut cycle, one of the great mythic themes recently revived and rejuvenated. . . . It is thus that Symphorien Champier composes successively a *Ship of Princes and Battles of Nobility* in 1502, then a *Ship of Virtuous Ladies* in 1503; there is also a *Ship of Health*, alongside Jacop van Oestvoren's *Blauwe Schute* in 1413, Brant's *Narrenschiff*, and Josse Bade's work, *Boats of Fools, Skiffs of Silly Women* (1498). Bosch's painting belongs, of course, to this dream fleet.

But all of these fictional [*romanesque*] or satirical vessels, the *Narrenschiff* is the only one that had a real existence, for they did exist [*ils ont existé*], these boats that carried their insane cargo from town to town. *Les fous alors avaient une existence facilement errante*. The towns drove them deliberately [*volontiers*] from their confines; they were allowed to run about in the distant countryside, when not entrusted to a group of merchants or pilgrims. The custom was especially frequent in Germany; in Nuremberg, during the first half of the fifteenth century, the presence of 62 mad had been registered; 31 were chased away. . . . Often [*souvent*], they were entrusted to boatmen: in Frankfort, in 1399, seamen were instructed to rid the city of a madman who walked about the streets naked. . . . Sometimes sailors disembarked these inconvenient passengers sooner than they had promised. . . . Often [*souvent*], the cities of Europe must have seen these ships of fools approaching.

(Foucault 1961: 10–11; Foucault 1972b: 18–19; Foucault 1973a: 7–8)

The discussion of ships of fools continues for several more pages, and the story gets more complicated. But we have enough of the text for our purposes here. Consider first what happens to '*Les fous alors avaient une existence facilement errante*' when one reads it in the context of the sentences that immediately precede and follow it. The preceding sentence conveys the idea that ships of fools *really did* exist ('*ils ont existé*'). With this idea in our heads, we are tempted to read '*Les fous alors avaient* . . .' as '*Therefore*, the mad had . . . a wandering existence'. In any case, whether one reads '*alors*' as meaning 'at that time' *and* 'therefore', or whether one reads it as meaning only 'at that time', the preceding sentence, with its insistence that ships of fools really existed, tends to push '*Les fous alors* . . .' in the direction of real existence also. The ships of fools did exist, and the mad (who were carried on them) led a wandering life. The progression of ideas seems clear. Thus, viewing the sentence in this context, we are pushed away from Gordon's rendering (that the existence of the mad *could easily* be a wandering one), and in the direction of Howard's rendering (that the mad led a wandering existence). And while Gordon is right to deny that '*une existence facilement errante*' should be read as 'an easy wandering existence', we can none the less see how the notion that it ought to be so read could emerge from the image of boatloads of mad people cruising up and down the 'calm' rivers and canals of medieval Europe, rather than running about in the countryside.

Let us move (at last) beyond '*Les fous alors* . . .' in order to contemplate the ambiguity of the passage more generally. The passage both denies and asserts that ships of fools had a real existence. As the reader can readily see, in the first three paragraphs Foucault characterizes the 'ship of fools' as a literary motif. Before even naming it, he identifies it as a 'figure' – indeed, as a 'symbolic' figure. It is an 'object', but one that appears in an 'imaginary landscape'. It is a 'literary composition', probably borrowed from the Argonaut cycle. Then, with the fourth paragraph, Foucault alters the emphasis. It turns out that unlike the ships of princes, of virtuous ladies, of health, and of foolish women, the *Narrenschiff* did exist. The rest of the paragraph provides a few scattered examples of the expulsion of mad people into the hands of sailors, and subsequent paragraphs continue discussing 'this circulation of the mad' (Foucault 1961: 11ff.; Foucault 1972b: 19ff.; Foucault 1973a: 8ff.).

We are now well along the road to seeing what sort of writer and thinker Foucault was. Note first how important a role works of art and literature play in the quoted passage. In *Histoire de la folie* generally, appeals to artistic and literary works are frequent. Often, these appeals provide the starting-point for a line of argument. This is certainly the case with the 'ship of fools' motif. It is unlikely that ships of fools would have figured in Foucault's text if there were not a famous painting by Hieronymus Bosch on the subject and a poem by Sebastian Brant, and if Tristan, feigning madness, had not been transported by a boatman over the sea. There are references also to Brant's *Narrenschiff* and Bosch's 'Temptation of St Anthony', not to mention (as one proceeds through the book) to *Don Quixote*, *Macbeth*, *King Lear*, Tasso, Racine, Swift, Diderot, Goya, Hölderlin, Nietzsche, Van Gogh, Roussel and Artaud. Foucault seems to have taken the works in question as emblematic of the 'experience of madness', which he saw as in some measure (although only uncertainly) retrievable from them.[2] At any rate, such appears to be the view that he held when he wrote *Histoire de la folie*. The view would have justified his giving to these artworks the role that he did. To be sure, even in the original edition of *Histoire de la folie* Foucault undercut this line of argument, for he also insisted that madness was 'the absence of the work', thus suggesting a gap between the experience of madness and the work and implying that the experience of madness was unrecoverable after all (Foucault 1961: v, 640–3; Foucault 1972b: 554–7; Foucault 1973a: 285–9). Here again, Foucault's ambiguity surfaces, as we shall see more clearly below.

To historians reading *Histoire de la folie*, it all too often seems that Foucault makes generalizations based on a striking image in a work of literature or art, without providing the additional arguments that would be necessary to establish persuasively that the image has broader significance. But the matter of Foucault's literariness goes deeper than this. It is not simply that Foucault relied heavily on artworks for ideas and evidence. Even more disturbing to historians (though they rarely recognize the problem for what it is) is that Foucault's own writing is highly 'literary'. Artists and creative writers – especially those close to the symbolist end of the literary spectrum – often aim for multiple possibilities of meaning. Artists in the symbolist mode *play* with words and images, setting up resonances between them. Foucault dealt extensively with this phenomenon in *Les Mots et les choses* (1966), under the rubric of 'the return of language' (Foucault 1973b: 42–4, 303–7, 382–7). In *Histoire de la folie*, he claimed that the decay of medieval symbolism (as represented, for example, by the figures carved on the walls of gothic cathedrals) was associated with a 'proliferation of meaning . . . a self-multiplication of significance', that occurred as the originally intended meaning disappeared (Foucault 1961: 22; Foucault 1972b: 28–9; Foucault 1973a: 18). It is clear that Foucault relished this kind of cultural situation, for, *mutatis mutandis*, precisely such a 'self-multiplication' is to be found in his own text.

As already suggested, in *Histoire de la folie* the multiplication most obviously manifests itself as ambiguity: hence the ambiguities that inhabit and surround '*Les fous alors avaient une existence facilement errante*'. But more can be said about the matter, for the ambiguity takes on a specific form: the form of reversal. In fact, *Histoire de la folie* is a kind of anti-Hegelian *Geistesgeschichte*. Foucault studied under the well-known Hegel translator and commentator, Jean Hyppolite (whose successor he would eventually be at the Collège de France). In the Hegelian system, particularly as interpreted by Hegel's left-Hegelian successors, an initial 'position' would be succeeded by a negation of that position, and the difference between the two would then be resolved in a higher synthesis. For example, Marx held that bourgeois society generates its contradiction, the proletariat, and that the contradiction is resolved through the emergence of a future classless society. Reversal is thus a dominant trope in Hegelian thought. Reversal equally plays a role in *Histoire de la folie* (it is less important in

Foucault's later writings, which stand further from his philosophical beginnings). But the reversal is different from the Hegelian sort, for it is an off-centre reversal, one that refuses to come together in the synthesis of a new beginning. Thus the opposition subsists, generating a 'dense' text. We end up not with Hegelian synthesis but with (for lack of a better term) 'postmodern' ambiguity.

Consider the chapter '*Stultifera navis*', which moves by a process of antithesis and progression – but always an imperfect antithesis and a broken progression. The chapter begins with an evocation of the disappearance of leprosy from the west (Foucault 1961: 3–7; Foucault 1972b: 13–16; Foucault 1973a: 3–7). By the end of the Middle Ages, Foucault contends, the old leprosaria, which had maintained leprosy in 'a sacred distance . . . a reverse exaltation', were empty (Foucault 1961: 6; Foucault 1972b: 15; Foucault 1973a: 6). In the fifteenth century the place of leprosy was 'at first' taken over by venereal diseases (Foucault 1961: 7–9; Foucault 1972b: 16–18). But the true successor to leprosy, Foucault claims, was not venereal disease but madness. Foucault then leaps forward: madness, he asserts, was 'mastered . . . toward the middle of the seventeenth century' (Foucault 1961: 9; Foucault 1972b: 18). By implication, madness must have been free at an earlier period: the opposition free/unfree comes into play. At this point Foucault gives us his 'ship of fools' discussion (Foucault 1961: 10–16; Foucault 1972b: 18–24; Foucault 1973a: 7–13), which comes in, one is initially tempted to think, as an emblem of this freedom. (In view of the apparent structure of the argument, it is again easy to see why one might be tempted to read '*une existence facilement errante*' as 'an easy wandering existence' – for here 'easy' would be the equivalent of 'free'.) But Foucault quickly thwarts the expectation that we are about to be treated to an account of earlier freedom, for it turns out that the mad are not only sent packing from the towns but are also imprisoned – as, for example, in Nuremberg, which Foucault had earlier mentioned as a town that expelled madmen (Foucault 1961: 12; Foucault 1972b: 20–1; Foucault 1973a: 9–10). Thus the antithesis wandering/imprisoned comes into play, only to be blurred. Some of the mad are imprisoned at the gates of towns, and so are placed 'at the interior of the exterior, and vice versa' (Foucault 1961: 14; Foucault 1972b: 22; Foucault 1973a: 11). Thus the opposition outside/inside is blurred. And so it goes. A particular aesthetic consciousness is at work here, a machine for the generation of ambiguity from decentred antitheses. Only if one opens one's mind to the complexity does one really see what is going on in *Histoire de la folie*. The work might be considered an instance of 'sophistic' historiography, if by 'sophistic' one wishes to suggest a commitment to antithesis, parataxis and disruption of continuity (Jarratt 1987).

II

A common move by professional historians is to condemn Foucault because he is 'rhetorical', an unserious *littérateur*. But professional historiography has its rhetoric also (Megill and McCloskey 1987). Thus we ought not to distinguish between a 'rhetorical' Foucault and a professional historiography that is unrhetorical. Nor should we try to rehabilitate Foucault by overlooking his particular rhetoric, as Gordon tends to do in his 'flat' reading of Foucault's text.

We can address the question of competing rhetorics by considering what Gordon says about the notion of 'experience' in *Histoire de la folie* and by comparing Gordon's reading of Foucault with the complexities of the text when read in a more detailed and textured way. Gordon's essay is in one of its aspects a defence of Foucault's project in *Histoire de la folie* against a criticism offered by Jacques Derrida in his essay '*Cogito et histoire de la folie*' (1963). Here Derrida claimed that Foucault's intention in writing *Histoire de la folie* was to write 'a history of madness *itself*', a task that Derrida went on to argue was impossible to carry out (Derrida 1978: 33−5). Gordon notes that a number of other critics have also seen Foucault's project in *Histoire de la folie* as involving an attempt to get back to the 'experience' of madness. Consider, for example, one critic's assertion that *Histoire de la folie*

> is an attempt . . . to come to grips with the true reality of madness. . . . Foucault proposes to return to 'that zero point in the course of madness at which madness is an undifferentiated experience, a not yet divided experience of division itself'; and starting from this zero point he proposes to write a history, 'not of psychiatry, but of madness itself, in its vivacity, before any capture by knowledge'.
>
> (Megill 1979: 477−8)[3]

Against this interpretation, Gordon argues that Foucault's point was precisely the *impossibility* of any such theory. Thus, in Gordon's view, Derrida and others have attributed to Foucault an intention that was the opposite of his true intention. They have reversed Foucault's point, condemning him for wanting to do what he himself stated could not be done (Gordon 1990: 19−21).

It is worth pointing out, by the way, that Gordon's tactic here − of responding to a critic by claiming that the critic has inverted the work being criticized − was practised by Foucault himself. The tactic tells us something about the character of Foucault's text. As Gordon notes, Foucault complained, in an irritated reply to criticisms of his work by the historian Lawrence Stone, that several of Stone's reproaches 'consist in repeating what I said while pretending I never said it' (Gordon 1990: 17; Stone 1982: 28ff.; Foucault and Stone 1983: 42). Technically, Foucault is here engaged in *apodioxis*, the indignant rejection of an argument as impertinent or absurdly false; he defends himself by accusing Stone of having engaged, at points, in an *inversio*. Under other circumstances, the observation that a critic has mistakenly inverted a statement that one has made might be offered in an irenic, concessive spirit, designed to bring writer and critic closer together. But there is no concession here: the implication is rather that the critic is an incompetent, and perhaps a conscious or unconscious plagiarist as well.

It cannot be denied (*concessio*) that critics misread, and that (even worse) they sometimes repeat an author's careful qualifications in such a way as to make it appear that the qualifications came first from the critic. I turn aside, however, from adjudicating the particular dispute between Foucault and Stone (*aposiopesis*: the breaking-off of an argument), for the concern here is not to determine what was or was not the case in early modern Europe but rather to gain some insight into the rhetorical structure of Foucault's text. The form of the criticism and the form of the text have a more than accidental relation, as the above discussion of '*Les fous alors*' ought to have prepared us to see. Let us continue a little further with Foucault's response to Stone. According to Foucault, those of Stone's criticisms that were not repetitions of Foucault's own points consisted 'in turning round, word for word, what I said and ascribing to me the subsequent thesis which has become untenable' (Foucault 1983: 42). In response to Foucault, one can only say that it is no wonder that Stone should have fallen into such an error, for Foucault's text invites misreading of *exactly* this sort. The anthropologist, Clifford Geertz, has written of Foucault's 'terse, impacted style, which manages to seem imperious and doubt-ridden at the same time' (Geertz 1978: 3). Midelfort and Dominick LaCapra also note, in their different ways, the antithetical character of the Foucauldian text (Midelfort 1990: 42; LaCapra 1990: 35). The combination of certitude and doubt, of assertion and subversion, of continuity and rupture, of repetition and change, is clearly one of the charms of *Histoire de la folie*, but it is also a fact that needs to be taken into account when discussion turns to the question of whether, on any particular point, Foucault has been misread.

To gain a yet fuller sense of the texture of Foucault's text, let us puzzle our way through two passages from the 1961 preface, both of which are concerned with the 'experience' of madness. In the second paragraph of the preface, following a short initial paragraph made up of two quotations, from Blaise Pascal and Feodor Dostoyevsky, Foucault declares that:

It is necessary to write the history of that other turn of madness – by which men, in a gesture of sovereign reason that confines their neighbors, communicate and recognize themselves through the merciless language of non-madness. To find again the moment of this exorcism [*conjuration*], before it was definitively established in the realm of truth, before it was revived by the lyricism of protest. To try to join up again, in history, with that zero degree of the history of madness where madness is an undifferentiated experience, a not yet divided experience of division itself. To describe, from the start of its trajectory, that 'other turn' which, to the one side or the other with its gesture, makes Reason and Madness fall again, as things henceforth external, deaf to all exchange, and as if dead one to the other [*Décrire, dès l'origine de sa courbure, cet 'autre tour', qui, de part et d'autre de son geste, laisse retomber, choses désormais extérieures, sourdes à tout échange, et comme mortes l'une à l'autre, la Raison et la Folie*].

This is doubtless [*sans doute*] an uncomfortable region. To traverse it we must renounce the comfort of terminal truths, and never let ourselves be guided by what we think we know [*pouvons savoir*] of madness. None of the concepts of psychopathology, even and especially in the implicit play of retrospections, can play the organizing role. What is constitutive is the gesture which divides madness and not the science that establishes itself, once this division is made, in the area of restored calm. What is primal [*originaire*] is the caesura that establishes the distance between reason and non-reason. . . . It is therefore necessary to speak of this primitive debate without presupposing a victory, or the right to a victory. . . .

Then and only then will the domain be able to appear where the man of madness and the man of reason, separating themselves, are not yet separate, and in a language that is very primal, very crude, far earlier than that of science, begin the dialogue of their rupture, which testifies in a fleeting way that they still speak to each other. Here, madness and non-madness, reason and non-reason, are confusedly implicated with each other. . . .

Modern man, in the midst of the serene world of mental illness, no longer communicates with the mad person. . . . There is no common language, or rather, there is no common language any more; the constituting of madness as mental illness, at the end of the 18th century, attests to a broken dialogue, posits the separation as already effected, and thrusts into forgetfulness those imperfect words, without fixed syntax and a bit stammering, in which the exchange between madness and reason was carried out. The language of psychiatry, which is a monologue of reason about madness, was able to establish itself only on the basis of such a silence.

I have not wished to write the history of this language, but rather the archaeology of that silence.

(Foucault 1961: i−ii; 1973a: ix−x)

The passage is complex, striking discordant notes. On the one side, Foucault expresses the wish to get back to the 'zero degree of the history of madness where madness is an undifferentiated experience'. On the other, he wants to write the history of the 'gesture of sovereign reason' by which men confined the mad. Thus he seems to envisage both a history of the experience of madness and a history of the confinement of the mad. At an early stage, he suggests, the two were joined together. But nowadays the language of psychiatry – which is surely part of reason's confinement of madness – is 'a monologue of reason about madness' that totally excludes communication with the mad themselves. Against psychiatry, Foucault tells us in the striking sentence that ends the quoted passage, that he wishes to write the 'archaeology' of madness's silence. At this point Foucault seems clearly to suggest, *contra* Gordon, a concern with the primal experience of madness, although it is an experience having a structural and not a substantive character since it is apparently constituted by the experience of the division itself. Yet at the same time Foucault undercuts his statements along this line. For example, he speaks only of 'trying' to reach the 'zero degree of the history of madness', not of actually reaching it; and what exactly *would* the 'archaeology' of a silence be?

It is important when reading Foucault to hold on to the density. Gordon notes that 'things are more complicated, and the facts more elusive than they might appear' (Gordon 1990: 19), but he seems insufficiently attentive to just *how* complicated and elusive matters are. In this regard let us consider our second passage from the 1961 preface (Gordon rightly characterizes the preface as 'among the most remarkable things Foucault wrote' (Gordon 1990: 19)). Here the characteristic Foucauldian pattern of forcefulness and doubt, manifested in successive assertion and denial, is particularly evident. Derrida's commentary on *Histoire de la folie*, and Gordon's counter-commentary, are emanations of this pattern:

it is not at all a matter of history of knowledge [*connaissance*], but rather of the rudimentary movements of an experience. A history not of psychiatry, but of madness itself, in its vivacity, before any capture by knowledge [*savoir*]. It would therefore be necessary to bend one's ear, to lean towards that mumbling of the world, to try to perceive so many images that have never been made into poetry, so many phantasms that have never achieved the colors of wakefulness. But that is doubtless [*sans doute*] a doubly impossible task: because it would require us to reconstitute [*reconstituer*] the dust of those concrete woes, of those words void of meaning that are unattached to time; and above all because these pains and these words are given to themselves and to others only in the gesture of division which already condemns and dominates them. It is only in the act of separation and starting out from it that one can think of them as a dust that is not yet separated. The perception that seeks to seize them in their wild state necessarily belongs to a world that has already captured them. Madness's freedom extends only as high as the walls of the fortress in which it is held prisoner. . . .

Accordingly, to write the history of madness will mean: to carry out a structural study of the historical ensemble – ideas, institutions, legal and police measures – which holds captive a madness whose wild state can never be restored [*restitué*] in itself; but for want of the inaccessible primitive purity, structural study must go back toward the decision which at the same time links and separates reason and madness. . . . Thus the momentous [*fulgurante*] decision, heterogeneous to the time of history yet ungraspable outside that time, will be able to reappear.

(Foucault 1961: vii)

On the side of assertion, Foucault tells us that his concern is with 'the rudimentary movements of an experience', with the 'history . . . of madness itself'. On the side of denial, he suggests that since the relevant sources are lost or perhaps never existed, and since in any case (as he contended in the extract from the preface quoted previously) madness is constituted only by the 'gesture' or 'caesura' that divides madness from non-madness, and moreover since, as he argues in another passage immediately preceding the one just quoted, western perception refuses to recognize that the words of madness ought even to be counted as language (even though the '*necessity of madness*' in our history 'is linked . . . to *the possibility of history*' (Foucault 1961: vi)), the history of madness itself cannot be written.

The complexity of the sentence just finished is intended to suggest something of the complexity of Foucault's text. The pattern – of assertion and denial – is obvious. But the denial is not a matter of simple retraction. Notice, for example, the *sans doute*, a phrase that also appeared in the two previous extracts from *Histoire de la folie*. What does *sans doute* mean? As with the English 'undoubtedly', the phrase is often used when quite a bit of doubt is felt. The French, being more subtle in such matters than English-speakers, acknowledge this in their dictionaries by giving *sans doute* the secondary meaning of 'probably'. Thus the phrase has a range of possible meaning, running from a certitude that none the less lacks the self-confidence to keep its mouth shut, to the opposite of the literal meaning: *with* doubt. And what are we to make of the subsequent paragraph? It appears that, while the 'wild state' of madness cannot be 'restored', we *can* 'go back' to the 'decision' by which madness was constituted. The decision in question (1) will be able to reappear; (2) is 'heterogeneous' to historical time, and is thus presumably outside historical time in some sense; and (3) cannot be grasped outside historical time. But can it be grasped *inside* historical time? Foucault appears to say neither yes nor no. Much suggests no. Much else suggests yes.

For example, Foucault's concern with 'structural study' can be read, not as a denial of the search for 'madness itself', but as a move from a substantive definition of madness to a structural definition (and thus to a definition that is necessarily plural, since different situations will generate – as Gordon emphasizes – different experiences of madness). After all, Foucault does retain, unerased, the initially stated intention of attempting a history of the 'zero degree of the history of madness' where madness is a 'not yet divided experience of division itself'. Moreover, at the end of the preface he writes of holding himself in a 'relativity without recourse', of employing a 'language without supports' that would somehow allow the words of madness to make their appearance (Foucault 1961: ix−x). Finally, in a passage from his *Maladie mentale et psychologie* that we can take as a restatement of his position in the period of *Histoire de la folie*, Foucault envisages 'the destruction of psychology itself and the discovery of that essential, non-psychological because nonmoralizable relation that is the relation between Reason and Unreason'. This relation, he claims, is 'present and visible in the works of Hölderlin, Nerval, Roussel, and Artaud'; it holds out, moreover, 'the promise . . . that one day, perhaps, [man] will be able to be free of all psychology and be ready for the great tragic confrontation with madness' (Foucault 1987: 74−5).[4]

Gordon questions the notion that 'experience' played an important role for Foucault in the period of *Histoire de la folie*. He states that 'the terms "experience of madness" and "experience of unreason" abound in *Histoire de la folie*' but that they almost always refer to the experience of ' "the sane or reasonable subject" ' (Gordon 1990: 21). The term carries 'little connotation of any mantic intuition of essences', Gordon contends; and it does not refer to 'one particular and uniquely true experience of madness' (Gordon 1990: 22). Gordon's assertions seem to be largely based on Foucault's treatment of 'experiences of madness' in the chapter of that title, which deals with madness after its 'capture' by Reason. But in Foucault's first chapter, '*Stultifera navis*', we are told of the rationally undifferentiated experience of madness, represented best by images of Bosch, Brueghel and Dürer (Foucault 1961: 21−2, 31; Foucault 1972b: 28−9, 36−7; Foucault 1973a: 18, 28). It is 'the tragic and cosmic experience of madness', which will find itself masked by the exclusivity of 'critical consciousness', but which will none the less reawaken from time to time − as in 'the last words of Nietzsche' and 'the last visions of Van Gogh' (Foucault 1961: 35; Foucault 1972b: 39−40). It is the threatening yet fascinating vision of esoteric learning, of forbidden wisdom and of man's hideous secret nature (Foucault 1961: 24−7; Foucault 1972b: 31−3; Foucault 1973a: 21−4). By contrast, the multifarious experiences of madness after the 'Great Internment' attract men but they do not fascinate, threaten or disturb them. 'All . . . is brilliant surface: no enigma is concealed' (Foucault 1961: 27−31, 51−3, quote at 29; Foucault 1972b: 33−6, 53−5, quote at 34; Foucault 1973a: 24−7, 35−7, quote at 25).

On the matter of 'experience' Gordon engages in a reductive reading of Foucault's text that goes against the spirit of his own astute comment that we 'may prudently respond' to *Histoire de la folie* with 'hesitation, diffidence and perplexity' (Gordon 1990: 23). He tries to resolve Foucault's ambiguities, in this case taking the denials seriously and allowing them to cancel out the assertions. Yet one of the charms of the work is precisely the fact that competing, even conflicting, voices are present in it (LaCapra

1990: 36). Moreover, there is further evidence, neglected or underrated by Gordon, to suggest that Foucault really did take 'experience' seriously in 1961. First, Foucault's writings of the 1950s show that he was considerably influenced by phenomenology in general and by Ludwig Binswanger's *Daseinanalyse* (existential psychology) in particular. Central to the phenomenological tradition is the preoccupation with getting back to 'the thing itself' – *die Sache selbst*. While it is clear that by 1961 Foucault had some doubts about the phenomenological tradition, the preoccupation remains as an important part of Foucault's concern in *Histoire de la folie*. The notion of 'experience' needs to be seen in the light of Foucault's interest in phenomenology.[5] Second, in *L'archéologie du savoir* (1969) Foucault's assertions that in *Histoire de la folie* he had been excessively concerned with 'experience' are more forceful than Gordon suggests. Foucault refers to the matter not once but several times. He goes out of his way to assert that he writes 'against an explicit theme of my book *Histoire de la folie*, and one that recurs particularly in the Preface'. He notes a need 'to suppress the stage of "things themselves" '. He declares, finally, that the aim of 'archaeology' is 'to free history from the grip of phenomenology' (Foucault 1972a: 47, 48, 203). All of this indicates a deep uneasiness on Foucault's part about the position that he had occupied in the earlier book.

III

The bemused reader might with some justification ask what the point is of this somewhat arcane discussion of Foucault's language in *Histoire de la folie* and of what his aims were when he wrote the work. If it were just a matter of arriving at a correct understanding of *Histoire de la folie* and of its place within Foucault's corpus generally, the discussion would be of relatively circumscribed interest. But our concern is really much wider than that. It is with the relation between Foucault's work (as exemplified in *Histoire de la folie*) and the work of more conventional historians. The wider topic, then, is the rhetoric of historiography, and indeed the rhetoric of academic disciplines generally.

One part of Gordon's argument is the claim that historians, particularly English-speaking historians, have misread *Histoire de la folie*. I largely agree with him. We have had some opportunity to see how ambiguous Foucault's text is; it is also difficult, gnomic, puzzling, paradoxical, suggestive, playful, erudite, recondite, learned and allusive (to choose only a few appropriate adjectives). As LaCapra has argued, historians tend to take a 'documentary' approach to texts – that is, they attempt to read *through* the text with the aim of getting at the reality that the text is presumed to cast light upon. They are generally not well attuned to the reading of 'complex texts – especially "literary" texts –', which 'are either excluded from the relevant historical record or read in an extremely reduced way' (LaCapra 1982: 54–5). It is only to be expected that in reading

Histoire de la folie historians should try to get some simple and direct propositions out of the work. But as we have seen, Foucault does not offer simple and direct propositions.

Another part of Gordon's argument is the claim that once historians come to know Foucault's work better, they will acknowledge him as one of their own. The claim, however, is questionable. Gordon greatly emphasizes a highly favourable review of *Histoire de la folie* by the historian Robert Mandrou, which appeared in the journal *Annales* in 1962, and to which Fernand Braudel, *chef* of the '*Annales*' historians, appended a similarly favourable note (Gordon 1990: 3–4; Mandrou 1962). Gordon takes these comments as unproblematic evidence in support of his assertion that French-speaking historians have been more receptive to Foucault than have English-speaking historians. He does not seem to have thought it necessary to investigate systematically the reception of Foucault by historians either in France or elsewhere. Yet, had he looked at subsequent issues of *Annales*, he would have found that in spite of the high praise of Foucault offered by Mandrou and Braudel, no one in the *Annales* community seems to have been moved to pay much attention either to Foucault or to *Histoire de la folie*. In the years 1963–9, only three extremely minor references to Foucault or his works appeared in the journal. In the period from 1970 onward, matters changed: Foucault's work *did* acquire a certain presence in *Annales*, with six references in 1970 alone and 36 through to 1981 (Megill 1987: 126, 130).[6] But the attention that *Annales* authors gave to Foucault's work after 1969 does not mean that it was being assimilated into the historical discipline in France. In 1975, at the time of the publication of Foucault's prison book, *Surveiller et punir*, the French historian Jacques Revel discussed the topic 'Foucault and the historians'; his decision to do so suggests that even the French saw the relationship between Foucault and conventional historiography as problematic. Revel characterized Mandrou's enthusiastic reaction to *Histoire de la folie* as a case of 'mistaken identity'. He claims that historians had been 'dumbfounded [*désarçonnés*] by *Naissance de la clinique* (1963), which they saw as a 'classic study of epistemology', and also by *Les Mots et les choses*, which they saw as metaphysics. As for *L'archéologie du savoir*, they did not bother to read it (Revel 1975: 13). So much for the favourable early reaction of French historians to Foucault's work.

To be sure, *Surveiller et punir*, which Revel saw as Foucault's 'most historical book' (Revel 1975: 11), opened up many paths between Foucault and conventional historians. But let us be perfectly clear about the relation between Foucault's kind of work and the work that prevails in the discipline of historiography (and in other disciplines as well). From the point of view of practitioners of the discipline, the main difficulty is not that Foucault draws on other fields in his writing of history, although it must be conceded that the presence in his work of elements drawn from diverse philosophical and literary traditions does make it harder to grasp.

Rather, the main difficulty is Foucault's antidisciplinarity. It is not that Foucault is an interdisciplinary writer, trying to link disciplines that have hitherto been kept separate, but rather that he is opposed to the very *idea* of a discipline. As one writer has noted:

> There is no discipline, with its institutions, journals, internal controversies, conceptual apparatus, methods of work, within which Foucault could carry out the task he had set himself. Indeed, there was a sense in which, like Nietzsche's, his work would have to be carried on outside, even against, the existing academic frameworks.
>
> (Sheridan 1980: 208)

Philosophers, historians and sociologists of science have increasingly been telling us that a discipline or subdiscipline is, among other things, a community of argument, or (perhaps better) a set of overlapping communities (Kuhn 1970; Toulmin 1972; Fleck 1979; Latour and Woolgar 1986; Knorr-Cetina and Mulkay 1983; Merton 1973; Merton 1988). The problem that Foucault raises for the 'community of argument' notion is that it is extremely difficult to argue with him, because it is extremely difficult to see what, exactly, he is arguing for. His ambiguity goes hand in hand with a kind of intellectual solitude. It is in literature, much more than in academic disciplines, that we are accustomed to seeing the creative ambiguity and suggestiveness that Foucault gives us in such large measure. This is not to say that the workings of a discipline are unliterary, for literary devices are of the utmost importance not only in the presentation of results but also in the very organization of research (Megill and McCloskey 1987; McCloskey 1985). Nor is it to deny that the disciplinary abhorrence of ambiguity is often more honoured in the breach than in the observance.[7] But it is to say that there is something central to the disciplinary project that seems thwarted in Foucault. It is as if, through his love of ambiguity, he has thrown a monkey wrench into the disciplinary machinery.

It is perhaps here that Foucault's work is most valuable. For disciplines are always faced by the danger of becoming sclerotized, self-contained operations. The process of producing and publishing a stream of articles, dissertations and books becomes routinized. But the aim of a discipline is the production of new knowledge, not simply the repetition of old. This aim stands in some tension with the fact that the production of new knowledge must fit itself into the already existing disciplinary framework, with its rules of thumb, acceptable begged questions, preferred focuses of research, and so on. In this context, Foucault's work must be seen as explosive, as dangerous to the sclerotization of the mechanism. It is, I think, a mistake to tone down Foucault in an attempt to make his work seem more acceptable from the point of view of 'normal' scholarly standards. It is not acceptable; and that is precisely the point.

ACKNOWLEDGEMENT

The author wishes to thank Kevin Burnett, Olivier Debarre, Rebecca Rogers, Shoggy Waryn and Trent Watts for their help.

NOTES

1 Howard's translation is of the French version condensed by Foucault himself (Foucault 1964), with some additional material restored from the original edition (Foucault 1961). Accordingly, some of the passages that I discuss in the present chapter do not appear in Howard's translation, or do so only in sharply abbreviated form.

2 To get something of the flavour of this effort, see Foucault 1961: 44–51, 415–26 and 634–43; Foucault 1972b: 47–53, 363–72 and 549–57; Foucault 1973: 28–35, 199–202, 279–89 (all the passages are abbreviated in the English translation).

3 The quotes within the quotation come from the preface to the first edition of *Histoire de la folie* (Foucault 1961: i, vii). Foucault deleted the first edition preface from the second edition of the work (Foucault 1972b). The first of the passages quoted is retained in the English translation; the second passage is not (Foucault 1973a: ix).

4 *Maladie mentale et psychologie* ['Mental Illness and Psychology'] was published in 1962. In its original form, it appeared in 1954 as *Maladie mentale et personnalité* (Foucault 1954a). The 1962 edition was an extensive revision of the 1954 book. The passage cited here appeared in a completely new chapter based on *Histoire de la folie*, which had been published, of course, in the preceding year (Foucault 1987: 64–75).

5 The relevant works are Foucault 1954b; Foucault 1954a; and Foucault 1957. For a discussion of Foucault's relation to phenomenology, see Megill 1985: 198–202 and especialy Dreyfus 1987: vii ff.

6 Megill (1987) provides a detailed analysis of the reception of Foucault's work, based on some rather thorough bibliographical and citational research. I take this opportunity to note that in researching the article I missed the three pre-1970 *Annales* references just referred to: Ehrard (1964); Anon. (1969); and Turin (1969). It turns out, however, that all are trivial. Ehrard refers to Foucault in passing, in the course of a review of Jacques Roger's *Les Sciences de la vie dans la pensée française due XVIIIe siècle*. Anon. gives us three lines on *L'Archéologie du savoir*. Turin refers to Foucault in passing, in the course of discussing sources relevant to the history of medicine in the Algerian national archives. Moreover, both Anon. and Turin go out of their way to describe Foucault as a philosopher – that is, as not a historian.

7 For an example of an ambiguity that professional historiography would reject, see Megill 1989: 640–1. But many ambiguities are acceptable in conventional historiography, because they are the ambiguities of 'common sense' and are thus not perceived *as* ambiguities by commonsensical readers.

BIBLIOGRAPHY

Anon. (1969) 'Le Choix des *Annales*' ['Some books of interest'], *Annales* 24: n.p.

Derrida, J. (1978) 'Cogito and the history of madness' in *Writing and Difference*, trans. A. Bass, Chicago: University of Chicago Press, 31–63.

Dreyfus, H. (1987) 'Foreword to the California edition', see Foucault 1987: vii–xliii.

Ehrard, J. (1964) 'Au XVIIIe siècle: Sciences de la vie et pensée française' ['The life sciences and French thought in the eighteenth century'], *Annales* 19: 947–52.

Fleck, L. (1979) *The Genesis and Development of a Scientific Fact* [1935], ed. T. J. Trenn and R. Merton, trans. F. Bradley and T. J. Wrenn, foreword by T. S. Kuhn, Chicago: Chicago University Press.

Foucault, M. (1954a) *Maladie mentale et personnalité* ['Mental Illness and Personality'], Paris: Presses universitaires de France.

Foucault, M. (1954b) 'Introduction', in L. Binswanger, *Le Rêve et l'existence* ['Dream and Existence'], trans. J. Verdeaux, Paris: Desclée de Brouwer.

Foucault, M. (1957) 'La Recherche du psychologue' ['Research in psychology'], in *Des Chercheurs français s'interrogent* ['French Researchers Reflect on their Research'], Paris: Presses universitaires de France, 173–201.

Foucault, M. (1961) *Folie et déraison: histoire de la folie à l'âge classique*, Paris: Plon.

Foucault, M. (1964) *Histoire de la folie* ['History of Madness'], Paris: Union Générale d'Editions.

Foucault, M. (1972a) *The Archaeology of Knowledge*, trans. A. M. S. Smith, New York: Harper & Row.

Foucault, M. (1972b) *Histoire de la folie à l'âge classique*, suivi de *Mon Corps, ce papier, ce feu* et *La folie, l'absence d'oeuvre*, Paris: Gallimard.

Foucault, M. (1973a) *Madness and Civilization: A History of Insanity in the Age of Reason*, trans. R. Howard, New York: Random House, Vintage Books.

Foucault, M. (1973b) *The Order of Things*, trans. anon., New York: Random House, Vintage Books.

Foucault, M. (1987) *Mental Illness and Psychology*, trans. A. Sheridan, foreword by H. Dreyfus, Berkeley and Los Angeles, Calif.: University of California Press.

Foucault, M. and L. Stone (1983) 'An exchange', *New York Review of Books*, 31 March: 42–4.

Geertz, C. (1978) 'Stir crazy', *New York Review of Books*, 26 January: 3–6.

Gordon, C. (1990) '*Histoire de la folie*: an unknown book by Michel Foucault', *History of the Human Sciences* 3: 3–26.

Jarratt, S. (1987) 'Toward a sophistic historiography', *Pretext: A Journal of Rhetorical Theory* 8: 9–26.

Knorr-Cetina, K. and M. Mulkay (1983) (eds) *Science Observed: Perspectives on the Social Study of Science*, London: Sage.

Kuhn, T. S. (1970) *The Structure of Scientific Revolutions*, 2nd edn, enlarged (orig. edn 1962), Chicago: University of Chicago Press.

LaCapra, D. (1982) 'Rethinking intellectual history and reading texts', in D. LaCapra and S. L. Kaplan (eds) *Modern European Intellectual History: Reappraisals and New Perspectives*, Ithaca, NY: Cornell University Press, 47–85.

LaCapra, D. (1990) 'Foucault, history, and madness', *History of the Human Sciences* 3: 31–8.

Latour, B. and S. Woolgar (1986) *Laboratory Life: The Construction of Scientific Facts*, 2nd edn (orig. edn 1979), Princeton, NJ: Princeton University Press.

McCloskey, D. N. (1985) *The Rhetoric of Economics*, Madison, Wisc.: University of Wisconsin Press.

Maher, B. and W. B. Mayer (1982) 'The ships of fools: *Stultifera Navis* or *Ignis Fatuus?*', *American Psychologist* 37: 756–61.

Mandrou, R. (1962) 'Trois Clés pour comprendre la folie à l'époque classique' ['Three keys to understanding madness in the classical period'], *Annales* 17: 761–72.

Megill, A. (1979) 'Foucault, structuralism, and the ends of history', *Journal of Modern History* 51: 451–502.

Megill, A. (1985) *Prophets of Extremity: Nietzsche, Heidegger, Foucault, Derrida*, Berkeley and Los Angeles, Calif.: University of California Press.

Megill, A. (1987) 'The reception of Foucault by historians', *Journal of the History of Ideas* 48: 117–41.

Megill, A. (1989) 'Recounting the past: "description", explanation, and narrative in historiography', *American Historical Review* 94: 627–53.

Megill, A. and D. N. McCloskey (1987) 'The rhetoric of history', in J. S. Nelson, A. Megill and D. N. McCloskey (eds) *The Rhetoric of the Human Sciences: Language and Argument in Scholarship and Public Affairs*, Madison, Wisc.: University of Wisconsin Press.

Merton, R. K. (1973) 'The Matthew effect in science' [1969], in *The Sociology of Science*, ed. N. Storer, Chicago: University of Chicago Press, 439–59.

Merton, R. K. (1988) 'The Matthew effect in science, II: cumulative advantage and the symbolism of intellectual property', *Isis* 79: 606–23.

Midelfort, H. C. E. (1980) 'Madness and civilization in early modern Europe: a reappraisal of Michel Foucault', in B. Malament (ed.) *After the Reformation: Essays in Honor of J. H. Hexter*, Philadelphia, Pa: University of Pennsylvania Press.

Midelfort, H. C. E. (1990) 'Comment on Colin Gordon', *History of the Human Sciences* 3: 41–5.

Revel, J. (1975) 'Foucault et les historiens' (interview with R. Bellour), *Magazine littéraire* 101: 10–13.

Sheridan, A. (1980) *Michel Foucault: The Will to Truth*, London: Tavistock.

Stone, L. (1982) 'Madness', *New York Review of Books*, 16 December: 28 ff.

Toulmin, S. (1972) *Human Understanding: The Collective Use and Evolution of Concepts*, Princeton, NJ: Princeton University Press.

Turin, Y. (1969) 'Médecine et archives algériennes' ['Medicine and the Algerian archives'], *Annales* 24: 1517–19.

Weightman, J. (1989) 'On not understanding Michel Foucault', *The American Scholar* 58: 383–406.

8   Reading and believing

On the reappraisal of Michel Foucault

H. C. Erik Midelfort

Colin Gordon makes the excellent point that too few of Foucault's English and American readers are familiar with the unabridged version of *Histoire de la folie*. For reasons best known to Foucault himself the short version in both French and English does not just leave out details but goes far to make transitions from one historical period to the next less intelligible than they were in the original, full-length study. I have long thought that Foucault permitted such fundamental changes because they corresponded better to his growing emphasis on cultural ruptures, an emphasis that came to fullest expression perhaps in *Les mots et les choses* and in *Surveiller et punir*. Certainly, it came as a surprise (perhaps even a disappointment) to some of Foucault's admirers that in 1983 he described his history of madness as 'entirely concerned with the *slow evolution* from one form of confinement, intended mainly for the poor, into a confinement involving medical treatment' (Stone and Foucault 1983: 42). In any event, Gordon is right that we need to consider the longer and fuller history.

I think that Gordon may also be right that I oversimplified Foucault's arguments when I subjected them to my critique. Gordon contends that I have misinterpreted Foucault with respect to the wandering life of the medieval mad. I confess that I too easily accepted the translation 'easy wandering existence' (*Madness and Civilization*, p. 8), but the point remains that Foucault grossly exaggerates the numbers of mad on the roads or in the ships of fools, ships fabricated by Foucault's symbol-seeking imagination. Did Foucault assert that ships of fools were a common, perhaps even a 'systematic practice in the medieval treatment of the insane'? What else could he have meant when he wrote: '*Souvent, les villes d'Europe ont dû voir aborder ces navires de fous*' (*Histoire de la folie*, 1972: 19); or

> *Et il se peut que ces nefs de fous, qui ont hanté l'imagination de toute première Renaissance, aient été des navires de pèlerinage, des navires hautement symboliques d'insensés en quête de leur raison: les uns descendaient les rivières de Rhénanie en direction de la Belgique et de Gheel; les autres remontaient le Rhin vers le Jura et Besançon.*
>
> (*Histoire de la folie*: 20)

Let us note that Foucault's few footnotes here, though more numerous than in the English translation, do not substantiate a single ship of fools. They speak of expulsions and deportations of individuals, as often by land as by river.[1] It is, of course, true that the mad were sometimes sent on a pilgrimage in hopes that they might recover, but in the Bavarian and Franconian cases I have studied closely, these madmen were not sent wandering; they were taken on a pilgrimage, they were led or carried to the shrine. Nor should we suppose that this practice was only medieval. Although statistics are hard to come by, it appears that just as many, and maybe more, pilgrims, including mad pilgrims, answered the call of baroque piety in the seventeenth century or of the resurgent Church Romantic in the nineteenth (Chélini and Branthomme 1982: 209–59, 295–53; Nolan and Nolan 1989: 80–114, esp. 99–105, 111–14).

Turning to the so-called great internment or great confinement, it seemed to me and still seems to me that Foucault exhibited an extraordinary capacity to quote and cite material that directly subverted his own con- clusions. Thus it is true enough that Foucault could acknowledge the existence of private madhouses and even of hospitals with therapeutic inten- tions in the eighteenth century, although for dubious (structuralist?) reasons he regarded such institutions as obsolete medieval relics, representa- tives of a supposedly declining ethos.[2] For Foucault the real innovation of the classical age was the institution of general confinement, the *hôpital général*, the workhouse, the *Zuchthaus*, a place of correction and punish- ment that had no medical purpose (*Histoire de la folie*: 137–8). So power- fully did these *maisons d'internement* capture Foucault's imagination that he allowed them to overwhelm his memory (and mine) when he contrasted the therapeutic intentions of the nineteenth century with the brutalizing age of reason:

> *A l'époque classique, au contraire, elle manifeste avec un singulier éclat le fait justement que* le fou n'est pas un malade. *L'animalité, en effet, protège le fou contre tout ce qu'il peut y avoir de fragile, de précaire, de maladif en l'homme.*
>
> (*Histoire de la folie*: 166; Foucault's emphasis)

This dramatic summary contradicts, of course, much of what Foucault tells us in his book. Of course the mad were often regarded as sick in the eighteenth century. Of course Foucault knew that. So what was he trying to say? I think that Foucault was so attracted to what I would call symbolic history, to a great subterranean movement of the symbols that in his view organize our attention and our affects, that he frequently allowed a shining symbol to blind him to what he otherwise knew. This could explain the 'ship of fools' and also his obsession with the '*grand renfermement*', a confine- ment mainly of beggars that included some mentally ill. Foucault knew of course that the mad were not locked up in large numbers until the nine- teenth century, but the image of the workhouse and of the *hôpital général* exerted so horrific an effect that Foucault rarely tells us how small a part the mad played in the repressive world of classical reason. (But see *Histoire de la folie*: 124.) Gladys Swain and Marcel Gauchet have pointed out that in France no more than 5,000 mentally disordered persons were incarcerated in the vast world of the *hôpital général* at the end of the eighteenth century. They represented a 'tiny minority of the mad who were still scattered throughout the interior of society'. On the eve of the First World War, by way of contrast, the incarcerated mad numbered *c.* 100,000 in France, or twenty times as many (Mongin 1983: 79).[3] The age of massive confinement of the mad was the nineteenth century. Again, Foucault knew this, but many readers have drawn other conclusions.

Gordon explains that with the great confinement of 1656–1800 Foucault was outlining the origins of the concept of deviance, as if the mad had previously been confined in *Narrenhäuser* and other cages and cells specially built for them. But any acquaintance with the history of hospitals would have shown Foucault that the mad of the late Middle Ages and the Renaissance were frequently lumped indiscriminately together with other unfortunates: orphans, the indigent, the crippled, the elderly, the blind. They received room and board and sometimes medical care as just one more variety of the socially helpless. It is not true that the mad were jumbled together with other categories of the poor and idle only after 1656, and Foucault must have known that it was not true. The correctional mood that overtook many national states in the seventeenth century did represent a major shift in the treatment and punishment of public poverty, but it is only incidentally and very indirectly a part of the history of madness. Surely Foucault knew that the moral condemnation of begging and unemployment, of madness and enthusiasm, of prostitution and blasphemy had a long history in the west. I doubt that their sudden arrival in the hospitals of absolutism marks the strange and sudden birth of deviance.

In other respects I find Gordon's clarification of Foucault's intentions helpful. It is now clearer to me what Foucault was trying to achieve with respect to deviance theory and the notion of mental illness. Here I would only remark that while canon law did indeed have a long tradition of finely shaded judgements about the degrees of personal responsibility and judicial competence, this was not much of a *medical* tradition before about 1600. Foucault's treatment of Paolo Zacchia is, therefore, misleading (*Histoire de la folie*: 139–40) because that Roman forensic physician did not so much sum up 'the whole of Christian jurisprudence concerning madness' (139) as preside over a forced marriage between medicine and law in this and in many other previously separate matters (see Midelfort 1988: 254–5). Legal medicine was actually a new field in the seventeenth century, and one that was so popular that by the mid-eighteenth century Jacob Ernest Friedrich Crell, a German jurist, charged that many a criminal suspect rushed to find compliant physicians who might testify to their madness in order to secure release from serious punishment (Crell 1737). Kant and Heinroth were not impartial or adequate sources from which to draw so far-reaching a conclusion, as Foucault seems to imply (*Histoire de la folie*: 140). I agree with the project that Gordon describes (p. 12) as the development and description of an 'institutional epistemology' taking account of various institutional perspectives, but when we deploy such an epistemology, we will find, I think, that the theologians and physicians of the period before 1600 or even before 1800 did indeed draw (in their own terms) a 'meaningful distinction . . . between physical medications and psychological or moral medications' (*Madness and Civilization*: 181; Gordon, above, p. 9). So separate were these institutional ways of knowing that Foucault almost totally ignored the theological. He had his reasons for paying no attention to demonic possession throughout the *Histoire de la folie*,[4] but they are reasons that would have baffled exorcists and Renaissance physicians alike, who regularly struggled to determine whether a particular person was spiritually infected or physically disordered. Surely here was a discourse and a therapy 'whose epistemological texture . . . [was] quite distinct from that of contemporary general medicine', to borrow Gordon's clear description of what Foucault meant by mental illness (Gordon, p. 9). Of course physicians and clerics admitted also that body and spirit were connected and that a melancholy temperament, for example, might be an invitation to the devil. But Foucault systematically excludes the possibility that demonic possession might have been the earliest form of a truly mental illness, a psychological disorder 'in the domain of guilt' (as Foucault says of the asylum), but a guilt of Christian and Satanic proportions. Where are the demons in Foucault? This subject is far too large to expound here, and it would require an institutional epistemology to grasp it, one which Foucault did not provide.[5]

It may be doubted whether Foucault will be acceptable once we have his full account before us in accurate English, but we might then understand Foucault better, and that would be a step in the right direction.

NOTES

1 For an amusing objection to Foucault on this point see Maher and Maher (1982).
2 Roy Porter has strenuously argued that these private asylums springing up in the seventeenth and eighteenth centuries provided just the novel milieu and just the experience of managing the mad from which English psychiatry could emerge as a separate discipline (Porter 1987).
3 See also Azouvi (1983) and Raynaud (1983). These reactions were stimulated by the dramatically revisionist work of Swain (1977), and Gauchet and Swain (1980). Swain and Gauchet mount an attack on Foucault in the context of an analysis of Pinel and Esquirol.
4 The fullest explanation for the principled exclusion of demonic possession appears, I believe, in Foucault's *Mental Illness and Psychology*, where he blandly describes as an 'inaccurate prejudice – the people defined as possessed were mentally ill', and apodictically declares that 'the complex problem of possession does not belong directly to the history of madness, but to the history of religious

ideas' (64). He conceded that medicine 'intervened' in the problem of possession from 1560 to 1640 and from 1680 to 1740 (taking up almost half of the period 1500 to 1800, therefore), but he insisted that 'the annexation of all these religious or parareligious phenomena by medicine is merely an accidental episode . . . and, above all, it is not the product of an effort essential to the development of medicine' (64–5). This could be developed perhaps into a coherent if not defensible position, but it would require a curious exercise to determine which of medicine's efforts at expansion and annexation were 'essential to the development of medicine'. It might be worth asking whether the medical takeover of moral therapy in the nineteenth century was any more essential. For me it seems crucial to note that in fact throughout the period 1500–1800 physicians and clerics disagreed among themselves about the characteristics of true possession, both in abstract terms and in specific cases. Foucault's plea for the independence of religious experience thus cuts him off from one of the most important sources of the idea of a mental illness.

5 Roy Porter treats the theme of religious madness and its obsessions of guilt and sacrifice in his *Mind-Forg'd Manacles* (1987).

BIBLIOGRAPHY

Azouvi, F. (1983) 'Les ruses de la déraison', *Esprit* 11: 87–92.
Chélini, J. and H. Branthomme (1982) *Les chemins de Dieu. Histoires des pèlerinages chrétiens des origines à nos jours*, Paris.
Crell, J. E. F. (1737) 'Observationes de probatione sanae mentis [1737]', in Christoph Ludwig Crell (1775–84) *Dissertationum atque programmatum Crellianorum Fasciculi XII*, Halle: fasc. V. 731–46.
Foucault, M. (1974) *Mental Illness and Psychology*, Berkeley, Calif.
Gauchet, M. and G. Swain (1980) *La pratique de l'esprit humain. L'institution asiliaitre et la revolution démocratique*, Paris.
Maher, W. B. and B. Maher (1982) 'The ship of fools; *Stultifera Navis* or *Ignis Fatuus*?', *American Psychologist* 37: 756–61.
Midelfort, H. C. E. (1988) 'Johann Weyer and the transformation of the insanity defence', in R. Po-Chia Hsia (ed.) *The German People and the Reformation*, Ithaca, NY: 234–61.
Mongin, O. (1983) 'Un nouveau regard sur l'histoire de la folie. Entretien avec Marcel Gauchet et Gladys Swain', *Esprit* 11: 79–86.
Nolan, M. L. and S. Nolan (1989) *Christian Pilgrimage in Modern Western Europe*, Chapel Hill, NC.
Porter, R. (1987) *Mind-Forg'd Manacles*, Cambridge, Mass.
Raynaud, P. (1983) 'La folie à l'âge démocratique', *Esprit* 11: 93–110.
Stone, L. and M. Foucault (1983) 'An exchange', *New York Review*, 31 March 1983: 42–4.
Swain, G. (1977) *La sujet de la folie. Naissance de la psychiatrie*, Toulouse.

9 Misunderstanding Foucault

Geoffrey Pearson

Colin Gordon begins by describing Foucault's *Madness and Civilization* as 'a famous book'. He might also have added that Foucault remains an extremely elusive author. Gordon's approach to these elusive qualities in Foucault's work, together with a number of controversies which have surrounded it, is to brand these as 'misunderstandings' which can then be corrected by a return to textual foundations and a 'correct' reading.

Something goes wrong in any translation – see, for example, the public scandal surrounding the first French edition of the complete works of Freud. Colin Gordon therefore has a point. One, moreover, which might arguably have particular relevance for a work such as *Histoire de la folie*, which appeared in English in such an emaciated form. Even so, it would be difficult to pretend that Foucault's work has not proved elusive and controversial in a much more general sense. So that, although it is welcome that we now have available one more of the several chapters excised from the English version of *Histoire de la folie*, it does not follow that the most useful response is (as Gordon does) to set about rescuing Foucault from his critics. Especially when the lifeline which is thrown to Foucault is one based around the notion of 'mis-reading' and 'misunderstanding'. To approach the controversy provoked by *Madness and Civilization* as if misunderstanding was the root difficulty implies an extraordinary passivity in both text and reader. It might almost be offered as a parody of Foucault's own self-parody in the rewritten preface to *Histoire de la folie*: '*Je suis l'auteur: regardez mon visage ou mon profil. . . . Je suis le nom, la loi, l'âme, le secret, la balance de tous ces doubles.*'

One must also ask, would things have been made any easier if from the outset the English-reading public had had access to the unabridged volume? On the contrary, if one allows an active emphasis to the process by which texts are read, even in the sense of people 'reading in' certain things, it seems more than likely that if the entire text of *Histoire de la folie* had been made available in English translation, it would have struck an Anglo-American audience as even more outrageous and prompted even more 'misunderstandings'. Colin Gordon laments 'the progressive erosion of meaning by commentary'. But is this not precisely the likely outcome when in an attempt to understand 'misunderstandings' the chosen tactic is that readings are corrected by appeals to the correct reading, so that criticism is devoured by counter-criticism, words play across each other as the text closes in upon itself, and meanings are grasped as 'essences' rather than as social constructions and thus obscured and eroded? The 'meaning' of Foucault's *Madness and Civilization* is what it meant to those who read it, both when it first appeared and in subsequent appropriations of Foucault's work to a variety of projects. It is to these scattered meanings (rather than to a textual essence) that I will address myself.

Let us assume, to follow Gordon, that in the beginning was the text and that the text was misunderstood. But then, let us suppose that misunderstandings are a vital means through which human beings communicate and recognize their differences from each other. Perhaps, even, to follow Adorno, misunderstandings are a means through which the incommunicable is communicated. Then it becomes necessary to remember that at the point at which *Madness and Civilization* appeared – such a famous, maddening and incomplete book – in many diverse aspects of western European and North American intellectual life and culture, there was a groping search for an incommunicable alteration in social affairs and in human self-understanding. It was a search which announced itself under diverse banners and ventures – 'antipsychiatry', 'deviance theory', 'labelling theory', 'counter-culture', 'history from below' – through which it was hoped that human nature and history would at last, liberated from the shackles of reified conceptions of conformity and mechanical systems of causality, speak for themselves. Set against this, there was a beleaguered professional establishment – Criminology, Psychiatry, History – which pressed back against these new claims, and reasserted the positivist scientific virtues, the set-in-concrete systems of classification, the sense of a true history ordained by ruling elites, and a culture bound and protected by tradition. And here, a man who had the audacity to confront one of the permanences of nature – madness, which had only quite recently been brought within the bounds of civilization, classified, understood and placed under effective treatment by a true medical science, as a true mental illness – and to establish this madness as a terrain upon which earlier cultures and civilizations and sciences had trespassed, bringing their own forms of understanding (and misunderstanding) to bear through their own authentic means. Although, crucially, theirs was not to be understood as a 'misunderstanding' of madness – neither as a pre-Enlightenment primitivism, nor as a romanticized 'Golden Age'. It was to be understood as a perception of madness fashioned within a fundamentally altered cultural landscape – '*sur un autre ciel*' is how Foucault expressed it. Whose side must this man be on, in this groping towards a different vision of humanity? No need to ask the question. And here, obviously, there was another misunderstanding: that the radical anti-humanist Michel Foucault could be mistaken for a humanist!

In order to clarify the reception of Foucault's *Madness and Civilization*, rather than returning to the text, we need to return it to the world which embraced it. What is required is an attention to what at one time, in *The Deviant Imagination*, I called the 'smell' of theory. That is to say, the extent to which theoretical enterprises, however they might be conceived, run up against and resonate with, or enter into abrasive contact with, wider currents of moral–political assumption and exchange. An obvious case in point is the way in which *Madness and Civilization* came to be appropriated to the antipsychiatry project – or, to be more specific, the English anti-psychiatry project associated with R. D. Laing. Colin Gordon acknow-ledges this as an issue, while evidencing little curiosity about the matter, although it was indeed one of the oddities of the reception of Foucault into an English-speaking audience that it was initially through a series on 'The World of Man' edited by R. D. Laing. (Commercial considerations in the world of publishing can be excused for the even larger oddity that *The Order of Things* and *The Archaeology of Knowledge* appeared within the same edited series.) David Cooper's ecstatic foreword to the book – 'Madness has in our age become a sort of lost Truth' – guaranteed a certain kind of initial readership with a certain cast of mind. The central thrust of antipsychiatry in this period of its development was the critique of medical appropriations of madness and associated methods of institutional confine-ment, classification and treatment. Whether or not Cooper's exclamation is a fair record of Foucault, the book was nevertheless entirely sympathetic to the antipsychiatry project – if only because it is a sound idea to attend to the origins of a system of thought and practice, if the object is to bring about its downfall. There is also, on any reading, a romantic residue in Foucault's work at this stage of a 'properly understood' sphere of madness – one situated within literary and dramatic forms, rather than being thrust to the margins of the culture where it is subject only to the gaze of medicine and science. The positioning of Nietzsche, Van Gogh and Artaud in the final paragraph of *Histoire de la folie* was scarcely intended to discourage thoughts of this kind.

And yet, the antipsychiatry appropriation of Foucault in itself fails to explain anything. Because it is, then, the reception of antipsychiatry which demands explanation. Very few medical psychiatrists were in sway of R. D. Laing in Britain in 1967. The rapturous welcome came from different sources among the younger generation – 'mindless militants' in the student movement; protesters against the genocide in Vietnam; cranks and scribblers around underground newspapers such as *International Times* who were already warning of the possibilities of environmental catastrophes and ecological planetary collapse – amidst stirrings of some older Reichian psycho-politics, and the new 'encounter groups', 'gestalt groups' and 'human potential centres'. It was possible within this structure of feeling to define madness as non-existent: merely, that is, as something manufactured by society. The radical libertarian texts of Thomas Szasz further encouraged such an attitude. Szasz's applications of Gilbert Ryle and Peter

Winch in *The Myth of Mental Illness* had been an engaging intellectual exercise. The political emphasis of his writing on law, liberty and psychiatry had sometimes been of a different kind, with a belligerent right-leaning radical libertarian stance. Szasz's 'historical' work, *The Manufacture of Madness*, developed a direct and compelling (and ultimately false) argument around the historical associations of madness and witchcraft, where Szasz's blunt no-nonsense approach stood in direct contrast to Foucault's oblique and self-enveloping literary stance. No prizes for guessing who defined the wider readership and understanding of the dawning historical shapes of lunacy and its treatment and control. Indeed, Foucault was now in some dodgy company. Although other historical work of a more scholarly nature joined the fray: David Rothman's *The Discovery of the Asylum* with its intriguing observations on asylum architecture; Andrew Scull's forays into the field of madness and psychiatry, which often seemed to adopt as an organizing principle a 'conspiracy theory' of the medical profession; Robert Castel's *L'Ordre psychiatrique*, which owed much to Foucault; Elaine Showalter's exposure of the gender divisions within this history; or Michael MacDonald's *Mystical Bedlam* which, although it distanced itself from Foucault's philosophy and method, nevertheless acknowledged the need to 'travel in the spreading wake of Michel Foucault's famous book'. But whatever different shades of emphasis one might easily discern between this empirical history and Foucault's own project, the 'Whig history' approach to the advancement of medical domination in the field of psychiatry (perhaps best exemplified in Kathleen Jones's work) was steadily pushed back from the central field of vision. And, whichever way one cared to look at it – indeed, whichever way one cared to look – Foucault's *Madness and Civilization* was there, as a commanding, looming presence.

By the time that Peter Sedgwick had summoned up his fatal blow to the antipsychiatry project, in his *Psycho-Politics*, antipsychiatry had given up the ghost. Indeed, it is one of the tragedies of Sedgwick's life that his earlier, scintillating essays on Laing from the early 1970s took so long to bear their final fruit. There remained only a dogged negativism in Sedgwick's opposition to any suggestion that the mentally ill were not in need of care and assistance, recklessly mixing its criticism of the quite different projects of Laing, Szasz and Foucault. From where we stand now, in fact, we can begin to see that the antipsychiatry movement is in need of an urgent reassessment: rejection of Laing has degenerated into little more than a knee-jerk spasm of fashion. It is a reassessment which, in its time, will no doubt redouble misunderstandings of Foucault.

Meanwhile, Foucault had become embroiled in a development approximately contemporary to that of the antipsychiatry project, in the shape of a critique of criminology. Indeed, this had been part of the same counter-cultural 'misfit paradigm' which had assisted the popularity of antipsychiatry. Drawing its inspirations from the same kind of rethinking of social institutions and the specific forms of knowledges, prevailing conceptions of 'normality' and conformity, together with socially constructed definitions and negotiations of the contours of madness, criminality and other forms of 'deviance', there had been a gathering together in both North America and Britain (and later some parts of Europe) of the 'sociology of deviance' through the work of such contrasting figures as Becker, Goffman, Scheff, Lemert, Matza, Schur, Douglas and Erikson. But here again there was something more at stake than simply a reshuffling of texts, since any number of the 'seminal' texts had been available, and unacclaimed, since the early 1950s. Rather, this was part of the same cultural tendency, the structure of feeling, which had embraced and promoted antipsychiatry beyond the boundaries of the clinic.

A core dimension of this sociological reappraisal of criminology involved attempts at an overarching theory of 'deviance' (to encompass not only crime and madness, and the conventional ground of criminology and psychiatry, but also sexual affairs, physical and social comportment in the form of 'manners', etc.). And here again in Foucault there was an appearance (indeed, the actuality) of a fellow traveller along this 'new' path; someone who was clearly interested in and devoted to this larger enterprise of the regulation of morality, which was incapable of being addressed from within the disciplinary straitjackets of criminology, psychiatry, psychology, law, etc. A further core preoccupation was the so-called 'labelling theory' (again dormant in the early work of Lemert and Becker since the early 1950s) which was concerned with the defining powers of the state and the collectivity on what should count as 'deviance' and 'normality'. If antipsychiatry had not found itself in sympathetic collusion with this shift of emphasis within North American sociology, it would have been strong-armed into service by the radical National Deviancy Conference of the early 1970s. Reified definitions, classifications and statistics of 'deviance' were anathema to this misfit sociology of the 1970s, whether in the form of the positivistic criminologies inherited from the past or medical assumptions which imposed 'disease' models on both crime and madness. In the 'appreciative' stance recommended by David Matza, as opposed to the dead weight of understanding pledged to a 'correctional' purpose, deviance was a free bird. 'Zoo-keepers of deviance' was a slogan summed up to characterize the past; for the present, the new radical deviancy theorists preferred safari parks. And M. Foucault was standing in the wings, as an accomplice in this relativizing venture, calling into question the facticity of both inherited institutional forms and the knowledges and practices with which they cohered.

A further set of related debates and disputes in which Foucault then became involved flowed from both the ways in which this new 'sociology of deviance' latched on to historical forms of understanding as part of its reconstruction of the terrain, together with new departures in Anglo-American history which had begun to address the question of a 'history from below' which often involved its own reconstructions of crime and punishment, together with a variety of aspects of popular culture and sentiment. This revitalized social history was to become a close companion to subsequent developments within British and North American approaches to 'deviance and social control', well exemplified in the collected edition on *Social Control and the State* by Stanley Cohen and Andrew Scull. In the late 1960s, there had been little more within this tradition than Musto's historical analysis of drug policies in the USA, together with historical vignettes such as Erikson's account of the Salem witch-trials. Meanwhile, Edward Thompson's *The Making of the English Working Class* had put down a monumental landmark of a history of a new kind. And then, in the mid 1970s, the appearance of Thompson's *Whigs and Hunters* and its companion volume *Albion's Fatal Tree* (Hay *et al*. 1975) signalled that the new social history of crime and punishment had come into full bloom. Moreover, the renewed interest by historians in matters of crime and punishment, together with the regulatory forms surrounding madness, offered a number of points of sympathetic alliance within the structure of feeling which addressed questions of 'deviance' and 'conformity'. On the one hand, history was an ideal vehicle for the empirical demonstration of the shift and change of social definitions of deviance and conformity. (Social anthropology had long provided a rich field of anecdote, rather than any serious basis for the analysis of comparative forms.) On the other hand, the new 'history from below' resonated with the implicit underdog sympathies of both the antipsychiatry and deviancy wings of the 'misfit paradigm' of the 1960s and 1970s.

Colin Gordon regrets the fact that Foucault was not accepted within the Anglo-American historical establishment, and seems somewhat bemused by the contrasting reception from French historians. And yet, even the most cursory understanding of the traditions of Anglo-American history would have predicted that even if Foucault had not been found in the company of such a rag-taggle-gypsy entourage as the student movement and antipsychiatry, with radical deviancy theorists in tow – flavoured with a whiff of the *événements* of 1968 – his work would still have received a frosty welcome in the English-speaking community of historians. Because if so far I have only mentioned the sites of sympathetic attachment between Foucault's work and the 'misfit paradigm', then it becomes necessary to put grit in the oyster. We can highlight a number of the ways in which Foucault's project was on a collision course with the English historical tradition, whether in its establishment or radical modes.

Setting Foucault to one side for a moment, the interest shown by sociologists in history (and by some historians in sociology) had violated an ancient taboo in the intellectual firmament of English historical scholarship. The two disciplines of sociology and history, with one or two notable exceptions such as Smelser's deployment of historical materials in his theory of 'collective behaviour' (i.e. social disorder), had passed each other by like ships in the night. It was, to mix a metaphor of Fernand Braudel, a 'dialogue of the deaf'. So that this co-mingling of historians and sociologists prompted not only areas of scholarship of mutual benefit, but also conflicts and crude territorial disputes and disciplinary feuds. Foucault in a sense fell foul of this.

Another fundamental source of difficulty lay in the distinctively different styles of address and scholarly display in England and France. A particularly severe distinction is maintained within the English tradition between 'science' and 'literature'. One of the problems with sociology and other forms of social scientific understanding is that they are often seen as grey areas between these two separate cultures, two nations of intact discourse within the same nation. The French relaxation of these corsets of knowledge and expression, which Foucault represents *par excellence*, offends these English puritan habits of thought no less than 'sociologists'. There is also that marked reluctance within English history to theorize, or to be seen to be theorizing. Foucault transgresses these interlocked taboos, whereby a privileged status is allowed to modest empirical obscurantism in English history and small-scale ventures are preferred to the total history of a Braudel. Foucault did not only feel like a fellow traveller to the radical sociologists of the 1960s and 1970s; he looked like a sociologist fellow traveller to the English historical establishment. When we are told, as recently as 1982, in the radical *History Workshop Journal* that Foucault 'is ultimately interested not in "the past"', his project is a 'history of the present' – this is damning with faint praise.

In order to see the differences between these two habits of thought and scholarship – the Anglo-American historian's devotion to a small-scaled focus of detailed sources and evidence; the French *élan* for the broad sweep of a total history – one need only set side by side Foucault's *Discipline and Punish* and Michael Ignatieff's *A Just Measure of Pain*. They are ideal companion volumes, both concerned with the same historical question: the emergence of the penitentiary in the course of the eighteenth and early nineteenth centuries. The one is written with the same all-embracing, elusive and provocative force which we so rightly identify with *Histoire de la folie* and its little Franco-Britannique cousin *Madness and Civilization*. The other offers an equally scintillating narrative of the emergence of the penitentiary amidst the English industrial revolution, but within the traditions of E. P. Thompson and his brilliant empiricism. Ignatieff grudgingly acknowledges Foucault on the last page, where he judges that Foucault's work is flawed by its 'fatalism' (i.e. structural tendencies and 'sociology') whereas Ignatieff advocates an emancipatory role for historical research, which in terms of the historical necessity of the prison was something which could liberate us from 'this suffocating vision of the past that legitimizes the abuses of the present and seeks to adjust us to the cruelties of the future'. Misunderstanding Foucault?

Perhaps. The important point surely is to acknowledge that just as the reception of his earlier publications such as *Histoire de la folie* was surrounded by both hostile rejection and romantic moon-gazing, his later and often less accessible work would continue to provoke argument, cement agreement in some quarters, divide opinion in other quarters, pass unnoticed elsewhere. Foucault's work was a major source of inspiration to the late twentieth century, making available a different way of thinking, a different way of looking, a different way of feeling about European history. The knock-on effects – whether in terms of dedicated applications, loose deployments, or those pale 'Foucauldian' imitations which have been fashionable with a generation of postgraduate students – have been formidable. It is, moreover, perfectly appropriate that work of the stature of Foucault's should generate such a ferment of controversy and provocation. The attempt to squeeze this ferment back into its original textual confines, to put the lid back on as it were, is a doomed pursuit. In spite of the fact that he renounced the author's sovereignty of the text (perhaps because of it) Foucault knew that the arguments provoked by the 'miniscule event' of the publication of a book would rebound against themselves and redouble unceasingly and ambiguously among his fellow travellers in an ambiguously finite universe. Scholars would trudge off into what they imagined to be the forests of the unknown, find false leads and follow false trails, return to base and strike out on a new path, meet people already trudging back. . . . The rewritten preface of *Histoire de la folie* already knew the score, of an incessant swarm of conjecture which surrounded its arguments, sometimes making them unrecognizable to the author himself, but in the final analysis 'neither delusion nor identity': '*Un livre se produit, événement miniscule, petit objet maniable. Il est pris dès lors dans un jeu incessant de répétitions; ses doubles, autour de lui et bien loin de lui, se mettent à fourmiller . . . les commentaires le dédoublent. . . . La réédition en un autres temps, en un autre lieu est encore un de ces doubles.*' ('A book appears, a minuscule event, a handy little object. From then on, it is taken into an unceasing game of repetitions; its doubles begin to swarm about it, near and far . . . commentaries split it in two. . . . A new edition, in another time, in another place, is again one of these doubles.')

BIBLIOGRAPHY

Castel, R. (1988) *The Regulation of Madness: The Origins of Incarceration in France*, Oxford: Polity Press.

Cohen, S. and A. Scull (eds) (1983) *Social Control and the State*, Oxford: Martin Robertson.

Erikson, K. T. (1966) *Wayward Puritans*, Chichester: Wiley.

Foucault, M. (1972) *Histoire de la folie à l'âge classique*, Paris: Gallimard.

Hay, D., P. Linebaugh, J. G. Rule, E. P. Thompson and C. Winslow (1975) *Albion's Fatal Tree: Crime and Society in Eighteenth-Century England*, London: Allen Lane.

Ignatieff, M. (1978) *A Just Measure of Pain: The Penitentiary in the Industrial Revolution*, London: Macmillan.

Ignatieff, M. (1983) 'Recent social histories of punishment', in S. Cohen and A. Scull (eds) *Social Control and the State*, Oxford: Martin Robertson.

Jones, K. (1955) *Law, Lunacy, and Conscience 1744–1845*, London: Routledge & Kegan Paul.

Le Rider, J. (1989) 'Freud et ses faux amis traducteurs', *Le Monde*, 28 February.

MacDonald, M. (1981) *Mystical Bedlam: Madness, Anxiety, and Healing in Seventeenth Century England*, Cambridge: Cambridge University Press.

Matza, D. (1969) *Becoming Deviant*, New York: Prentice-Hall.

Musto, D. (1973) *The American Disease: Origins of Narcotics Control*, New Haven, Conn.: Yale University Press.

Pearson, G. (1975) *The Deviant Imagination*, London: Macmillan.

Rothman, D. (1971) *The Discovery of the Asylum: Social Order and Disorder in the New Republic*, Boston, Mass.: Little, Brown.

Scull, A. T. (1975) 'From madness to mental illness: medical men as moral entrepreneurs', *European Journal of Sociology* 16.

Scull, A. T. (1976) 'Mad-doctors and magistrates: English psychiatry's struggle for professional autonomy in the nineteenth century', *European Journal of Sociology* 17.

Scull, A. T. (1979) *Museums of Madness*, London: Allen Lane.

Sedgwick, P. (1971) 'R. D. Laing: self, symptom and society', *Salmagundi* 16.

Sedgwick, P. (1972) 'Mental illness *is* illness', *Salmagundi* 20.

Sedgwick, P. (1982) *Psycho-Politics*, London: Pluto.

Showalter, E. (1985) *The Female Malady: Women, Madness and English Culture, 1830–1980*, New York: Pantheon Books.

Smelser, N. J. (1959) *Social Change in the Industrial Revolution*, London: Routledge & Kegan Paul.

Szasz, T. S. (1961) *The Myth of Mental Illness*, New York: Harper & Row.

Szasz, T. S. (1973) *The Manufacture of Madness*, London: Paladin.

Thompson, E. P. (1968) *The Making of the English Working Class*, Harmondsworth: Penguin.

Thompson, E. P. (1975) *Whigs and Hunters*, London: Allen Lane.

Weeks, J. (1982) 'Foucault for historians', *History Workshop* 14.

10 Foucault's great confinement

Roy Porter

On first reading *Madness and Civilization*[1] twenty years ago, I was bewitched, bothered and begrudging. Since then, my admiration, for both its erudition and its vision, has grown with every rereading. Time has proved it by far the most penetrating work ever written on the history of madness (and, above all, the history of reason). Colin Gordon's paper (1990) evokes the dazzling originality of Foucault's analysis, and there is no need here once again to detail its qualities. As Gordon emphasizes, the standard criticisms have often been the products of prejudice, misunderstanding and ignorance (not least, ignorance of those parts of *Folie et déraison* omitted from the English translation).[2]

In this brief chapter I shall reconsider a few of the problems Foucault discusses. I shall concentrate on developments in England during Foucault's 'classical age' (roughly from 1650 to 1800, the time of Pinel and Tuke). I shall suggest some alternative readings, based, I hope, on a familiarity with Foucault's complete text, on the findings of subsequent research, and, not least, on the suggestions afforded by Foucault's own later works (what sort of a *Folie et déraison* would the author of *Surveiller et punir* or *La volonté de savoir* have gone on to write?). Space restrictions force me to be long on assertion and short on nuance and evidence; for documentation I refer the reader to the subsequent scholarship listed in the notes.

Central to Foucault's interpretation of the successive construals and exclusions of madness is the idea of a 'great confinement', a great internment, activated, from the mid-seventeenth century, in context of political absolutism and Enlightenment rationality (Foucault 1965: 61). Foucault treats the 'great confinement' as a European movement, though one assuming diverse institutional forms in different monarchies (Foucault 1965: 43, 49). Those whose lives affronted bourgeois rationality – beggars, petty criminals, layabouts, prostitutes – became liable to sequestration higgledy-piggledy with the sick and the old, the lame and lunatic.[3] Such problem people, though *different* from normal citizens, were *identical* among themselves. Their common denominator was idleness. The mad did not work; those who did not work were the essence of unreason.[4]

If this is an honest, albeit desperately simplified, summary of key features of Foucault's 'great confinement', it is a concept which I do not find especially applicable to England (less still, one might add, to Scotland and Ireland).[5] Take 'confinement' first. What happened in post-Restoration England to the kind of social flotsam and jetsam, whose destiny in France, according to Foucault, lay in the *hôpital général*? Of course, some such people ended up in that institution's English 'twin city', the workhouse. Research has confirmed the spread of the workhouse during the Georgian century as a solution to problems of social policing (Thomas 1971; Rose 1971). But the vast majority of the poor and the troublesome were not interned within institutions, remaining at large in society, under the administrative aegis of the Old Poor Law. Or, one might say, they *were* 'confined', but confined only within the bounds of their parish of settlement. The perpetuation of such costly and lax outdoor relief enraged later reformers. A better symbolic date for an English 'great confinement of the poor' might be 1834, with the advent of the New Poor Law and its compulsory workhouse.

This applies no less to the mad. Michael MacDonald has demonstrated how rarely the mad were formally confined in early Stuart England (families, of course, shut up their mad relatives in cellars and barns) (MacDonald 1981a; 1981b; 1982a; 1982b). The signs are that such informal arrangements remained extremely common in the century after the Restoration. The work of Fessler and Regan on Lancashire, and Rushton on the North-east, shows that lunatics typically remained at large, the responsibility of their family under the eye of the parish (Fessler 1956; Regan 1986; Rushton 1987; cf. Jimenez 1987).

Of course, some 'mad folks' (however defined) ended up under lock and key, and the institutionalized population grew. But I am not convinced that it makes much sense to label this process a 'great' confinement. Before 1774, private asylums were under no legal obligation to keep admissions records, and, even thereafter, little reliance should be placed upon official returns; but it seems reasonable to suggest that perhaps not many more than 5,000, and certainly fewer than 10,000, people were confined as mad in England by the early nineteenth century, in all types of institution (private, public and charitable madhouses, gaols, workhouses, etc.) (Porter 1987a, Chaps 1, 3; Parliamentary papers 1819). In what Foucault called the 'classical age', the growth in the practice of excluding the mad was gradual, localized and piecemeal. The curve on the graph becomes steep only in the nineteenth century; by 1900, the tally of inmates had leapt to almost 100,000. This should not surprise us: for it was not till the nineteenth century that Parliament made the erection of public lunatic asylums mandatory. For England, it makes better sense, numerically and conceptually, to call not the eighteenth century, but its successor, the period of the 'great confinement'. Before 1800, the handling of lunacy remained largely local and responsive to market forces; thereafter the state seized the initiative.[6]

Central to Foucault's reading of the 'great confinement' is the claim that the mad were confined without distinction alongside all other 'offensive' people: all were 'Unreason' (Foucault 1965: 83). There is value in Foucault's insistence that madness was not, at this stage, defined by specialist psychiatric criteria, being rather a negative projection of Reason. Yet this picture of indiscriminate confinement does not seem accurately to match what actually happened in England. Few lunatics were kept in gaols, and workhouse superintendents resisted their admission, fearing they would be disruptive of order and labour.[7] By contrast, the practice developed of farming out dangerous parish lunatics to specialist private asylums (perhaps a function of England's more sophisticated market economy) (Parry-Jones 1971).

In other words, the tendency in England was not to lump but to split. This is graphically demonstrated by practice in London. The sister corrective institutions, Bethlem and Bridewell, had histories that were closely intertwined; they were managed by the same governors. Yet scrupulous care was taken to reserve Bethlem for lunatics and Bridewell for the disorderly (initially misplaced inmates were sometimes transferred). It would be profoundly misleading, in other words, to see Bethlem as anything like a London equivalent to the *hôpital général*. Whatever its grim faults, Bethlem was run, throughout the classical period, as a medical institution, under a physician, for treating those considered, after medical examination, clinically insane.[8]

Foucault's use of the category 'unreason' brilliantly captures the ontological and social alienation of the madman in contemporary discourse: he was like a wild animal (not a human), he was idle (not a bourgeois) (Foucault 1965: 72). Two comments are, however, called for. First, about labour. I do not find prominent in eighteenth-century English discourse the couplings Foucault emphasizes between sanity and work, madness and sloth.[9] Less still was there any concerted attempt to put the asylum population to work (the contrast with nineteenth-century practice is stark indeed).[10] In later studies, especially *La volonté de savoir* (1976), Foucault detached himself from those who interpret the disciplines of modernity (e.g. sexual restraint) as responses to the 'work ethic' supposedly demanded by capitalist rationality. In his earlier emphasis upon the union of rationality and labour we have, I suggest, an instance of Foucault offering the kind of 'ideological' interpretation he was later to dismiss as glib Freudo-Marxism.

Second, about the madman as subhuman – an identification whereby Augustan reason dramatically re-enforced the scapegoating of the mad as 'other'. Andrew Scull has recently reaffirmed the frequency with which the lunatic was characterized as a 'brute' in eighteenth-century formulations.[11] Another image, however, became prominent in the Enlightenment, one scarcely acknowledged by Foucault: the madman not as emblematic of the full 'animality of madness', but as he who reasons wrongly – and who may therefore be capable of re-education and reform (Porter 1987a: Chap. 4).

As Foucault rightly stresses, it was this latter concept of insanity which became central to the 'moral therapy' reformism of Pinel and the Tukes at the close of the eighteenth century.[12] I wish to suggest, however, that it was influential within English theory and practice notably earlier. John Locke's contention that madness arose from the (mis)association of ideas was eagerly and explicitly taken up by numerous Georgian writers and mad-house keepers, especially William Battie and Thomas Arnold (Porter 1987a: Chap. 4; Hoeldtke 1967; Arnold 1782–6). Indeed, the pamphlet battle waged in the 1750s between Battie and John Monro, the physician to Bethlem, hinged precisely on this issue. Monro contended that madness was a radical and dehumanizing vitiation of the will; citing Locke, Battie by contrast embraced the optimistic view that it was, very frequently, a per-fectly curable error of the reasoning processes (Battie 1962). Peculiarly, Foucault barely mentions Locke, and entirely omits the immensely influen-tial Battie. This may account for his otherwise quite mystifying remark that in the eighteenth century 'psychology did not exist'.[13] In the pedantic and trivial sense, this may be true – the term itself was not used to label a discipline. But a Lockeian 'psychology' (call it what you like) was a vast significance in British writings on madness from Battie through to Connolly.[14]

Which brings me to my concluding point, Foucault implies that the 'moral therapy' of the Tukes (kindness, humanity, reason) marks an authentic break in England, much as the reforms of Pinel in France. I shall not here discuss the general issue of continuities *versus* discontinuities in history, nor Foucault's tendentious reading of Tukean psychiatric 'kind-ness' as an internalized intensification of repression.[15] I believe, however, that to see the Tukes as constituting a major discontinuity is uncritically to accept their own propaganda and that of nineteenth-century reformers who routinely blackened their predecessors. The research of the last generation has revealed the extent of the preaching and practice of forms of 'moral' treatment, drawing upon Locke's psychology, in the era preceding the Tukes (Porter 1987a: Chap. 4). Foucault was right to perceive that the history of madness cannot be understood without tackling the history of reason. These few remarks have attempted to show that the modalities of 'reason' of England in the classical age still need further scrutiny.[16]

NOTES

1 Foucault (1965). This is a translation of the abridged (1964) French edition of (1961) *Folie et déraison: histoire de la folie à l'âge classique* (Paris: Plon).
2 In this paper, I have consulted M. Foucault (1961) *Folie et déraison: histoire de la folie à l'âge classique* (Paris: Plon) alongside the English translation men-tioned in note 1. I have quoted from the (abridged) English version where possible. Otherwise I have quoted from the 1961 (full) French edition.
3 Foucault (1965), 48: Foucault speaks of an 'undifferentiated mass'.

4 Foucault (1965), 45, 51, 57: Foucault writes of inmates 'subject to the rules of forced labour'.
5 See Rice (1981); Finnane (1981). Public confinement of the mad was rare in either country before the nineteenth century; the insane remained the responsibility of their families.
6 For nineteenth-century developments see Scull (1979; 1981; and 1989). Scull (1989) is a collection of essays, among which the following are specially relevant; 'Humanitarianism or control? Some observations on the historiography of Anglo-American psychiatry', 31–53; 'From madness to mental illness: medical men as moral entrepreneurs', 118–61; 'The asylum as community, or the community as asylum: paradoxes and contradictions of mental health care', 300–30.
7 Delacy (1986), 117–19. Most lunatics in gaol were apparently criminal lunatics; for the fight between workhouses and asylums at a later date, see Hervey (1987).
8 Andrews (1991). Andrews conclusively demonstrates that Bethlem was exclusively for the insane, and that admission was by medical criteria. See also Allderidge (1985); O'Donoghue (1914; 1923). Foucault shows that the *hôpital général* was *not* a medical establishment, and contends that in the classical age the 'madman was not a sick man' (Foucault 1965: 40, 74). Foucault recognizes that Bethlem was only for the mad (1961: 138), but he does not comment on the bearing of this fact for his general vision of internment.
9 By contrast it was often complained that profit-seeking within the commercial economy was the cause of insanity. *Cf.* Beddoes (1802–3), Volume 3, essay 10, p. 77.
10 The idleness of the inmates of the traditional asylum was a frequent cause for complaint. See Parliamentary Papers (1815). For the order of labour in the *nineteenth*-century asylum see Hunter and Macalpine (1974).
11 Scull (1989) 'The domestication of madness', 54–79. See also Dudley and Novak (1972).
12 Foucault (1965), Chap. 9, 'The birth of the asylum'. For modern assessments of the Retreat see Digby (1984; 1985; 1986a; 1986b; 1987); Scull (1989) 'Moral treatment reconsidered', 80–95.
13 For Foucault's remark, see (1956), 197; for psychology, see Fox (1987), 1–22. Locke receives but one passing mention from Foucault (1961: 238), Battie none at all.
14 For the enduring power of associationism, see Porter (1987b).
15 Foucault's implication that 'kind' psychiatry is even worse than 'cruel' confinement is clearly not empirically refutable. For what it is worth, the work of Anne Digby has shown that a high proportion of the inmates of the York Retreat recovered their senses, left the asylum, and were grateful for the treatment they had received. These facts may, of course, be adduced to prove Foucault's point. See Digby (1985; 1986a; 1986b; 1987).
16 For the 'reason' of eighteenth-century England, see Porter (1981); Rousseau and Porter (1990).

BIBLIOGRAPHY

Allderidge, P. H. (1985) 'Bedlam: fact or fantasy?', in W. F. Bynum, Roy Porter and Michael Shepherd (eds) *The Anatomy of Madness*, 2 vols, London: Tavistock, ii, 17–33.
Andrews, J. (1991) 'A history of Bethlem Hospital *c.* 1600–*c.* 1750', Ph.D. thesis, University of London.

Arnold, T. (1782–6) *Observations on the Nature, Kinds, Causes and Prevention of Insanity*, 2 vols, Leicester: Robinson & Cadell.

Battie, W. (1962) *A Treatise on Madness*, and John Monro, *Remarks on Dr. Battie's Treatise on Madness*, introduction by R. Hunter and I. Macalpine, London: Dawsons.

Beddoes, T. (1802–3) *Hygeia*, 3 vols, Bristol: J. Mills.

Delacy, M. (1986) *Prison Reform in Lancashire 1700–1850*, Manchester: Chetham Society.

Digby, A. (1984) 'The changing profile of a nineteenth-century asylum: the York Retreat', *Psychological Medicine* 14: 739–48.

Digby, A. (1985) 'Moral treatment at the York Retreat', in W. F. Bynum, Roy Porter, and Michael Shepherd (eds) *The Anatomy of Madness*, 2 vols, London: Tavistock, ii, 52–72.

Digby, A. (1968a) *Madness, Morality and Medicine*, Cambridge: Cambridge University Press.

Digby, A. (1986b) *From York Lunatic Asylum to Bootham Park Hospital*, York: Borthwick Papers, no. 69.

Digby, A. (1987) 'Quantitative and qualitative perspectives on the asylum', in R. Porter and A. Wear (eds) *Problems and Methods in the History of Medicine*, London: Croom Helm, 153–74.

Dudley, E. and M. E. Novak (eds) (1972) *The Wild Man Within*, Pittsburgh, Pa.: University of Pittsburgh Press.

Fessler, A. (1956) 'The management of lunacy in seventeenth century England. An investigation of quarter session records', *Proceedings of the Royal Society of Medicine* 49: 901–7.

Finnane, M. (1981) *Insanity and the Insane in Post-Famine Ireland*, London: Croom Helm.

Foucault, M. (1961) *Folie et déraison: Histoire de la folie à l'âge classique*, Paris: Plon.

Foucault, M. (1965) *Madness and Civilization: A History of Insanity in the Age of Reason*, trans. R. Howard, New York/London: Random House/Tavistock (1967). This is a translation of the abridged (1963) French edition.

Foucault, M. (1976) *La volonté de savoir*, Paris: Gallimard; trans. by R. Hurley as *The History of Sexuality*, Volume 1, *Introduction*, London: Allen Lane (1979).

Fox, C. (1987) 'Defining eighteenth-century psychology. Some problems and perspectives', in C. Fox (ed.) *Psychology and Literature in the Eighteenth Century*, New York: AMS Press, 1–22.

Gordon, C. (1990) '*Histoire de la folie*: an unknown book by Michel Foucault', *History of the Human Sciences*, 3: 13–26.

Hervey, N. (1987) 'The Lunacy Commission 1845–60, with special reference to the implementation of policy in Kent and Surrey', Ph.D. thesis, University of Bristol.

Hoeldtke, R. (1967) 'The history of associationism and British medical psychology', *Medical History* 11: 46–65.

Hunter, R. and I. Macalpine (1974) *Psychiatry for the Poor, 1851. Colney Hatch Asylum, Friern Hospital 1973: A Medical and Social History*, London: Dawsons.

Jimenez, M. A. (1987) *Changing Faces of Madness. Early American Attitudes and Treatment of the Insane*, Hanover/London: University Press of New England.

MacDonald, M. (1981a) *Mystical Bedlam: Madness, Anxiety and Healing in Seventeenth-Century England*, Cambridge: Cambridge University Press.

MacDonald, M. (1981b) 'Insanity and the realities of history in early modern England', *Psychological Medicine* 11: 11–25.

MacDonald, M. (1982a) 'Religion, social change and psychological healing in England 1600–1800', in W. Sheils (ed.) *The Church and Healing*, Oxford: Basil Blackwell, 101–26.

MacDonald, M. (1982b) 'Popular beliefs about mental disorder in early modern England', in W. Eckhart and J. Geyer-Kordesch (eds) *Heilberufe und Kranke in 17 und 18 Jahrhundert*, Münster: Burgverlag, 148–73.

O'Donoghue, E. G. (1914) *The Story of Bethlem Hospital from its Foundation in 1247*, London: T. Fisher & Unwin.

O'Donoghue, E. G. (1923) *Bridewell: Hospital, Palace, Prison, School from the Earliest Times to the End of the Reign of Elizabeth*, London: Bodley Head.

Parliamentary Papers (1815) *Reports from the Committee on Madhouses in England*, House of Commons.

Parliamentary Papers (1819) *A Return of the Number of Houses in Each County, or Division of the County, Licensed for the Reception of Lunatics*, House of Commons.

Parry-Jones, W. L. (1971) *The Trade in Lunacy, A Study of Private Madhouses in England in the Eighteenth and Nineteenth Centuries*, London: Routledge & Kegan Paul.

Porter, R. (1981) 'The Enlightenment in England', in Roy Porter and Mikuláš Teich (eds) *The Enlightenment in National Context*, Cambridge: Cambridge University Press, 1–18.

Porter, R. (1987a) *Mind-Forg'd Manacles. A History of Madness from the Restoration to the Regency*, London: Athlone.

Porter, R. (1987b) 'Bedlam and Parnassus: mad people's writing in Georgian England', in G. Levine (ed.) *One Culture. Essays in Science and Literature*, Madison, Wisc./London: University of Wisconsin Press, 258–80.

Regan, M. (1986) *A Caring Society. A Study of Lunacy in Liverpool and South West Lancashire from 1650 to 1948*, Merseyside: St Helens and Knowsley Health Authority.

Rice, F. (1981) 'Madness and industrial society. A study of the origins and early growth of the organisation of insanity in nineteenth-century Scotland *c.* 1830–1870', Ph.D. thesis, University of Strathclyde, 2 vols.

Rose, M. (1971) *The English Poor Law 1780–1930*, Newton Abbot: David & Charles.

Rousseau, G. S. and R. Porter (1990) 'Introduction' to G. S. Rousseau (ed.) *The Languages of Psyche. Mind and Body in Enlightenment Thought*, Berkeley, Calif. and Los Angeles: University of California Press.

Rushton, P. (1987) 'Lunatics and idiots: mental disability, the community and the Poor Law in north-east England, 1600–1800', *Medical History* 32: 34–50.

Scull, A. (1979) *Museums of Madness*, London: Allen Lane.

Scull, A. (ed.) (1981) *Madhouses, Mad-doctors, and Madmen: the Social History of Psychiatry in the Victorian Era*, London: Athlone Press.

Scull, A. (1989) *Social Order/Mental Disorder. Anglo-American Psychiatry in Historical Perspective*, London: Routledge.

Thomas, E. G. (1971) 'The treatment of poverty in Berkshire, Essex and Oxfordshire 1723–1834', Ph.D. thesis, University of London.

11 Foucault, rhetoric and translation
Figures of madness

Anthony Pugh

> *translation is like history (. . .) to the extent that history is not to be understood by analogy with any natural process.*
>
> (de Man 1986: 83)

The debate over Colin Gordon's attack upon what he portrays as certain historians' misreading or even non-reading of the original, untranslated and unabridged version of Foucault's *Histoire de la folie* illustrates among other things how attitudes to the role of rhetoric in the human sciences have shifted in the period since the work first appeared. Of particular interest are difficulties arising from Foucault's idiosyncratic attitude to both historical references in the form of other texts and historical 'referents' such as recorded events, dates, persons and places, for it is clear that those who see 'referents' primarily as words and those who see them as 'things' read the 'same' book and its rhetoric differently.

Folie et déraison, to give the book its original title, was always an unusual piece of *writing* as well as an unconventional work of history, but French theorists of the 1960s and 1970s were frequently more interested in the problem of the relationships between signs, signifiers, tropes and 'figures' within the fictional worlds of literary texts than in the role of rhetoric in apparently more 'referential' ones (Genette 1966: 209) such as 'histories'. Barthes had decoded novelists' use of the past historic tense in provocatively ideological terms and used the term *'écriture'* to describe a kind of writing whose essential content was in fact embodied in its 'style' (Barthes 1953), but it was some time before he made explicit the significance, for both his cultural critique and his personal poetics, of rhetoric, old and new (Barthes 1966; 1970). Though emergent neologisms like 'textuality' and Kristeva's *'signifiance'* (Kristeva 1969)[1] highlighted the 'play' of surface forms in the creation of meaning, the emphasis was still literary, and Barthes's remarks on traditional fiction's parasitical position in relation to the 'Order' of bourgeois history achieved more prominence than his equally significant essay on historical writing (Barthes 1967). Discussions of rhetoric tended meanwhile to be very technical (Groupe μ 1970), while Genette's edition of *Fontanier* (Genette 1977) stressed the obscure nineteenth-century rhetorician's discreet professionalism, as if it were just a matter of putting rhetoric back into the curriculum (as has subsequently been done in impressive textbooks like *Le Français au lycée* (Pagès 1984). Only when Michel de Certeau and Paul Veyne, following very much in Foucault's wake, turned the spotlight on the *writing* of history (de Certeau 1975; Veyne 1971), did the problem of the relationship between rhetoric and reference or 'referentiality' reappear on the theoretical agenda. However, such was the havoc wrought by ideologues who insisted upon 'the materiality of the signifier' and deconstructors who saw no end to the twists and turns of rhetoric that the renewal of interest in referentiality was described by one linguist as akin to the return of the repressed, the rediscovery of an obscene, degraded notion (Kerbrat-Orecchioni 1982: 28).

Gradually, then, the focus moved back towards rhetoric's actual function (the persuasion of the reader) as opposed to its intrinsic or extrinsic status in relation to language – only to reveal that both critical theory and philosophy had also repressed another crucial problem: the uncertain protocols governing the reception of texts (Scholes 1989). Again, the Freudian law (Freund 1987: 132–3) revealed the systematic way emphasis on one 'face' of language (whether form, meaning or reference) can conspire to conceal the other(s). All of which would tend to support Foucault's theses regarding discourse, 'knowledge' and power, and, in particular, the tendency for discourse about language to mimic the circular negotiations by means of which his 'mad poets' had exposed the '*non-sens*' present in, beneath or behind all discourse. But it took the appearance of revisionist histories and dubious autobiographies to force French philosophers and theorists to look again at language, rhetoric, reference and reading in the context not so much of 'history' as 'temporality' (Ricoeur 1983; 1984; 1985).

Jean Bessière's recent 'counter-reading' of contemporary discourse about rhetoric makes the point concisely:

> writing and reading are acts; acts that are always in the present, and as a consequence self-referential and in some degree systematic since the acts they stand for close the system while putting it into motion. . . . Reading rhetoric is not so much reading the possibility of its meaning or lack of meaning as noting the relationship that the speaking, writing and reading subject maintains with the other. . . . The contemporary ideology of rhetoric invites a reading of rhetoric in terms of a recuperation or loss of what is enunciated. . . . But the questioning that rhetoric brings about is first of all a questioning of the removal of both the text and the subject as writer or reader from the problem.
>
> (Bessière 1989: 7–8)

Such then is the broad historical and theoretical context for what follows, but I also wish to explore some of the implications for the debate over *Histoire de la folie* of a memorable remark by Foucault concerning reading:

A nightmare has pursued me since my childhood: I have before my eyes a text which I cannot read, or of which only a small part is decipherable; I pretend to read it. I know that I am inventing it; then the text suddenly blurs entirely . . .

(Foucault, quoted in Gane 1986: 1)

Authentically autobiographical, fictional or apocryphal, this memory allegorizes beautifully the inherent difficulties of the translator's task by transposing the problematic into an oneiric context where the absence of an 'original text' (in the sense of a set of primary meanings) is taken for granted. For as more than one theorist of translation has remarked, the better the translation, the more clearly is the mythical nature of the 'original' revealed. Discussing his study of Walter Benjamin's 'The Task of the Translator', Paul de Man demonstrated the point by quoting devastating examples of misunderstandings and mistakes by Benjamin's distinguished translators, and ended up claiming that translations do not 'translate' meanings from one language to another at all. Neither metaphors for an original nor copies, they remained 'intralinguistic' in that they functioned not between or across languages but 'between one linguistic function and another' (de Man 1986: 61). The result could however be positive if it resulted in new readings of the source text: '[T]he translation canonizes, freezes, an original and shows, in the original a mobility, and instability, which at first one did not notice' (de Man 1986: 61).

Nowadays, against the background of an extreme theoretical position such as the one represented by a controversial figure such as de Man, what were first seen as quirks of style and a confusing use of referents and references in *Histoire de la folie* are read rather differently; at first construed as strange tensions between the tropological and the literal levels of a text ostensibly about properly historical matters (dates, sources, facts, an explanatory narrative of cause and effect), stylistic peculiarities in Foucault's text are also viewed in terms of new thinking concerning the relationship between historicity, narrativity and an altogether less theoretical thirst for autobiographical clues. Critical theory has always cultivated misreading in the sense of reading 'against' the text (or the ideologies that control their reading) and, as Foucault himself remarked, it is only in retrospect that the calculated strangeness of a writer's mannerisms can be defined as a recognizable 'style'. Judgements concerning any 'evolution' in a 'style' are, however, themselves also subject to Foucault's catch-22 rule, if indeed the concept of 'evolution' applied to writing is just another instance of a discursive reflex that contrives to conceal the final issue of silence and writing-for-death beneath a scientistic, humanistic belief in progress towards something other than death.

This is why even the significance of stylistic details can be problematic, as when Foucault italicizes the word '*continuité*' in the opening pages of Chapter IV (in reference to the classical period's treatment of the insane) and goes on to claim that the 'experience' described was *'homogène'* despite the multiplicity of terms used to classify the mad. While Foucault's use of italics remains perfectly coherent in the context of the antitheses at work in his text ('Il ne s'agit pas de repérer l'erreur qui a autorisé pareil *confusion*, mais de bien suivre la *continuité* que notre manière de juger a maintenant rompue') the pre-echo of what would become key notions in critical theory in the 1960s and 1970s, such as discontinuity and heterogeneity, is bound to affect our reading now: they have become, retrospectively, clues to the negative epistemology Foucault would enunciate in his subsequent writings. Readers in 1961 (including professional historians – see Castel in Chap. 4 of this book) would, however, have considered such details as insignificant and incidental to the main argument of *Histoire de la folie*, a work which, in its complete version, appeared as solidly based upon historical evidence (in the form of references to documents and other histories) as any reader of a more conventional 'history' might wish. There is little point in asserting that Foucault's *real* purpose was to explain our difficulty in understanding the kinds of judgements that were used to lock away the mad in the seventeenth and eighteenth centuries in terms of discontinuities in diagnostic criteria reflected in unstable terminologies corresponding to arbitrary classifications, or that modern 'mental medicine's' prestige is a consequence of a combination of technology and 'knowledge as power' (as in the uniformization of treatment of forms of 'unreasonable/irrational' behaviour by means of drugs), for most of these points emerge, *indirectly* and *ironically*, 'between the lines'. So although we cannot really object to remarks to the effect that Foucault's emphasis on discontinuities in *Histoire de la folie* was 'in part a rhetorical device' designed to undermine unquestioned concepts like 'human nature' or 'progress' (Donnelly, in Gane 1986: 17), such rhetorical devices are not reducible to a single, literal, 'intentional' meaning. Instead, they remain open to new readings and interpretations corresponding to new preoccupations that might just represent the 'return' of older ones.

While *Histoire de la folie* obviously has to be approached both as a chronicle that reproduces or refers to certain documented 'facts' and as a highly wrought text clearly significant in terms of Foucault's future development as a *writer*, the translator must nevertheless take care not to impose too much in the way of retrospective judgements upon details. While acknowledging that the reception of the work in the context of critical theory and literary history as well as history 'proper' is an integral part of the story of misreading charted in this volume ('rewriting' is only half the problem), the implications of 'transitory' and retrospective reading (Ricardou 1972: 34) should be thought out in terms of a dialectic with no positive terms: no original meaning, no final meaning – just what readers have made and will make of an original text, what translators try to make of its difficulties, and what readers of translations do with what they derive from them.

Returning to the question of rhetoric and autobiographical clues, it is interesting to note that it was on a historian's writings that Barthes had tested, a few years before the publication of *Histoire de la folie*, the hypothesis that the tropological patterns of texts corresponded to an author's 'personal mythology' (Barthes 1954), but it was not until much later that Hayden White, using Kenneth Burke's Vico-inspired quartet of 'Master-tropes', argued that historians' comic, tragic, tragi-comic, romantic or ironic world-views might be echoed by characteristic figural patterning and tropological choices (White 1973). It is hardly necessary to summarize the ensuing moves: the undoing of tropes leads to the questioning of the very notion of readability; translatability becomes a major philosophical problem, and, finally, all we have left is endless rewriting. Indeed, if the history of madness is being rewritten and *Histoire de la folie* retranslated now, it is precisely because pathological attitudes towards rhetoric and rhetoricity have been revealed by cultural contradictions specific to the late twentieth century, as evidenced by the simultaneous flight away from and back to referentiality in historiographic theory and popular culture (Baudrillard 1981: 69–76). What this boils down to is that history-writing has no privileges over other types of discourse, and if Foucault's status as a historian remains questionable it is because the questions he asks historians about their assumptions and methods remain critical in all manner of discursive practices including critical theory.

One of my contentions is therefore that misreading, when it is not merely a matter of professional prejudice or political posturing, is as it were built in to reading: it is an experience common to all, simply because writing, reading, interpreting and rereading are all diachronic, and thus involve forgetting and repressing. There is in other words a pathology of reading that has yet to be explored, for whether we like it or not we are all inscribed, as writers, in the phenomenon we are examining. Here, it is discourse on language and, specifically, discourse about (Foucault's) discourse on the language used to classify the insane. The readings of *Histoire de la folie* discussed in this volume go back thirty years and the readings of *Madness and Civilization* cover more than twenty; long enough for all of those concerned to have experienced a number of shifts, even radical alterations, in their own attitudes towards language, theory, thought, history and possibly translation too. In fact, *not* to have undertaken *some* rethinking in at least one or two of these areas would in itself betoken an uncanny resistance to the strangeness of the postmodern condition.

Certainly, the view that the problem of *Histoire de la folie*'s chequered career in the Anglo-Saxon world lies in 'mistranslation' alone is a chimera. As Colin Gordon points out, Richard Howard's rendering of what was already an abridged version in French is good enough, and, while I have drawn attention to some slight disagreements I have with Howard's rendering of the opening of Chapter IV (Foucault 1991: 20–1), I do not consider, for reasons outlined above, that his translation constitutes or ever constituted a barrier to some 'truer' understanding of an original that it somehow travesties. Happily, Gordon's 'Response' (see Chap. 14) has also disposed of the notion that Foucault, by authorizing the publication of a truncated text in translation, was attempting in some way to control its reception by English-speaking readers. My own contacts with Foucault's publishers confirm Gordon's view that Foucault neither discouraged nor encouraged a 'rectification' of the situation. Quite simply, no British or American publisher was sufficiently interested, until recently, in the idea of going back to the original and completing the job. Now that this process has commenced, however, the situation is different; it is possible to re-examine in detail both the quality of the historical 'evidence' (the references), the use Foucault makes of it, and, as a by-product of the process of translation, look more closely at some of the more noteworthy narratological, rhetorical and stylistic features of the text. As Gordon admonishes: 'Foucault's work does not need an armed guard . . . some things become no longer sayable about *Histoire de la folie*, and . . . others become seeable'; '[W]hy worry about Foucault's reception by "the historians"?' (see Chap. 14).

A penetrating essay by Hayden White depicted catachresis as the dominant trope in Foucault's writing (White 1979), but the 'Master-trope' (White 1973; Burke 1969) that gives *Histoire de la folie* its unique tone is surely Irony; catachresis, or the 'improper' use of terms, is, like any other figure of rhetoric, a meaningless device until read: what counts is its effect upon the subject as reader, and all readers read 'intentionally', both in terms of what they think the writer's intentions were and their own particular preoccupations. The problem is that both they and '[H]uman authors exist in time. Their intentions change . . . and often these intentions are vague and incomplete to begin with'. The reader produces 'a textual interpretation that is the product of two consciousnesses, finding meanings that neither could be said to have "intended" before they were found but that both would find appropriate' (Scholes 1989: 53–4). Here, however, the theorist goes just too far, as if nostalgia for a mythical meeting of minds via texts had momentarily clouded his analysis, for we can only *claim* that in Foucault's writing irony has the 'purpose' of revealing the empty spaces of a historical time around familiar or uncritically accepted terms and that misnaming the mad was an abuse of language carried out by a 'superior' power calling itself 'reason'; none of this is guaranteed by any superior authority.

Foucault's 'history' of madness can of course also be read as a *parody* of rationality's own linguistic and rhetorical devices, showing how reasonable it was to confine and punish, and then medicate and infantilize those manifesting the signs of unreason. Hyperbole and hypallage (altering the construction and application of words) would be among the many tropes besides irony which could be read as serving this purpose. There is a danger here though: a too accomplished parody runs the risk of defeating its own object if it resembles its target too closely. As Jonathan Culler has pointed out, irony is not always easy to pin down, since an ironic statement cannot be ironic *per se*: it requires, like parody, a context or the memory of another text, not to speak of a reader or addressee (Culler 1974: 188). Which means that if we think we perceive irony as a trope in Foucault's text, it is either in reference to what we assume on the basis of other reading to be authorial intentions or other expectations deriving from some intertext we recognize as a 'ground' against which the ironic meaning can be seen as 'really' ironic (the Greek root for 'irony' is *eiron*, meaning to dissemble) – or some combination of all these elements. Expectations vary from reader to reader, and different readers obviously read different texts, which inevitably (and ironically) means that the only ground one can be sure of sharing is that occupied by rhetoric's 'commonplaces'. In the present context this means the syntagms imposed by the contingencies of communication, consumption and exchange in today's intellectual marketplace, such as the 'jargon' of critical theory or any other of the social/human sciences. To say, with Foucault, that there is no 'place' outside discourse though there is infinite space within it, is thus both a commonplace of a certain postmodern discourse and a statement that sums up some of what we think we know and a lot of what we do not know about discourse. As interest in rhetoric in the human sciences has grown, moreover, the 'same' problematic has been seen to occur across a range of disciplines, such as psychology, whose claims to knowledge about knowing are deflated in the last chapter of the original *Histoire de la folie*, entitled *'Le cercle anthropologique'*. Psychology, says Foucault, is just another instance of the 'dialectic of modern man grappling with his truth, which comes down to saying that it [psychology] will never exhaust what it is at the level of true knowledge' (Foucault (1961) 1972: 549, my translation).

The last lines of the passage in question (which immediately precedes the section that became the 'Conclusion' with the much-cited praise of poetic folly in the abridged version and in Howard's translation) are also worth quoting, since the problem of translating them forces the reader/interpreter/ translator to choose between good and bad rhetoric (if it is not improper to talk of a proper use of rhetoric in the first place): *'Mais dans ces engagements bavards de la dialectique, la déraison reste muette, et l'oubli vient des grands déchirements silencieux de l'homme'* (Foucault (1961) 1972: 549). In translating this, interpretative choices have first to be made, such as deciding that the sentence in fact 'makes sense', for it is immediately clear that a 'literal' rendering will produce non-sense. There is in any case no absolute literal ground upon which to build, since the signifier *'engagements'* could be rendered as either 'encounters' or as a military metaphor, 'skirmishes', while *'grands déchirements silencieux'* means something half-way between 'great silent rendings' or 'great silent conflicts'. Choosing between these variants, the translator is bound to try to 'homogenize' the language to some extent, in the interest of readability. A literal translation of a putative 'original' being impossible we could nevertheless opt for a *relatively* unadorned version: '[B]ut in these chattering dialectical encounters unreason remains silent, and forgetting comes from man's great, silent conflicts'. We might, however, prefer a more elaborate style involving some transpositions: 'But throughout the chatter of dialectical encounters unreason remains mute, and from the huge silence in man comes forgetfulness'. If both versions were felt still too obscure, a causal element could be introduced (or stressed, if felt somehow to be 'already there'). This would make 'forgetfulness' (or should it be 'forgetting'?) a more explicit *result* of man's *'grands déchirements silencieux'*: '[B]ut throughout the chattering skirmishes of the dialectic reason stays mute, as the silent, rending conflicts in man obliterate its memory'. We should not forget either that the whole sentence could also be in the past tense in English, since Foucault is still referring to nineteenth-century psychiatry.

It is translation as such that fails here, not just translators, for in a literal rendering concerned with clarity rhetorical effects reinforced by grammatical twists may have to disappear while others are introduced. In the sentence quoted above, for example, the two clauses are linked by *'et'*, but the conjunction appears also to function like a copula articulating subject and predicate: unreason, personified, is made to appear a cause of the *'grands déchirements silencieux de l'homme'* from which comes *'l'oubli'*. The conjunction has fused the two independent statements; now they are linked by an inexorable logic. In classical rhetoric, the omission of a connecting particle between clauses was called *asyndeton*, or *dissolutio*; in Foucault's sentence, the connecting particle seems, on closer examination, to be hard to justify on grammatical grounds. Rhetorically, however, it reinforces the paradox being explained (psychology's self-ignorance) by demonstrating the difficulty of explaining it adequately with the same discourse as used by psychology to assert its mastery over unreason: the gap in the logic is emphasized by being filled, gratuitously. The figure of *dissolutio* is thus effectively reversed in a kind of *mise en abyme* of rhetoricity, a reversed mirror-image of rhetoric as the 'double' of a non-existent 'proper' language: something within language that dissolves sense and that grammar can undo.

To come after Flaubert, Kierkegaard and Nietzsche is to live in the 'age of suspicion', and the 'ground' against which Foucault's text projects (what we read as) ironic effects of meaning is therefore already that of a shared cultural prejudice in favour of dubitative attitudes and wariness before over-confident rejoicing in the power of words. Foucault's ironic style in *Histoire de la folie* is thus no mere affectation, and a lot more than a 'rhetorical device': it reveals by refraction the crucially distorting prejudices shared by those who assume they already know what history is and who also assume that 'unreason' is to reason as negative is to positive or darkness to light. Ironizing constantly on this counter-enlightenment theme, Foucault's writing draws attention to a message better left implied than spelled out, for to draw attention too explicitly to a basically *contradictory* argument whose hidden agenda consists of demolishing from within both the assumptions and the methodology of conventional histories would have been counter-productive for initial readability in 1961. Subverting a rationale based on absolute distinctions between reason and a purely grammatical opposite called *'dérasion'* requires some subtlety if the argument is not to be dismissed as the token oppositionalism that came a little later to be known as *'contesta-tion'*. This is perhaps why Foucault uses the word *'déraison'*, which 'unreason' translates adequately, but not wholly accurately, as the mor-phology of the French word reveals reason's own role in constructing not its absolute *negative* but a kind of shadow of itself, a dimly recognized Other; not so much 'unreason' as a desertion from it, a falling away from reason that cannot be defined other than on reason's own terms.

Such an example shows why irony is not a 'figure' in the sense that it is recognizable as a typical syntagm; as we have seen, all we can do is describe what we think an ironic statement might mean, in relation to a literal one that we have to construe in between or behind the lines. This difficulty was recognized early on by Gérard Genette: '[R]hetorical form is a surface, that sets the boundaries between the present signifier and the absent signifier' (Genette 1966: 210). The reading of the term *'déraison'* described above is therefore in a sense perfectly gratuitous, for the type of irony in which Foucault specializes hollows out a distance between the literal surface of the text (which is in fact the only dimension where 'figures' or tropes can be perceived as such) and a putative literal *meaning* that is *never* spelled out: the reader does not discover, uncover or 'recover' such meanings for they are not inherent in the text (or elsewhere) but are produced by the 'play' (in the sense of looseness) in 'the internal space of language' between signs and meaning (Genette: 209). Speaking 'for' but not of course quoting the mad, Foucault can only express the pathos of their plight by means of rhetoric, but he finds a way of circumventing the classical age's 'interdiction' of the insane and of making their voices heard and their pain felt by repeated use of the metaphors *'visage'* and *'figure'*. Because in French *'figure'* can mean both 'face' and figure in the rhetorical sense, the *translatio* or metaphoriza-tion of meanings is reinforced by play on an accident of language, across a semantic gap between synonymous terms. The result is a series of quasi-oxymorons: invisible faces (*'les visages de la folie'*) silently screaming at the reader out of the gathering darkness of the European enlightenment (Foucault (1961) 1972: 149).

Thus by contriving to write a history of a phenomenon whose reality he doubts and whose aetiology as charted by conventional historians he views as totally imaginary, Foucault unsettles previous accounts of the history of madness, undoing narrative sequences and dissolving crucial 'events' back into the void of pre-discursive 'experience'. His own tale of madness subverts the cause and effect logic of narrative sequence by opening up all manner of gaps between the literal signifier and its 'absent' meaning: it is not a history that is being constructed or even a story that is being unfolded:

it is more like a 'mis-story' being untold. The mistelling is what inevitably produces 'misreading'. The reading that *Histoire de la folie* invites must therefore itself be an 'unreasonable' one, and this irony is felt throughout. Perceiving the effect does not, however, help in the construing of individual sentences, which is the level at which the translator necessarily operates.

The effect of reading Foucault's 'mis-story' is in fact like listening to a very long unfinished joke: there is not just an ever-increasing time-lag between reading and comprehension, but no cathartic release at all, no revelation of meaning that might restore sense to the world of appearances and misnomers. Whereas simple irony involves a doubling back in time to an 'original' or literal meaning in an effort to 'correct' the sense of the ironic statement which, logically, must be partly or wholly untrue, exaggerated or understated in order to be perceived as ironic at all, Foucault's irony (like Flaubert's) has a 'cosmic' quality, for he (his writing) sends us 'back' on a wild goose chase in pursuit of imaginary referents we can only describe and analyse according to the terms laid down by our present concerns and using the words current in our present discourses. While the consequences for translation are disturbing, the recognition that translation does only operate 'intralinguistically' (de Man 1986: 82) can nevertheless help to determine what the practical possibilities of translation are, as opposed to the absolute impossibilities.

A sentence early in Chapter IV of *Histoire de la folie* illustrates the difficulty of finding a precise locus for the literal meaning we aspire to discover behind the irony of uncertainty, catachresis and parison (symmetrical clause structures). *'Elle [la folie] est déjà en porte-à-faux à l'intérieur de ce monde de la déraison qui l'enveloppe de ses murs et l'obsède de son universalité'* (Foucault (1961) 1972: 157).[2] Literally, this means that madness (is) was 'already in an awkward position ('out on a limb' is a rough equivalent of *'en porte-à-faux'*) in the world of unreason that wrapped it in its walls and overwhelmed it by its universal character'. My final version of this sentence reads as follows: 'It was already in a precarious situation in this world of unreason, whose enveloping walls were an overwhelming reminder of its universality' (Foucault 1991: 3). While I am reasonably confident of having rendered the essential and 'rationally' explicable meaning of the complex image of a personified madness wrongfully imprisoned, I can hardly claim to have reproduced its intricate, interrelated (if not entangled) rhetorical features. For example, the personification loses some of its vigour through the sacrifice of the idiomatic expression *'en porte-à-faux'*. And, in their turn, the equally personified walls hemming madness in become less threatening. Finally, the paradoxical process by which unreason 'obsesses (or overwhelms) madness with (or by) its universality' is made to seem all too 'reasonable'. As it happens, an earlier more 'literal' (in fact more respectfully figural) version of this sentence was roundly criticized by one of the many specialists who have contributed to this volume, and, although he had totally misunderstood the sentence anyway, I decided to compromise, sacrificing the strangeness and near illogicality of Foucault's image for a partial 'explanation' that retained at least the form of the personifications, if not the full impact of the metaphorical substitutions that produce, in French, a striking sense of language itself 'out on a limb'. Indeed, the more one looks at it, the stranger it becomes, and it is here that we can see translation as itself a metaphor for a certain type of deconstructive reading. Parodying Paul de Man, therefore, we reach a point (a point of no return, or of aporia) where the image reads as a demonstration of *'paradoxisme'* (Fontanier/Genette 1977: 137) verging on non-sense, a *mise en abyme* of both the figure of madness and the madness of figures, which is to say, rhetorically, chiasmus, or the figure in which word order is reversed, as in a mirror. Whether the *mise en abyme* is literal, as in chiasmus, or symbolic, as in the example of unreason faced by madness, unable to explain its difference, the immediate effect of the passage is to make the reader too feel trapped by a language that defers, rather than refers, refusing to make immediate sense.[3] The irony in the rhetoric is once again the simple fact that it is the 'same' language which, in the name of reason, the law and, later, science, confines, imprisons, interns and 'treats' the insane.

Irony can signal either doubt and uncertainty or their opposite, depending upon contexts and intertexts, but if ironic effects in *Histoire de la folie* are sometimes ambiguous it is because a discourse about language that questions language's right to name must avoid implying over-confidence in linguistic paradigms; if the narrative dimension of the book is dominated by metaphor, as it chronicles all the different names given to the 'same' symptoms of madness, the effect is systematically anti-realist, since metonymy is the basic of both realist narrative and conventional history. Add to this an argument that is neither coherent nor incoherent, but which is nevertheless persuasive, and we have at first sight just a paradoxical demonstration of language's power to create something out of nothing other than substitutions and what one might call 'dissemblance' (dissemble + resemblance). The by-product — the unsettling of the reader — is, however, a positive effect in relation to the author's own thesis concerning discourse and power, for by means of the *indirect* discourse of irony, both philosophical and ethical points could emerge out of the writing's self-referential rhetorical artifices. If rhetoric is already a 'misuse' of language, then the misuse of language by reason can only be illustrated by a 'double' misuse of rhetoric, as revealed in the *mise en abyme*. Again, such effects do not have to have been 'intended'; they are only 'there' to the extent that reading (and translation) attentive to gaps and indeterminacies produce them.

When Foucault refers to previous historians of madness as 'doctor-historians' (Foucault (1961) 1972: 131; 1991: 7), he is referring to attempts to demythologize the notion that the French Revolution brought an end to the criminalization of the mad but also mocking histories that implicitly justify 'mental medicine' as practised ever since. The irony thus works in at least two directions, emphasizing both the ease with which history can be written in order to validate the present and the way it (re)organizes the past. Because of this dual focus, I felt obliged to add to Howard's version of a sentence from the beginning of Chapter 4 of *Histoire de la folie*, while also altering the style. Foucault writes: *'Laissons au jeu des archéologies médicales le soin de déterminer s'il fût malade ou non, alinéné ou criminel, tel qui est entré à l'hôpital pour "le dérangement de ses moeurs" ou tel autre qui a "maltraité sa femme" et voulu plusieurs fois se défaire'* (Foucault 1972: 124). Howard gives: 'We leave it to medical archeology to determine whether or not a man was sick, criminal or insane who was admitted to hospital . . . and tried several times to kill himself' (Foucault, trans. Howard 1967: 65). My version reads: 'We can leave it to the whims of medical archeology to determine whether the man who . . . and tried several times to make away with himself was ill, deranged or criminal' (Foucault, trans. Pugh 1991: 1, 21). The addition of 'whims' points up the references backwards and forwards in Foucault's text to 'doctor-historians'; the use of 'make away with himself' restores the hidden quotation with its period language; the reordering of the syntax and the change to the definite article ('the man', in place of Howard's 'a man') constitutes an attempt to retain the distancing and exemplifying effect of the use of the French comparative *'tel'* (*'tel qui est entré . . .'*) without using the cumbersome English equivalent of 'such and such who . . .'. But as these examples show, the relationship between the original text and its 'intended reader', already dependent upon how effects we can only *assume* to be ironic are received (and by whom), becomes even harder to establish when translators write out little local difficulties in the original, thus turning into mere stylistic idiosyncrasies or 'devices' what are actually parts of a total rhetorical package. All of which makes one wonder whether *Histoire de la folie*, though it is indeed a (kind of) history of madness, was ever 'intended' for anyone professionally interested in insanity other than social historians and theorists? Was it written *against* all the professions whose power over individuals and groups was so dramatically reinforced (according to Foucault) by the political and symbolic act he calls 'the great confinement' ('doctor-historians', psychiatrists, psychoanalysts)? The point is, of course, that irony as a rhetorical device can always backfire, especially when there is uncertainty at the level of intended readership, and Foucault's need to quote and refer to so many 'doctor-historians' and jurists does mean that some of the effects of irony referred to above, as well as the effects of what Fontanier called non-tropes or figures of style such as *'dubitation'* and *'paradoxisme'* (Fontanier/ Genette 1977: 444, 137) may remain unnoticed or be discounted by readers concerned mainly with the accuracy of statements, the quality of inferences and the believability of the 'story' told in *Histoire de la folie*. Indeed, the somewhat tetchy argument between Gordon and the historians seems to demonstrate just this.

Irony appears therefore very much a figure of reading, rather than of writing, a figure of uncertainty and distance. While often thought to signify authorial mastery, or authors' desire to control reading, irony can also create a climate of doubt by signalling the absence of the referent and the power of the rhetoric filling the void between the words read now and things past or present. Thus, while *Histoire de la folie* is a work embodying a remarkable degree of rhetorical energy, it does not seem to emanate from an 'author'. Instead, by repeated use of impersonal phrases and the first person plural it envelops the reader within a collective contemporary 'we' standing for all readers, and, in particular, ourselves as deluded and alienated 'others', reliant upon reason and the objective language of science, the irony being that we cannot recognize ourselves as the others of the Other represented by the man of unreason.

Later, denouncing the concept of authorship as an ideological fiction, Foucault argued that reading, in our literary/historical culture, is always oriented 'back' towards a father-figure (Foucault (1963); 1977). Such a relationship, based on a *presumption* of responsibility (like paternity as described by Freud), is also unsettled by translation. Studies by reception theorists indicate moreover that readers constantly *invent* authorial intentions corresponding to what they think the text ought to mean in terms of their expectations (as all teachers of literature know, students tend to perceive irony in terms of authorial mastery: 'what he really meant was . . .'). Translation is thus a practical workshop for reading as rhetorical deconstruction: betraying the original, it reveals how misreading and cultural remapping occur, while also adding temporal layers to the text. In *Histoire de la folie*, for example, a whole shift of tenses (from the French historical present, used insistently by Foucault, to the English simple past) is required.

Differences between French and English grammar, syntax and usage can be overstated, but there is no doubt that questions of tense usage regularly create serious difficulties for translators – especially when there is so much interest in the 'original' as here. I would argue, for example, that Foucault's use of the historical present throughout the *Histoire de la folie* does not merely correspond to a French grammatical and literary convention but reflects and concentrates his very special sense of the interrelatedness of 'then' and 'now' in relation to the history of madness. Readers' sense of their rationality and their place in history is shaken by the story being replotted using spatial metaphors. A paradigm of figures of displacement and distance, proximity and remoteness, contagion and immunity replaces the cause and effect relationships inherent in conventional narrative discourse, emphasizing the 'strangeness' of a new metaphorical landscape. The 'misrecognitions' produced by 'our distinctions' (Foucault 1991: 2) between reason and unreason are thus demonstrated by another substitution as opposed to being ex-plained, this time within rhetoric itself (metaphor for metonymy).

In a way, the ideal translation would, like Foucault's history, be a translation into the present rather than back to the past; it would carry with it no residue or memory of its starting point. Neither copy nor palimpsest, a translation is a movement away from the source text, in both temporal and spatial terms, so when source text and what I might call the 'derived' text are brought back together again and superimposed the distance produced by a process that is already a species of rhetorical transformation is abolished. This is why, in translating Chapter IV of *Histoire de la folie*, I made decisions intended to make up for losses such as described earlier. By retaining certain Gallicisms, especially syntactic ones, and by reproducing certain metaphors that sound very odd in English, I wanted to remind readers of the original rather than make it fade. As the previously mentioned suggestions for 'improvements' to an early draft all too clearly showed, the attempt was doomed to fail: what the specialists want are recoverable meanings and recognizable figures in the weave of the text.

The comical argument among Gordon, Scull and Megill over the meaning of *'les fous avaient alors une vie facilement errante'* (Foucault 1972: 19) – which for my money should be rendered quite simply as 'the mad may well have led a wandering life at that time' – is thus both exemplary – because it shows sensitivity to the problems of translation – and rather extraordinary in that it puts the spotlight on a rather trivial example of a mistranslation resulting from a failure to perceive how idiomatic syntax affects literal meaning. A full-blown academic row over it would seem hardly worth while – unless, that is, one also pays attention to the rhetorical dimension of the phrase in relation to its context, for Foucault's wording could be read as implying that he does not really care whether the proposition is literally true or not, so long as the image of the wandering medieval madman, as portrayed in poems such as Beroul's *Tristan*, gels in the reader's mind or attaches itself to an existing stereotype. He is dealing, after all, not so much with literal truth as with the images of the mad that conditioned and still condition our attempts to imagine their 'experience' and governed (and still govern) our decisions about their place in, outside, or on the margins of society. There is no recognizable trope involved in *'avaient alors une vie facilement errante'*, just a sense of dislocation from the literal produced by an unusual or unexpected word order and an idiomatic use of the adverb.

To sum up, Foucault's style involves both complex uses of rhetoric, and very simple ones, such as repetition whose effects are not always so simple to analyse. Evoking in Chapter IV the powerlessness of a class of people already silenced by confinement but sometimes rendered doubly speechless by the decree of 'interdiction', he emphasizes the cruel irony of such punishment by constant use of the word *'expérience'*, echoing the chapter-heading *'Expériences de la folie'*. This same phrase is used repeatedly thereafter, so often in fact, that the reader ends up wondering what it really means. For the translator, there is a moment of hesitation (one of many): in some cases the word *'expérience'* might be rendered by 'experiment'. The men of reason thought they had the right words to qualify the men (and women) of unreason; now we in our turn try out others to describe their common but undefinable 'experience'. We too experiment, but with a language that we no longer trust, whose 'normal' meanings dissolve to reveal what Genette called the 'internal space of language' and Foucault *'les grands déchirements silencieux'* in man. But this, as we say, is the point: the impossibility of defining the essence of a condition that cannot ever be a recognizable entity 'in itself'.

If there is a moral to this story it is therefore that the 'experience' of madness which is described in *Histoire de la folie* is *also* that of the 'doctor-historians' who have tried to arrest unreason by naming it. And the experience is beginning to be shared by otherwise reasonable, rational, late twentieth-century readers whom the work makes aware of the madness of figures and the folly of translation.

NOTES

1 The relevance of this concept for translation theory has recently been underlined by Annie Brisset, whose enquiry into the relationship between translation and parody emphasizes what happens in the 'gap' between source text and target text. Brisset likens this space to the domain of the semiotic and the symbolic, as explored by Kristeva, '(. . .) it is in the gap, or the excess, separating source text and target text that one can observe how the translating subject engages [*embraie*] and assigns meaning. This is the reason why one can say that the difference constitutes a privileged place in the cognitive process and in critical endeavour' (Brisset 1985: 207, my translation). To this analysis I would only add that both Kristeva and Barthes, like Foucault himself, as well as other theorists such as Louis Marin, see this space as the privileged, atemporal zone of the 'pathological' subject of the unconscious.

2 The relationship between madness and unreason is explained at greater length by Foucault himself in the following chapter, *'Les insensés'*: *'Dans les maisons d'internement, la folie voisine avec toutes les formes de la déraison qui l'enveloppent et définissent sa vérité la plus générale; et pourtant, elle est isolée, traitée d'une manière singulière, manifestée dans ce qu'elle peut avoir d'unique comme si, appartenant à la déraison, elle la traversait sans cesse par un mouvement qui lui serait propre, se portant d'elle-même à son plus paradoxal extrême.'* (Foucault (1961) 1972: 173–4). 'In the houses of confinement, madness cohabits with all the forms of unreason which envelop it and define its most general truth; and yet madness is isolated, treated in a special manner, manifested in its singularity as if, though belonging to unreason, it nonetheless traversed that domain by a movement peculiar to itself, ceaselessly referring from itself to its most paradoxical extreme.' (Howard 1967: 82–3). '[R]eferring from itself . . . to' is in my view misleading here, and should be replaced by 'carried by its own momentum to . . .'.

3 '(. . .) isn't translation the operator of differance [sic], deferring and differing that which makes it possible?' (Derrida 1985: 114).

BIBLIOGRAPHY

Barthes, R. (1953) *Le Degré zéro de l'écriture*, Paris: Editions du Seuil.
Barthes, R. (1954) *Michelet*, Paris: Editions du Seuil.
Barthes, R. (1966) 'L'Analyse rhétorique', *Littérature et société*, Brussels; Editions de l'Institut de Sociologie de l'Université libre de Bruxelles.

Barthes, R. (1970) 'L'Ancienne rhétorique: aide-mémoire', *Communications* 16: 172–229.

Baudrillard, J. (1981) *Simulacres et simulation*, Paris: Editions Galilée.

Bessière, J. (1989) 'Rhétoricité et passages de la distance: pour une contre-lecture des idéologies contemporaines de la rhétorique avec l'aide de Paulhan, Queneau et Handke', *Texte* 8/9, Toronto: Trinity College.

Brisset, A. (1985) 'La traduction comme transformation para-doxale', *Texte* 4, 191–207, Toronto: Trinity College.

Burke, K. (1969) *A Grammar of Motives*, Berkeley: University of California Press.

Culler, J. (1974) *Flaubert and the Uses of Uncertainty*, London: Elek Books Ltd.

de Certeau, M. (1975) *L'Ecriture de l'histoire*, Paris: Editions du Seuil.

de Man, P. (1986) *The Resistance to Theory*, Minneapolis: University of Minnesota Press.

Derrida, J. (1985) *The Ear of the Other. Otobiography, Transference, Translation* (ed. C. McDonald), trans. P. Kamuf, New York: Schocken Books.

Donnelly, M. (1986) 'Foucault's Genealogy of the Human Sciences', in Gane (1986).

Fontanier, P. (ed. Genette) (1977) *Les Figures du discours*, Paris: Flammarion.

Foucault, M. (1961) *Folie et déraison: histoire de la folie à l'âge classique*, Paris: Gallimard.

Foucault, M. (trans. R. Howard) (1967) *Madness and Civilization*, London: Tavistock.

Foucault, M. (1972) *Histoire de la folie à l'âge classique*, Paris: Gallimard.

Foucault, M. (1991) 'Experiences of madness', trans. Anthony Pugh, *History of the Human Sciences* Vol. 4, no. 1.

Freund, E. (1987) *The Return of the Reader*, London: Methuen.

Gane, M. (ed.) (1986) *Towards a Critique of Foucault*, London: Routledge & Kegan Paul.

Genette, G. (1966) *Figures*, Paris: Editions du Seuil.

Groupe μ (1970) *Rhétorique générale*, ed. J. Dubois, Paris: Larousse.

Kerbrat-Orecchioni, C. (1982) 'Le Texte littéraire: non-référence, auto-référence, ou référence fictionnelle?', *Texte* 1, Toronto: Trinity College.

Kristeva, J. (1969) *Semiotikè: Recherches pour une sémanalyse*, Paris: Editions du Seuil.

Pagès, A. (1984) *Le Français au lycée*, Paris: Fernand Nathan.

Ricardou, J. (1972) 'Penser la littérature aujourd'hui', *Sud* 8.

Ricoeur, P. (1983) *Temps et récit*, tome 1, Paris: Editions du Seuil.

Ricoeur, P. (1984) *Temps et récit*, tome 2, Paris: Editions du Seuil.

Ricoeur, P. (1985) *Temps et récit*, tome 3, Paris: Editions du Seuil.

Scholes, R. (1989) *Protocols of Reading*, New Haven and London: Yale University Press.

Veyne, P. (1971) *Comment on écrit l'histoire*, Paris: Editions du Seuil.

White, H. (1973) *Metahistory: The Historical Imagination in Nineteenth-Century Europe*, Baltimore: Johns Hopkins University Press.

White, H. (1979) 'Michel Foucault', in *Structuralism and Since*, ed. J. Sturrock, Oxford: OUP.

12 Of madness itself

Histoire de la folie and the object of psychiatric history

Nikolas Rose

A history of madness itself . . . Michel Foucault spoke of such a project in the preface to the first French edition of *Histoire de la folie*. Many have quoted these words as if they both encapsulated the romantic dream that inspired Foucault's project and condemned it to incoherence.[1] Even Foucault was later to suggest that he was prey to a certain epistemological naïvety in *Histoire de la folie*, tempted to found his analysis upon something intrinsic to the wild power of madness prior to its capture by the knowledges and apparatuses of society.[2] How could one recover the past experiences of madness itself when they are known to us only in the forms in which they have been structured by reason and can be grasped only through our present rules of sense? How could one write of madness itself without transforming it by those forms of reason in which writing partakes? How could Foucault, whose whole work is committed to the radical historicity of the objects of knowledge and power, speak of madness itself?

Of course, *Histoire de la folie* is, self-evidently, not a history of madness itself, if that implies a 'history of the referent'. As Colin Gordon points out, Foucault raises this option only to dismiss it: it would be impossible to rescue lost sufferings from the historical reason that has already subjected them to an order without appeal.[3] Instead, for *Histoire de la folie*, a history of madness will mean 'a structural study of the historical ensemble – notions, institutions, juridical and police measures, scientific concepts – which hold captive a madness whose wild state can never in itself be restored'. Yet, Foucault continued, 'short of this inaccessible primitive purity, structural study must ascend back to the decision which at once joins and separates reason and madness; it must strive to discover the perpetual exchange, the obscure common root, the originary affrontment which gives meaning to the unity as much as to the opposition of sense and senselessness'.[4] If we are to understand the lasting power that *Histoire de la folie* still exercises over both new and old readers, we might reflect on these two inseparable dimensions of its analytic project. And, I suggest, we might find that the power of the book arises precisely from its concern, in all senses of the word, with what is specific to *madness itself*.

To pose the matter this way is to distinguish *Histoire de la folie* from the two bodies of literature to which it has frequently been annexed: the social history of psychiatry and the sociology of deviance. Madness, in *Histoire de la folie*, is not the mere conceptual and practical focus of certain institutions, professions, beliefs and individuals that are the precursors of psychiatry, and whose vicissitudes may be imagined according to the schema familiar from the history of other social phenomena. Neither is madness merely a form of categorization used in certain societies, by certain persons, in certain contexts, with certain consequences, to a violation of norms of conduct, thought or emotion, through processes that are fundamentally common whatever norms are in question. For *Histoire de la folie*, madness, rather, exists in a constitutive relation with 'civilization'. It is ungraspable outside the integral ties that divide it from, and bind it to, reason. And it forms an indispensable 'other side' to the multitude of dreams, programmes, projects and laws that have constituted 'society' as a historically specific assemblage of positive knowledges of the soul and 'the social', of technologies for the policing of conduct, and of rules for the government of the self.

MADNESS ITSELF: I

Unlike much critical sociology, *Histoire de la folie* does not ground a critique of the social role of psychiatry upon an alternative ontology of madness. Instead, it suggests that the modes of problematizing existence that we know as madness are formed in the same historical movement that constitutes psychiatry as the instance that will identify and govern them. *Histoire de la folie* thus seeks to describe the historical ensemble which brings our modern perception of the territory of psychiatry into existence. Hence the history of madness it undertakes is neither a history of different beliefs about madness nor an account of the different ways in which the mad have been treated. It is a history of the divisions within which madness has been formed and re-formed, of the ways in which diverse problematizations of existence along a range of political, social, ethical and philosophical dimensions have been linked together and rendered intelligible in terms of madness. What we term 'psychiatry' becomes possible only once a system of relations is established between a range of persons, conditions and judgements, such that they can form the object of a single, though heterogeneous, field of representation and intervention. To term this a 'system' is not to imply that it is unitary and clearly distinguished from other systems, so much as to suggest that it is characterized by a certain commonality of problems, and that it is constantly seeking the principles upon which these problems and their solutions might be unified and unambiguously differentiated from what they are not. The question that critics so often address to psychiatry – what is madness and how is it to be known – is the very question that structures the disputatious territory of psychiatry itself: the quest for a knowledge of madness that will integrate its subjects and rarify its existence.

Perhaps, here, in proposing to reconstruct an 'experience' of madness, *Histoire de la folie* sometimes confuses more than clarifies, suggesting some kind of structural coherence underpinning the apparent diversity of the forms in which madness is thought and treated within a certain field of space and time. Foucault was in part, no doubt, seeking to counter the anachronistic retrospective judgements of orthodox psychiatric histories, that condemn the past for its confusion in not sufficiently differentiating the mad from the criminal or the immoral.[5] But his analysis nevertheless constantly reminds us of the difficulty of accommodating the forms of recognition and regulation of madness within a single vocabulary or a single perception. Certainly, the classical age was no more 'confused' about madness than we are today, but, as today, no single gaze or gesture alienated madness, no single institution encompassed and governed the mad, no single knowledge embraced them. The system of thought we need to reconstitute has the regularity of a dispersion: it is heterogeneous not only with our own discursive formation of mental illness but also within itself.

To point to dispersion is not merely to celebrate heterogeneity, but to suggest that the coherence of what we could term 'the psychiatric system' is neither a matter of institutional homogeneity nor of theoretical consistency. Rather, it lies in three shifts that *Histoire de la folie* exquisitely documents. First, in the new linkages established between madness as illness, madness as derangement of the self, and madness as social violation. Second, in the emergence of a medico-juridical system of confinement, the first of a whole family that will operate under the aegis of an authority whose claim to social legitimacy is grounded in the possession of sanctioned expertise. Third, in the formation of new institutional sites under a diagnostic gaze, within which practices are organized for the rationalized normalization of pathological persons to the status of social citizens.

The sociological conception of 'the medicalization of deviance' is little help in understanding the conceptual and practical processes which assembled psychiatry's subjects. The inhabitants of the territory of psychiatry were first gathered together under the aegis of a system of thought that cannot be split according to the retrospective application of definitions of what pertains to 'law', what to 'medicine', not least because each would be fundamentally transformed in the process. Paradoxically, for those who suggest that a humane and enlightened 'moral treatment' was defeated by a mechanistic and brutal 'mental medicine', it was the birth of the *moral* order as a single conceptual and practical space that allowed the unification of the insane, the furious, the demented and the maniacal with the licentious, the blasphemer, the gambler, and with others who violated their obligations as the subjects of their familial or 'social' worlds. These personages suffered from conditions that were moral in the sense that they could be seen, at least in part, as personal consequences of the transgression of standards for conducting a virtuous life – from onanism, vanity, religious fanaticism, excesses of food and drink, to shocks to the spirits consequent upon sudden changes in circumstance. They were moral in that their troubles emanated from a disorder of an interior domain between the fibres, nerves and ducts of the body and the phenomenology of ravings, delusions, misconducts and vices. And they were moral in that their problems were susceptible to a systematic regime of treatment in which the institution of confinement became itself the means of reform, through the immersion of the inmate in an unbroken regime of normalized judgement in the hope that the sufferer might be re-attached to the values of civilization – moderation, diligence, order, regularity of habits and self-control. It was this assembly that psychiatry sought – and still seeks – to organize by means of a coherent classificatory system that would simultaneously reveal the unity of the objects that appear in it and underpin its powers over them.

As *Histoire de la folie* makes clear, our contemporary world of madness was born here. The institution of a uniform regime of confinement, scrutiny and reformation for this assembly of persons and troubles was neither the origin of a medical knowledge of madness nor the inauguration of the medical practice of the cure: both long preceded these events. Its significance is somewhat different. First, it institutionalizes the boundaries, limits and contours of what we, today, have come to contemplate as mental illness. Second, these newly associated subjects of madness can come under the remit of an authority that fuses moral prestige and technical skill within a single personage. Third, a new psychiatric epistemology can arise out of the material and technical conditions of the asylum itself: a range of troubles can become the objects of a continuous diagnostic and systematizing gaze that construes them alike as evidencing psychopathology, that can document and normalize them, that can aspire to organize their heterogeneous disturbances within a single tranquil space of knowledge. And fourth, the subjects of psychiatry can become the target of systematized programmes structured by the aspiration to rehabilitate.

This new dispensation is no simple 'medicalization'; we might, rather, think of it as the transfer of madness to a 'clinical' field. It inaugurates a complex process of contestation over the proper practical distribution of antisocial acts among various apparatuses and procedures of regulation – the school, the prison, the asylum, the child guidance clinic, the court, social work – and their proper cognitive distribution among the positive sciences – medicine, psychiatry, criminology, jurisprudence, psychology, sociology. What unifies this systematization is not so much medical hegemony, as the fact that tragic, wild, scandalous, distressing, incomprehensible acts are accorded a new intelligibility, simultaneously given a purely negative status as pathology, and placed at least potentially within a domain where they can be considered as the outcome of some fault inhering within the subject of those acts amenable to a positive knowledge and a rational calculus of transformation.

Sociological interpretations of these processes in terms of deviance and its control invert the point at issue: the relation of madness to the infraction of norms is less a sociological truism than a historical achievement. What *Histoire de la folie* demonstrates is what Colin Gordon felicitously terms 'the reciprocal disenchantment of transgression': new ways in which conduct is problematized and linked together as *no more than* the violation of a social standard for the comportment of the self that is consequent upon individual pathology. This disenchantment of transgression is itself conditional upon a transformation of political rationalities that occurs in most European states in the nineteenth century, in which the problem of good government is reformulated, in part, in terms of the reconciliation of the freedom of subjects with the need for social order, by means of a multitude of programmes for the moral improvement of individuals. The asylum, like the prison, emerged as the reciprocal of these projects that recast the questions of public tranquillity, wealth and happiness as problems of the moral constitution of free citizens: the mad would be those who could not operate that regulated freedom that made up society, who could not bear their obligations as social citizens.

Histoire de la folie reveals how the modern territory of madness as mental illness was linked to citizenship in another way that is not grasped in sociological explanations couched in terms of medical entrepreneurship. If doctors gained mastery over the world of confinement, this was related to a difficulty produced by the juridical transformations that conferred the obligations, duties and status of citizens equally upon all a nation's subjects. The medical remit over the asylum emerged as a solution to the problem of reconciling the constitutional requirement that all constraints upon the freedom of citizens be guaranteed by law, with the social requirement for the confinement of those whose infractions were not of law but of the moral responsibilities of citizenship. The confinement of the mad person as a citizen had to satisfy the double requirement of social protection and constitutional justification. As Chapter 4 of *Histoire de la folie* – 'Experiences of madness' – implies, the legal authorization of confinement under a medical mandate was to satisfy this double requirement; it was also to respond to the demands of constitutionality in so far as, from this time forth, psychiatry would promise the restoration of the insane and disenfranchised inmate to the capacity of functioning citizen, subject of law and morality. Hence, Foucault argues, our current experience of madness unifies in the form of an illness that which was brought together first at the 'meeting point between the social decree of confinement' of those who perturbed the tranquillity of family or street and 'the juridical knowledge which designated the capacities of the subject as a legal entity', and hence required a particular warrant for the deprivation of a citizen's liberty. 'The ''positive'' science of mental illness, and the humanitarian sentiments which promoted the madman to the rank of human being, were only possible once this synthesis was solidly established. It forms, in a way, the concrete *a priori* of all our psychopathology's claims to scientific status.'[6]

It is in these ways, I suggest, that *Histoire de la folie* charts the history of 'madness itself', not as a stable referent, but as a network of relays within which the vicissitudes of individual suffering have become related to a whole range of confrontations between authorities and that which affronts them, and have been organized within a clinical domain structured by claims to positive knowledge and efficacious technique. In this process, the testimony of the mad person is disqualified as reason and requalified only as the mark of a pathology to be remedied by subjection to expertise. Against the self-images of an age that would see this as enlightenment, *Histoire de la folie* seeks to describe the diverse, heterogeneous and often ignoble surfaces of its emergence, and the price paid in the distance we establish between madness and all that is entailed in 'civilization'. The 'history' of *Histoire de la folie* is inescapably 'critical'; its aim is to enable us to think madness *differently*: as arising from and conditioning particular and historically variable arrays of conceptual and practical relations among ethics, politics and truth. If *Histoire de la folie* is a history of madness itself, this is not in the sense that it seeks to put everything in its rightful place within a serene unity of past and present, but in the sense that it disturbs and fragments the very territory which has made possible not only medical psychiatry, but all those other forms of expertise over the mad which contest its power.

MADNESS ITSELF: II

Histoire de la folie explores the constitutive relation between madness and civilization in another way that makes it of enduring and disturbing significance. Our experience of madness, suggests Foucault, was born in a division and relation that perpetually undergirds the forms of life and reason that make up the history of '*l'homme européen*' since the beginning of the Middle Ages: the history of madness is carved out upon that division in all its diverse forms. In this second, and perhaps more profound, sense, madness *itself* is the object of *Histoire de la folie*. Madness is neither a natural universal nor socially relative, it is the inescapable other side brought into being through all those heterogenous but interlinked gestures in which reason, sense and civility have constituted themselves by dividing themselves from that which they are not. By according a kind of trans-historical historicity to those acts of division, *Histoire de la folie* can signify, without attempting to reconstruct, that *disruption* which madness proffers to its other, the *disruption* that reason incessantly seeks to divide from itself. In giving recognition to that incessant affront that constitutes the inspiring and tragic specificity of madness itself, *Histoire de la folie* – even in its reduced English version – achieves that disturbing power that distinguishes it from the multitude of sociological histories of psychiatry that have followed it.

Madness *disturbs*, and in tracing the forms of this disturbance *Histoire de la folie* is as much a work of philosophy as of history: its concern with the past is more than a fusty or ingenuous antiquarianism or a repetitive pedagogy of sociological relativism. In tracing that something that perpetually escapes and entices the multifarious projects of rationality and propriety, *Histoire de la folie* reminds those who would speak of madness of the fragility of the webs that constitute selves and hold them within the bonds of sense, self-management and social reciprocity. The text, that is to say, forces us to recognize, without romanticizing, that *something* that is the inescapable price that is exacted from each of us by civilization, that something from which reason has progressively alienated itself, in the form of medicine and the name of a positive science, for some two hundred years.

It is fashionable to decry the radical critiques of psychiatry of the 1960s, retrospectively unified as antipsychiatry, and hence to associate or distinguish *Histoire de la folie* from those movements, depending upon whether one wishes to damn or praise it. And yet, what was most radical but most pragmatic about those times was neither a denial of madness nor a wish to abolish psychiatry, but simply the aspiration to (re)open a dialogue between reason and those whom it considered mad. R. D. Laing was only the most visible of those many writers, activists and patients who sought to draw attention to the strange yet fundamental fact that in a world where so many 'experts' had something to say about madness, the only voices not heard, or heard only as symptoms, were those of the mad themselves. It is entirely in the spirit of all his subsequent writings that Michel Foucault should have treated this question historically, and sought to document the conditions under which this monologic relation about the mad became possible, indeed appeared enlightened and almost inescapable. As Foucault puts it in the most moving paragraph of *Histoire de la folie*, 'the constitution of madness as a mental illness . . . thrusts into oblivion all those stammered, imperfect words without fixed syntax in which the exchange between madness and reason was made. The language of psychiatry, which is a monologue of reason *about* madness, has been established only on the basis of that silence'.[7] In writing 'an archaeology of that silence' the power of *Histoire de la folie* lies in the hope it offers that the arrogance, however humane it may be, with which the personage of expertise approaches the subject of pathology is a fact of history and not a mark of edification, the hope that one day we might be able to listen again to that which madness testifies and, in doing so, transform our relations with those we call mad.

To read *Histoire de la folie* in this way is not to suggest that it be exempt from historical criticism and correction. But it does mean that it is a text whose aspirations are as much ethical as historical, concerned with the relations that we have established between reason and unreason within our systems of thought and value, the practical relations we have established between ourselves and those whose modes of existence we separate from us by deeming mad, and the ways of thinking about madness and normality that inform our relations with ourselves. Scholars may wish to disencumber the history of psychiatry from such concerns. So much the worse for those who, in seeking to write a dispassionate account of that self-satisfied triumph of reason over madness, merely reduplicate it. It would indeed be ironic if, in our renewed attention to the history of psychiatry, we were to forget the processes that brought its object into existence and inscribed it into our modern imagination as pathology, negativity, incompetence and deficiency: the processes that still today, in their different ways, continue to thrust all that we call madness, and all those we call mad, into oblivion.

NOTES

1 The most prominent, and perhaps the most wilful, was Jacques Derrida. The reader is referred to Colin Gordon's account in '*Histoire de la folie*: an unknown book by Michel Foucault', *History of the Human Sciences* (1989) 3: 3–26. My comments throughout are indebted to Gordon's discussion.
2 See, for example, *The Archaeology of Knowledge*, London: Tavistock, 1972, p. 16, p. 47.
3 Gordon, op. cit.
4 *Histoire de la folie*, p. vii. I quote the translation from Gordon, op. cit., p. 19, and the reader is referred to his discussion.
5 See, for example, the remarks at the beginning of Chap. 4 entitled 'Experiences of madness'. ˉ
6 *Histoire de la folie*, p. 63.
7 *Histoire de la folie*, p. ii, quoted from R. Howard's translation in *Madness and Civilization*, London: Tavistock, 1967, p. xii.

13 A failure to communicate?

On the reception of Foucault's *Histoire de la folie* by Anglo-American historians

Andrew Scull

In view of some of the critical things I shall have to say about *Madness and Civilization* (Foucault 1965; 1972), I think it is appropriate to begin by acknowledging that almost all those who have worked on the history of psychiatry during the past two decades and more owe multiple debts to the late Michel Foucault. On a purely mundane level, it was surely the reception accorded to Foucault's work and the stature he came to occupy in both the academy and café society, that played a major role in rescuing madness from the clutches of drearily dull administrative historians and/or psychiatrists in their dotage, giving the whole topic the status of a serious intellectual subject and thus attracting us to it in the first place. More broadly, whatever else he may have suffered from, Foucault did not lack for intellectual daring, and most of the best work in the field for the past fifteen or twenty years can be seen as responding, at least in part, to the intellectual challenges he threw down.

That said, how well has *Madness and Civilization* stood the test of time? And how far is its clearly mixed-to-negative reputation among most Anglo-American scholars a reflection of their lack of acquaintance with the full text of Foucault's argument? How far, to put it another way, are complaints in English-speaking academia about deficiencies in Foucault's scholarship objections which can be turned back with interest on the complainers, whose starting point may not be the complete and authentic version of Foucault's own argument, but rather the severely truncated (and occasionally inaccurate) English translation?

Regrettably, one must concede that there is some truth to these allegations. Foucault's defenders can point, for instance, to Lawrence Stone's (1987: 274) attack on Foucault in the *New York Review of Books* for being 'unconcerned with historical detail of time or place or with rigorous documentation'. Remarkably, for criticism emanating from so eminent a quarter, this turned out to be an assault which was itself so carelessly constructed as to leave Stone open to a quite devastating riposte, one which Foucault himself hastened to deliver.[1] Alternatively, Foucault's supporters can cite the treatments of *Madness and Civilization* in Peter Sedgwick's *Psycho Politics* (1982) and in J. G. Merquior's volume on *Foucault* (1985) for the Modern Masters series, both of which rely unapologetically on the abbreviated English text and on rehashing the criticisms of others.

The implication seems to be that the publication of a complete version of Foucault's argument, references and all, would suffice to alter the verdict of most Anglo-American specialists that *Madness and Civilization* is a provocative and dazzlingly written prose poem, but one resting on the shakiest of scholarly foundations and riddled with errors of fact and inter- pretation. To the contrary, I predict the reverse would happen: access to the complete text would serve to strengthen conventional historians' doubts, and to remove the most effective defence mounted by members of the Foucauldian cult. And this would not be (as Foucault's more sophisticated supporters would have it) because one could anticipate persistent mis- readings of the master's *oeuvre*, the product of the ignorance of an audience unacquainted with the subtleties of continental scholarship and in con- sequence condemned to view his work 'literally out of context, [as] an isolated archipelago of studies lost in a sea of staunch empiricism and pragmatism' (Guédon 1977: 245; see also Leary 1976). Rather, the problem is the very genuine deficiencies and vulnerabilities of Foucault's historical scholarship, defects which would only become the more visible in a complete version of his text.[2]

Claims that

> [Foucault's] erudition, if one challenges its authenticity (e.g. on the selec-
> tion of sources) is at least as authentic as anything one will find employed
> anywhere else to back up more orthodox theses in the history of ideas
> (Peters 1971: 637)[3]

can perhaps persuade the credulous and give the monolingual critic some pause, so long as one can wave airily in the direction of a thousand and more absent and untranslated footnotes. They are likely to lose their pro- tective powers when one realizes that the whole of Foucault's discussion of lunacy reform in nineteenth-century England, for instance, rests on essen- tially two sources, Samuel Tuke's *Description of the Retreat* of 1813 (S. Tuke 1813), and Hack Tuke's 1882 *Chapters in the History of the Insane* (D. H. Tuke 1882); or, again, that virtually his only source for his dis- cussion of English and Irish poor law policy in the sixteenth, seventeenth and eighteenth centuries is the dated and long-superseded work of Sir George Nicholls (1781–1865).[4]

Erik Midelfort's objection that Foucault has wrongly assumed 'that confinement of the mad by the state was uniform all over Europe [in the classical age]' (Midelfort 1980: 257) and Lawrence Stone's similar com- plaint that Foucault had ignored the 'enormous differences in the degree and organization of incarceration from country to country' (Stone 1987: 271) have been dismissed by Foucault and his followers. The master himself retorted that, in the unabridged French edition of his book, 'on pages 67–74 and 483–96, I insist on the pronounced differences between a country like France and a country like England' (Foucault in Stone 1987: 285). Similarly, Colin Gordon (1990a: 15) cites a brief passage on pp. 405–6 of the French edition (Foucault 1972) to 'prove' that Foucault was aware and took adequate account of the differences between France, Germany, Austria and England. Again, the existence of a complete English translation will only expose the threadbare quality of these defences. Of the two passages Foucault himself cites, one is devoted solely to a comparison of the Pinelian and Tukean versions of moral treatment, and is simply irrelevant to the issue at hand; while the other contains a few desultory comparisons of responses to poverty and dependency in Protestant Europe and France, essentially tangential to the larger argument Foucault is bent on constructing.[5] The passage to which Gordon refers simply regurgitates a list of names and dates on which various institutions were founded – for England, drawn from Hack Tuke (1882) and Tenon's (n.d.) contemporary report on English hospitals and prisons, and for Germany and Austria from a similarly restricted group of nineteenth-century sources. The notion that this brief listing, which is coupled with some misleading comments about the absence of a medical presence in eighteenth-century institutions like St Luke's,[6] constitutes a satisfactory discussion of the issue of cross-national variation in the resort to confinement simply won't stand scrutiny. A full translation of *Histoire de la folie* would make this only too apparent to an English-speaking audience. Moreover, and contrary to the impression most readers would derive from Gordon's commentary, Foucault's remarks entirely fail to mention the phenomenon of the growth of private madhouses in eighteenth-century England, though this is precisely one of the major developments which Midelfort had criticized Foucault for overlooking.

In any event, Foucault and his followers are caught in a bind here, because for years, not just his critics, but also his supporters had cited his discussion of the Great Confinement of the classical era as one of the more original and important contributions of his study. As one can scarcely avoid noticing, there are all too many passages in *Histoire de la folie* which insist on the sudden emergence and the universality of the impulse to confine: the spread of 'an entire network' of places of confinement 'across Europe . . .'; an associated shift in meaning,

which had so hastily, so spontaneously summoned into being all over Europe the category of classical order we call confinement. . . . There must have formed, silently and doubtless over the course of many years, a social sensibility, common to European culture, that suddenly began to manifest itself in the second half of the seventeenth century; it was this sensibility that suddenly isolated the category destined to populate the places of confinement. . . . Confinement, that massive phenomenon, the signs of which are found all across eighteenth-century Europe. . . . Throughout Europe, confinement had the same meaning . . .

and so on (Foucault 1965: 45–7, 49; 1972: 66–7, 75, 77). Critics like Erik Midelfort and sympathetic voices like Ian Hacking (1986: 29) have scarcely erred when they complained of Foucault's 'predilection for French examples projected on to European history. . .'. Nor are they mistaken to see in this cavalier propensity to over-generalize a source of grave interpretive errors. (For some further discussion of this point, see Scull 1989: Chap. 1).[7]

Foucault's discussions of the periods before and after the classical age are at least equally vulnerable to criticism, and, once again, the appearance of a complete transaction is unlikely to help his defenders. Tuke and Pinel play a central role in his account of the era of moral treatment, which has as its crucial subtext the changing nature and extent of medical involvement in the management of the mad. As Colin Gordon (1990a: 8) recognizes, a vital part of Foucault's analysis is his attempt to represent

> the concept of mental illness as being comparatively recent in historical origin, constituted and made possible by a set of changes in thought and practice dating from the end of the eighteenth century.

In Foucault's own words, the world of the asylum which Tuke and Pinel created constituted *'l'apothéose du personnage médical'*. Of all the changes they instituted,

> *elle est sans doubt la plus importante, puisqu'elle va autoriser non seulement des contacts nouveaux entre le médecin et le malade, mais un nouveau rapport entre l'alienation et la pensée médicale . . . L'oeuvre de Tuke et celle de Pinel, dont l'esprit et les valeurs son si différents, viennent se rejoindre dans cette transformation du personnage médical.*

Where, on Foucault's account at least, the physician till the late eighteenth century *'n'avait pas de part à la vie de l'internement[, o]r il devient la figure essentielle de l'asile'*. Indeed, the asylum itself now becomes *'un espace médicale'* (Foucault 1972: 523–4; 1965: 269–70).

It is, of course, in a distinctly Foucauldian sense that the master concludes (Foucault 1972: 525; 1965: 271) that it was *'Tuke et Pinel [qui] ont overt l'asile a la connaissance médicale'*. Where earlier medical accounts of the origins of madness had been of a piece with medical theorizing about disease in general,[8] their accomplishment was to create a novel and quite separate species of mental medicine: *'apres Pinel et Tuke, la psychiatrie va devenir une médecine d'un style particulier . . . pour la première fois dans l'histoire de la science occidentale, [la médecine de l'esprit] va prendre une autonomie presque complète . . .'* (Foucault 1972: 527; 1965: 274–5). And within the new realm of a madness subordinated to a reconstituted medical authority, the speciality they created was one *'dont les pouvoirs n'empruntaient à ce savoir que leur deguisement, ou, tout au plus, leur justification'*; an enterprise whose true powers *'sont d'ordre moral et social . . .'* (Foucault 1972: 525; 1965: 271–2).

But, notwithstanding all the qualifications Foucault introduces here (including the claim that '[c]e *n'est pas comme savant que l'homo medicus prend autorité dans l'asile, mais comme sage*' (Foucault 1972: 524; 1965: 270), the central thrust of this line of argument is to assert an intimate, essential and positive linkage between the new reforms and the consolidation of medical jurisdiction over the treatment of the mad. And one must immediately object that, as it stands, this whole discussion is fundamentally misleading, obscuring – indeed threatening to render completely invisible – what I take to be perhaps *the* crucial contemporary implication of moral treatment for the relations between medicine and the insane. For Tuke was a layman, and the whole burden of his version of moral treatment constituted 'a rather damning attack on the medical profession's capacity to deal with mental illness' (Bynum 1981: 43). Moral treatment, at least in its English guise, was a *threat* to pre-existing medical involvement in the mad-business, and, as I have shown elsewhere (Scull 1989: 118–61), it took a concerted effort on the part of interested medical men to put down the challenge it posed to their emerging hegemony.

Similarly, although Pinel was an eminent physician, his experience convinced him that medicine was all but useless in madness, and he concluded that the success obtained in applying exclusively a moral regimen 'gives great weight to the supposition that, in a majority of instances [of insanity], there is no organic lesion of the brain nor of the cranium' (Pinel 1962: 5). Dora Weiner's (1984) and Jan Goldstein's detailed reconstructions of the circumstances surrounding Pinel's 'discovery' of moral treatment have demonstrated quite conclusively 'its non-esoteric, lay origins – which Pinel [himself] so proudly and defiantly proclaimed' (Goldstein 1987: 72–119). By his own account, his contribution was to convert this 'charlatanistic' technique developed by the lay *concierges* who had day-to-day charge of the insane 'into a respectable tenet of official medicine', a scientizing project he accomplished through philosophical specification of the mechanisms of both cause and cure, and through the application of statistical methods to measure and confirm quantitatively 'the efficacy of the treatment' (Goldstein 1987: 105, 101).

In Pinel's eyes,

> the lay *concierge*, as diligent, perceptive, and talented as he might be, was inalterably the intellectual inferior of the *médecin-philosophe*. The latter would take the rough-hewn commonsensical knowledge of the former and transform it into something refined, scientific, and esoteric; the elite professional confraternity, at one moment threatened with dissolution by Pinel, was thus fundamentally – and quickly – restored by him.
>
> (Goldstein 1987: 77)

But not always securely: as Ian Dowbiggin (1986) has shown, in France, too, moral treatment's implied or explicit denigration of the value of medical treatment on occasion threatened the legitimacy of the physician's presence in the asylum, a problem which long persisted and, even after it had apparently been solved, subsequently recurred, much to the discomfort of later generations of alienists. So the role of Pinel and Tuke in ushering in the Golden Age of psychiatry (Castel 1976; 1988) is at the very least far more complicated and indirect than the reader of *Histoire de la folie* would realize.[9]

Famously, in assessing moral treatment, Foucault stands Whig history on its head: this nineteenth-century 'reform' constitutes, in his eyes, the imposition of an ever-more thoroughgoing 'moral uniformity and social denunciation' – the historical moment at which the medical gaze secured its domination over mental illness, launching *'ce gigantesque emprisonnement moral, qu'on a l'habitude d'appeler, par antiphrase sans doute, la libération des aliénés par Pinel et par Tuke'* (Foucault 1972: 514, 530; 1965: 259, 278). Such ringing denunciations embody a rather complex set of assertions, some of which I think are defensible and correct, others quite dubious or wrong. Be that as it may (and the issues are too many and complex to deal with in a chapter as brief as this one),[10] Foucault's claims about the silencing of the mad under the dominion of alienism carry all the more force as polemic, since they contrast so pointedly with his portrait of the openness of medieval and early Renaissance society towards folly and unreason.

Foucault's floridly rendered portrait of a Continental equivalent of Merrie Olde England, an era in which folly flourished largely free of pernicious social restraint, is the last aspect of his discussion in *Histoire de la folie* to which I wish to give some attention. Erik Midelfort made these lyrical passages, with which Foucault launches his enquiry into the vagaries of the western response to madness, the focus of some of his harshest and most dismissive criticism. And Colin Gordon (1990a: 16, 17) has now tried to debunk this whole line of argument by suggesting that it is the compound product of the mistranslation of a single phrase and a refutation of something 'not actually asserted by Foucault'.

The phrase in question is Foucault's claim that, in the Middle Ages, *'Les fous alors avaient une existence facilement errante'* (Foucault 1972: 19; 1965: 8). In his text, Midelfort quotes Richard Howard's English rendering, that the mad 'led an easy wandering life', while quoting the French original, together with the related passages that follow it (*'Les villes les chaissaient volontiers de leur enceinte; on les laissait courir dans des campagnes éloignées, quand on ne les confiait pas à un groupe de marchands et de pèlerins'*) in a footnote. Gordon (1990a: 16) pounces: here is a 'piquant illustration of the scholarly hazards of translation'. The phrase, it seems, should rather be rendered: 'the existence of the mad at that time could easily be a wandering one'. Whether the wandering life would be an easy one, Gordon then claims, 'is on Foucault's account of the matter, extremely dubious' (1990a: 17). Thus, Midelfort's whole line of criticism is vitiated by his neglect of the French text.

What could provide a better demonstration of how a complete and accurate translation of *Histoire de la folie* would serve to disarm the misplaced criticism of Anglo-American academics? Except that Gordon's whole line of argument places a weight on '*facilement*' that it simply cannot bear. Foucault's chapter on the medieval and early Renaissance period extends for more than forty pages, and Midelfort's rendering of his views ranges across this whole text. As a complete translation of *Histoire de la folie* would make clear, and as Midelfort correctly concludes, the dominant thrust of Foucault's analysis is to emphasize the real presence of madness *within* society, in daily life as in art and literature, '*au coeur même de la raison et de la vérité*' (Foucault 1972: 25; 1965: 14). It is the openness of medieval society to folly and unreason, not its harshness and cruelty, that is at the centre of Foucault's account,[11] notwithstanding the glancing references to whipping[12] and to *Narrtürmer*. And it is in this context that one is asked to attend to '*un object nouveau [qui] vient de faire son apparition dans le paysage imaginaire de la Renaissance; bientôt il y occupera une place privilégiée: c'est la Nef des fous*' (Foucault 1972: 18; 1965: 7).

The myth of the Ship of Fools is quite crucial to the image of the medieval response to madness which Foucault wants us to embrace, and quite naturally, in consequence, *Stultifera Navis* is the title of his opening chapter. Before he turns to the plastic and the literary arts for evidence of a wide-ranging cultural fascination with Folly, it is in the *Narrenschiff* that Foucault sees and seeks to capture the essence of the medieval response to madness. The Ship of Fools is, he recognizes, '*une composition litteraire, empruntée sans doute au vieux cycle des Argonautes, qui a repris récemment vie et jeunesse parmi les grands thèmes mythiques*' (Foucault 1972: 18–19; 1965: 7) and, in literary circles, it has plenty of company:

> *La mode est à la composition de ces Nefs dont l'équipage de héros imaginaires, de modèles éthiques, ou de types sociaux, s'embarque pour un grand voyage symbolique qui leur apporte sinon la fortune, du moins, la figure de leur destin ou de la vérité.*
>
> (Foucault 1972: 19; 1965: 7–8)

But there is a major difference: unlike, say, the fashionable Ship of Princes, the Ship of Virtuous Ladies, or the Ship of Health, the Ship of Fools is something more than a literary or an artistic conceit.

Indeed,

> *de tous ces vaisseaux romanesques ou satiriques, le Narrenschiff est le seul qui ait eu une existence réelle, car ils ont existé, ces bateaux qui d'une ville à l'autre menaient leur cargaison insensée.*
>
> (Foucault 1972: 19; 1965: 8)

Having made this claim, Foucault then launches into a lengthy discussion of the practical and symbolic significance of these 'real' ships, with their floating cargo of madmen in search of their reason, parading up and down the Rhine, haunting the imagination of the entire early Renaissance, living symbols of *'la situation* liminaire *du fou à l'horizon du souci de l'homme médiéval'* (Foucault 1972: 22, emphasis on *'liminaire'* in the original; 1965: 11).

Unfortunately for all those enamoured of this romantic and delightfully delineated landscape, reality must be rendered in rather darker hues. As Erik Midelfort has pointed out, the ship of fools (like Foucault's other striking image of the medieval leprosaria, waiting across three centuries, *'solliciter par d'étranges incantations une nouvelle incarnation du mal, une autre grimace de la peur, des magies renouvelées de purification et d'exclusion'* (Foucault 1972: 13; 1965: 3), till they were populated by the mad) is simply a figment of the latter's over-active imagination: 'Occasionally the mad were indeed sent away on boats. But nowhere can one find reference to real boats or ships loaded with mad pilgrims in search of their reason' (Midelfort 1980: 254; see also Maher and Maher 1982). Where the mad proved troublesome, they could expect to be beaten or locked up; otherwise, they might roam or rot. Either way, the facile contrast between psychiatric oppression and an earlier almost anarchic toleration is surely illusory. And in the face of the magnitude of Foucault's distortions, and the significance of these passages for his argument, it is more than a trifle disingenuous for Colin Gordon (1990a: 16) to concede, grudgingly, that 'as far as I know . . . the denial that riverborne deportation was a systematic practice in the medieval treatment of the insane . . . may well be correct'; and then to attempt to minimize the importance of this concession by stating that 'the contrary is not actually asserted by Foucault'.[13]

Where does all this leave us? It is an interesting (and deplorable) variation on Gresham's law that the appearance of an abbreviated or otherwise defective translation of a major scholar's work seems to preclude or greatly delay the issue of a good one. Foucault is hardly the first to suffer such a fate,[14] and he is unlikely to be the last. Of course, then, one would welcome the appearance of a complete and accurate rendering of *Histoire de la folie* in English, and one gathers that Routledge are already planning to issue a revised edition of this sort.[15] Its appearance will doubtless provoke a reassessment of Foucault's work on the history of psychiatry. For the reasons I have sketched here (and not just among the adherents of the liberal public relations school of psychiatric history), I would wager a quite substantial sum that the judgement rendered in informed quarters will remain largely negative.[16]

ACKNOWLEDGEMENT

This essay was written while I held a University of California President's Research Fellowship in the Humanities. I should like to express my gratitude for this financial support, and for the helpful comments of Timothy McDaniel on an earlier draft. I incorporate here an earlier discussion of some of these materials, which appeared in *History of the Human Sciences* 3 (1990), 57–67.

NOTES

1 Stone reprints Foucault's reply, as well as his own ill-judged attempt to have the last word, in Stone 1987. See my discussion of this episode in Scull 1988. As I shall demonstrate in what follows, several of Stone's criticisms (e.g. that Foucault is careless with historical detail, neglects elementary conventions of historiography, and ignores the cross-societal *differences* in European responses to madness), though clumsily made and poorly documented, turn out to contain a substantial kernel of truth. Perhaps this explains the interesting publication history (or non-history) in France. Lawrence Stone has informed me that, before his exchange with Foucault was published in the *New York Review of Books* (and before he had seen Stone's reply), Foucault insisted that the exchange should also appear simultaneously in the French journal *Le Débat*. Stone and Robert Silvers, the editor of the *New York Review*, agreed these terms, subject to the proviso that the debate was to be reprinted in its entirety, and that Stone would be allowed to respond to any further comments by Foucault. To meet an urgent deadline at the French end, the galleys containing the exchange were rushed to Paris. But the planned French translation never appeared, because Foucault intervened at the last moment to prevent its appearance. (The key elements in Lawrence Stone's account of these events have been confirmed separately by Robert Silvers and by Pierre Nora, editor of *Le Débat*, in letters to me dated 13 July 1990 and 25 October 1990, respectively.) In acknowledging that the non-publication was at Foucault's insistence (*'Il m'a demande ensuite de ne pas le faire'*), M. Nora hastens to add that this was *'non par censure mais parce qu'il [Foucault] pensait que ce échange n'avait pas beaucoup d'intérêt et ne meritait pas . . . "le voyage transatlantique"'*. *Bien sûr*. Its 'triviality' and lack of intrinsic interest doubtless explain why the exchange is accorded so little significance by the English-speaking members of the Foucauldian cult.

2 Foucault's confession, in correspondence with Maher and Maher (1982: 759) that 'The documentation which I have utilized for *L'Histoire de la folie* comes in large part from the library at Upsala [sic]' perhaps explains – though it scarcely excuses – the shortcomings of his scholarship and the weakness of the evidentiary basis on which he relies throughout the book.

3 Compare, too, Jean-Claude Guédon (1977: 273): 'Moreover he generally uses a range of sources sufficiently wide to satisfy even the most demanding historian'. (One might object that simply referring to a wide range of sources is not the same thing as using them in ways that would satisfy 'the most demanding historian'; but in any event, the objection would be superfluous, for Guédon's claim is demonstrably false.)

4 Nicholls (1854) [Foucault cites the 1898 edition]; Nicolls (1856) [referred to in the text of *Histoire de la folie*, but omitted from the bibliography]. This tendency to rely on very selectively mined nineteenth-century sources of dubious provenance is a recurrent feature of Foucault's discussions. Indeed, Colin Gordon's defence of Foucault's scholarship refers on several occasions to his habit of plucking his 'facts' from such sources, without displaying any sense of unease or concern about the implications of this practice for the reliability of the evidentiary foundation on which Foucault's flights of fancy purport to rest.

5 It is precisely the essentially tangential character of this passage which allowed for its entire and unnoticed excision from the abridged French edition and subsequent English translation. Note, too, that in Foucault's view, the differences are largely temporary and transitional. In less than half a dozen paragraphs, he presents a brief discussion of Calvinist and Lutheran attitudes to poverty, and their impact in creating *'une forme nouvelle de sensibilité à la misère'* in northern Europe, then asserts that

Par des chemins différents − et non sans de nombreuses difficultés − le catholicisme arrivera . . . a des résultats tout à fait analogues. . . . Bientôt, le monde catholique va adopter un mode de perception de la misère qui s'était développé surtout dans le monde protestant.

(Foucault 1972: 69, 70, 71)

6 '*D'ailleurs, les nouveaux hôpitaux qui sont en train de s'ouvrir ne sont guère différents, dans leurs structure, de ceux qui les avaient precedés d'un siècle . . . pour être specialement destines aux insensés, les hôpitaux nouveaux ne laissent guère plus de place à la médecine*' (Foucault 1972: 406).

7 *Pace* Colin Gordon (1990b: 390−1), the difficulties here do not derive from the xenophobia of a bluff Anglo-Saxon historian, resistant to 'foreign' ideology and unwilling to grant 'French facts' the same peripheral weight as their English counterparts. It is not just that one can legitimately raise questions about the facticity of some of his facts (cf. Fairchilds 1976; Swain 1977; Gauchet and Swain 1980), and about the scholarly acceptability of what Jan Goldstein (1990: 334−6) suggests is 'a deliberate rhetorical strategy on Foucault's part' of vacillation and ambiguity on the question of 'whether [his book] is about France, or whether the France in its pages is supposed to represent the west'. More importantly, I would argue that it is in good measure through this substitution of rhetorical gamesmanship for a serious comparative examination of the European encounter with madness that Foucault is able to circumvent the difficult but crucial task of providing a systematic examination of the relevance of the economic and the political realms to the understanding ot the issues at hand.

8 '[*D*]epuis les grecs, [*le médecine de l'esprit*] n'était qu'un chapitre de la médecine, et nous avons vu Willis étudier les folies sous la rubrique des "maladies de la tête"' (Foucault 1972: 527; 1965: 275).

9 I have expanded on my discussion of this issue here (as compared with that offered in Scull 1990) in the first place because of the importance of spelling out the precise nature of Foucault's claims about the relationship between moral treatment and mental medicine; but also because Colin Gordon (1990b: 390−1) has objected that my earlier more truncated criticism had relied on selective quotation to prove its point (and had carelessly or stupidly failed to grasp that Foucault's analysis was actually identical to mine). In particular, he has claimed that in omitting the words '*on croit*' which immediately precede the phrase '*Tuke et Pinel on ouvert l'asile à la connaissance medicale*' in *Histoire de la folie*, I have played fast and loose with Foucault's text for my own disreputable purposes. Not so. As the much more extended passages quoted here make clear (and the reader is also referred to the complete discussion in Foucault 1972: 523−7), Foucault is unquestionably one of those who '*croit*' that this is so. As for Gordon's claim that 'Goldstein shows that Foucault's discussion of Tuke and Pinel, if read with a modicum of attentiveness, can be seen to expound the same view as Scull's on this matter' (Gordon 1990b: 390): I don't know whether to be flattered by the concession from a Foucauldian that I've at last got something right (albeit presumably by the neat trick of simultaneously misunderstanding and misappropriating the master); or bewildered by the creative (mis)reading of texts which allows him to make such a judgement. Goldstein, to my eyes, at least, claims nothing of the sort. She *does* suggest that Foucault was aware of Tuke's lay status (though she concedes that he fails 'to mention this seemingly important fact') (Goldstein 1990: 338); and I am sure she is correct on this point. (The lay origins of the English version of moral treatment are too blindingly obvious to be missed by anyone who reads the *Description of the Retreat* (Tuke 1813), as we know that Foucault did.) Her own creative account of what Foucault was up to (1990: 337−9) stresses his deliberate use of ambiguity as a

tool 'for breaking down conventional categories of analysis and thereby of defamiliarizing the past'; and, in a clever attempt to rescue a dubious line of argument, suggests that Foucault's strategy in emphasizing the way moral treatment transforms the asylum into 'a medical space' depends upon a deliberate blurring of two distinct senses of medicine – medicine as the generic relief of suffering, and medicine as the application of physical remedies. Whether or not one chooses to accept her analysis (and one should recognize that its adoption would simultaneously require the dangerous concession that Foucault 'revels' in ambiguity, but 'never stops to analyse it or to provide us with a sober definition of terms that would clarify it' (Goldstein 1990: 338)), even Goldstein would concede the gulf between Foucault's project and my own attempt to provide a coherent and persuasive account of how professional control over madness was secured by physicians. Let me insist again: on the crucial issue of the *threat* moral treatment posed to the medical monopolization of the treatment of the mad, Foucault is utterly silent, and, in my view, that silence cannot but be construed as a major misunderstanding of the significance of the events he purports to analyse.

10 See the more extended discussion in Scull 1989: 1–30.

11 An alternative text makes it abundantly clear that this is Foucault's central claim about madness in the pre-modern era. In 1962, a year after the publication of *Histoire de la folie*, Foucault's first book, *Maladie mentale et personalité* (1954) was reissued under the new title, *Maladie mentale et psychologie*. Its two new chapters on 'Madness and culture' contained Foucault's own précis of his argument, a text subsequently blessed by one of his epigones as 'a stunning ten-page summary of [*Histoire de la folie*]' (Dreyfus 1987: xxvii). Having noted 'the great prestige of madness' in the Renaissance, Foucault proceeds to stress that:

> Generally speaking, madness was allowed free reign; it circulated throughout society, it formed part of the background and language of everyday life, it was for everyone an everyday experience that one sought not to exalt nor to control. . . . Up to about 1650, Western culture was strangely hospitable to these forms of experience. About the middle of the seventeenth century a sudden change took place: the world of madness was to become the world of exclusion . . . madness, which had for so long been present on the horizon, disappeared. It entered a phase of silence from which it was not to emerge for a long time; it was deprived of its language; and although one continued to speak of it, it became impossible for it to speak of itself.
>
> (Foucault 1987: 67–9)

12 *Il arrivait que certains insensés soient fouettés publiquement, et qu'au cours d'une sorte de jeu, ils soient ensuite poursuivis dans une course simulée et chassés de la ville à coups de verges.*
> (Foucault 1972: 21; 1965: 10)

So far as I can tell, this is the only reference Foucault makes to whipping, and the modifiers in the passage are not without interest: it *happens* that *certain* madmen . . . in the course of *a kind of game* . . . *a mock race* . . . find themselves subject to the whip; and the chasing out of town, so we are informed in the next sentence, is '*un partage rituel*', a ritual exile. There is material here for our semiotic friends to play with.

13 It is telling that even a participant in this debate who is relatively sympathetic to Gordon's position (LaCapra 1990: 32, 38) recognizes the weakness of his argument here. In response, Gordon (1990b: 388) has now been forced to concede that Foucault 'elaborates his material with a certain degree of poetic

license, at times blurring together the possible symbolic meanings of material practices and cultural motifs'. But the same passage reveals a desperate attempt to rescue the reality of the ship of fools: I refer not just to the remarkable admission that Foucault may possibly have resorted to 'slightly hyperbolic usage' (wishful thinking is more like it – as Midelfort (1990: 42) comments, 'Foucault's few footnotes . . . do not substantiate a single ship of fools'); or even to the bathetic remark that 'What Foucault is saying, by saying that there were actual ships of fools in the middle ages, is that some mad people travelled, for various reasons, in boats along European rivers in the course of the middle ages' (Gordon 1990b: 387); but also to the Alice-in-Wonderland attempts to reverse the plain meaning of Foucault's own text. Foucault (1972: 19; 1965: 8) writes: *'Souvent, les villes d'Europe ont du voir aborder ces navires de fous'* – 'Often the cities of Europe must have seen these "ships of fools" approaching their harbors'. Gordon (1990b: 337–8) glosses: 'This "must" is probably one of the kind which actually . . . conveys a less than apodictic certainty'. Where 'must' is to be rendered 'may just possibly have' one has indeed entered, in Gordon's (1990b: 393) own words, 'a regime of commentary under which anything goes'. Perhaps conscious of the frailty of this line of defence, Gordon (1990b: 388, 387) tries in the alternative to downgrade the importance of the whole episode anyway: it lies, he suggests, 'at the extreme initial margin of [Foucault's] theme and period' and the passages in question 'cover six pages out of 600'. But this won't do either, for the claimed marginality is a myth. Any unprejudiced reading of Foucault's text 'must' (and I mean this in the ordinary, taken-for-granted, standard sense of the term) acknowledge the centrality of 'the ship of fools, . . . given the metaphoric and argumentative role of Foucault's correlation of the Renaissance with embarkation in contrast to the linkage to the classical age with confinement and the house of confinement' (LaCapra 1990: 32).

14 For instance, following the appearance of inadequate English versions of Durkheim's *The Division of Labor in Society* and of his *Rules of Sociological Method* in 1933 and 1938 respectively, corrected versions did not appear in print until the 1980s (Durkheim 1982; 1984); and the haphazard appearance of translations of bits and pieces of Max Weber's *magnum opus, Wirtschaft und Gesellschaft* (poor as some of them were) meant that a translation of the whole was put off for something close to half a century (Weber 1968). Durkheim and Weber had the excuse of being dead, and hence of possessing no means of rectifying matters; but it was Foucault himself who licensed the production of an abbreviated version of his argument in *Histoire de la folie* for English-speaking audiences, and who made no move to alter this situation over the space of more than twenty years, long after his status as a cultural icon would have made the issue of the complete version a financially viable proposition.

15 Elsewhere (Scull 1989: 15), I have pointed out that the reasons for the appearance of only an abridged text in English 'remain obscure' and have suggested that 'perhaps Foucault did not object too strenuously' to this state of affairs, since a truncated version of his argument, with its sometimes abrupt transitions, more readily accommodated itself to his later emphasis on historical discontinuities. I echoed here in tentative form a hypothesis first advanced by Erik Midelfort (1980). Colin Gordon (1990b: 386) attributes such suggestions to 'moments of genuine intellectual disorientation' occurring in what he, with uncharacteristic generosity, acknowledges to be 'otherwise lucid minds'. I do not want to make too much of this issue, since it is one on which I have always insisted that closure, or even a reasonable degree of certainty, is impossible. But I would point out that the idea that Foucault sought to influence the fate of his ideas through a strategic deployment and concealment of texts is more plausible than Gordon allows. One may instance several examples of him behaving in just

this fashion: the suppression of the publication in French of his exchange with Lawrence Stone (see note 1 above); his repeated refusals to allow the republication of his first book, *Maladie mentale et psychologie*, in French, and his unsuccessful attempts to prevent the appearance of an English edition (Gordon 1990b: 386); and his written instruction that no posthumous manuscripts of his were to be published (Rabinow 1990: 56). Moreover, his disciples, perhaps taking their cue from the notorious practices of the Freud Archives, have set up a Foucault Archive in Paris, open only to carefully pre-screened scholars, and only under the condition that no materials in the archive are to be reproduced! (Rabinow 1990: 56). Whatever one makes of these episodes, they certainly suggest that Foucault played a more active role in the management of his *oeuvre* and his image than Gordon is willing to acknowledge.

16 One last comment: Gordon (1990b: 381–2, 393) seeks repeatedly to impugn the honesty and scholarly bona fides of Foucault's critics, frequently resorting to what I can only describe as smear tactics (while protesting simultaneously that he is not motivated by 'the sad passions of the sectarian' and that he seeks to avoid 'the stale and gloomy incriminatorial mode'). We critical voices, the unwashed and unconverted, are, it seems, poor 'defensive' creatures, unwilling to face up to our own 'insecurities' – feebly trying to practise 'normal science . . . while teetering over an abyss'. Called to account for our failings, we persist in egregious error 'in ways which reveal an unusually drastic economizing of intellectual and scholarly means'. Doubts are even expressed about whether (unspecified) particular individual participants in the debate have, 'as a matter of fact, ever managed to find the necessary time to read [*Histoire de la folie*], let alone to reread it'. And, in consequence, our judgements about the work in question are, it seems, 'largely a matter of [in?]judicious guesswork'. One cannot help at least feeling a twinge of admiration for the chutzpah all this represents. Astonishing and incredible as it may seem to Colin Gordon, however, one may be acquainted with the full panoply of Foucault's history of madness without being tempted to embrace his oracular utterances as revealed truth.

BIBLIOGRAPHY

Bynum, W. F. (1981) 'Rationales for therapy in British psychiatry, 1770–1835', in A. Scull (ed.) *Madhouses, Mad-Doctors, and Madmen: The Social History of Psychiatry in the Victorian Era*, London/Philadelphia, Pa.: Athlone/University of Pennsylvania Press, 35–57.

Castel, R. (1976) *L'Ordre psychiatrique: l'age d'or d'alienisme*, Paris: Minuit.

Castel, R. (1988) *The Regulation of Madness: Origins of Incarceration in France*, Oxford/Berkeley: Polity/University of California Press. (Translation of Castel 1976)

Dowbiggin, I. (1986) *The Professional, Sociopolitical, and Cultural Dimensions of Psychiatric Theory in France, 1840–1890*. Unpublished Ph.D. dissertation, Rochester University.

Dreyfus, H. (1987) 'Foreword to the California Edition' of Michel Foucault, *Mental Illness and Psychology*, Berkeley, Calif.: University of California Press, vii–xliii.

Durkheim, E. (1982) *The Rules of Sociological Method*, New York: Free Press.

Durkheim, E. (1984) *The Division of Labor in Society*, New York: Free Press.

Fairchilds, C. C. (1976) *Poverty and Charity in Aix-en-Provence 1640–1789*, Baltimore, Maryland: Johns Hopkins University Press.

Foucault, M. (1965) *Madness and Civilization: A History of Insanity in the Age of Reason*, New York: Vintage.

Foucault, M. (1972) *Histoire de la folie*, Paris: Gallimard.

Foucault, M. (1987) *Mental Illness and Psychology*, Berkeley, Calif.: University of California Press.

Gauchet, M. and G. Swain (1980) *La Pratique de l'esprit humain. L'Institution asiliaitre et la revolution democratique*, Paris.

Goldstein, J. (1987) *Console and Classify: The French Psychiatric Profession in the Nineteenth Century*, Cambridge: Cambridge University Press.

Goldstein, J. (1990) ' "The lively sensibility of the Frenchman": some reflections on the place of France in Foucault's *Histoire de la folie*', *History of the Human Sciences* 3: 333–41.

Gordon, C. (1990a) '*Histoire de la folie*: an unknown book by Michel Foucault', *History of the Human Sciences* 3: 3–26.

Gordon, C. (1990b) 'History, madness, and other errors', *History of the Human Sciences* 3: 381–96.

Guédon, J.-C. (1977) 'Michel Foucault: the knowledge of power and the power of knowledge', *Bulletin of the History of Medicine* 51: 245–77.

Hacking, I. (1986) 'The archeology of Foucault', in D. C. Hoy (ed.) *Foucault: A Critical Reader*, Oxford: Blackwell.

LaCapra, D. (1990) 'Foucault, history, and madness', *History of the Human Sciences* 3: 31–8.

Leary, D. (1976) 'Michel Foucault: an historian of the *Sciences Humaines*', *Journal of the History of Behavioral Sciences* 12: 286–93.

Maher, W. B. and B. Maher (1982) 'The Ship of Fools: *Stultifera Navis* or *Ignis Fatuus?*', *American Psychologist* 37: 756–61.

Merquior, J. G. (1985) *Foucault*, London: Fontana.

Midelfort, H. C. E. (1980) 'Madness and civilization in early modern Europe', in B. C. Malament (ed.) *After the Reformation: Essays in Honor of J. H. Hexter*, Philadephia, Pa.: University of Pennsylvania Press, 247–65.

Nicholls, G. (1854) *A History of the English Poor Law in Connection with the Legislation and Other Circumstances Affecting the Condition of the People* 2 vols, London: Murray.

Nicholls, G. (1856) *A History of the Irish Poor Law*, London: Murray.

Peters, M. (1971) 'Extended review of Michel Foucault, *Madness and Civilization*, and of Jean Piaget, *Structuralism*', *Sociological Review* 19: 634–8.

Pinel, P. (1962) *A Treatise on Insanity*, trans. D. D. Davis, 1806; facsimile edition, New York: Haffner.

Rabinow, P. (1990) 'Truth and society', *History of the Human Sciences* 3: 55–6.

Scull, A. (1988) 'Keepers', *London Review of Books* 29 September 1988: 21–3.

Scull, A. (1989) *Social Order/Mental Disorder*, London/Berkeley, Calif.: Routledge/ University of California Press.

Scull, A. (1990) 'Michel Foucault's *History of Madness*', *History of the Human Sciences* 3: 57–67.

Sedgwick, P. (1982) *Psycho Politics*, London/New York: Pluto/Harper and Row.

Stone, L. (1987) *The Past and Present Revisited*, London: Routledge & Kegan Paul.

Swain, G. (1977) *La Sujet de la folie. Naissance de la psychiatrie*, Toulouse.

Tenon, J. (n.d.) 'Journal d'Observations sur les principaux hopitaux et prisons d'Angleterre', *Papiers sur les hopitaux* III, folios 11–16 (*c*. 1790).

Weiner, D. (1984) 'The Origins of Psychiatry: Pinel or the Zeitgeist', in O. Baur and O. Glandien (eds) *Zussammenhang: Festschrift für Marliene Putscher* vol. 2, Köln: Wienand, 611–31.

Part III
Review

14 Rewriting the history of misreading

Colin Gordon

Et pourtant d'autres, 'perdant leur chemin, souhaitent le perdre à jamais'.
(*Histoire de la folie*, 1972: 549)

A reviewer once wrote that trying to introduce Foucault's work into British intellectual life was like entering Cerberus at Cruft's. Several respondents have taken a similarly quizzical view of my effort to commend Foucault's book to English-language historians. Some (Scull, Midelfort, Merquior) doubt whether the work, even when it has been read in its full original form, can ever pass muster on straight historiographic criteria; others (LaCapra, Megill, Pearson) suspect that the very attempt is a kind of category mistake, a pedantic misrecognition of the three-headed nature of the beast.

For the same and other reasons, my contention that *Histoire de la folie* has been a largely unread or misread book has been perceived by some respondents as not so much perverse as obtuse. Can the fate of a book be reduced to a catalogue of rectifiable errors? Did not Foucault himself, in his 1972 preface to the second edition, disclaim any such correctional prerogative over the reception of this work? Even where many misreadings can be documented, can their cause or blame (Megill asks) plausibly be laid only on the side of the guilty readers?

I agree with Paul Rabinow that the stale and gloomy incriminatorial mode is best avoided. Foucault's work does not need an armed guard. An alternative course might rather be to try, by the adducing of interesting facts, to shift the limits of what has been seen and said of it. This was the aspiration of my essay: to help to bring it about that some things become no longer sayable about Foucault's *Histoire de la folie*, and that others become seeable. Without, I hope, yielding to the sad passions of the sectarian. But not without exercising a certain sense of the grotesque.

'FOUCAULT AND THE HISTORIANS'

Why worry about Foucault's reception by 'the historians'? Was he writing especially for them? If Foucault was not a historian, why read him as one? Was Foucault seriously interested in dialogue with historians? Has his work not chiefly been taken up by people doing those kinds of history seldom done in history departments (intellectual history, history of science, art history, histories of special social institutions and practices)? Was Foucault's work much better understood or received by French- than by English-speaking historians?

What historians have thought about Foucault matters partly because of why non-historians (or non-mainstream historians) take it to matter; and because it conditions views of what other kind of thinker or writer Foucault may actually have been. Take for example H. C. Erik Midelfort's findings, and their use by J. G. Merquior, or Peter Sedgwick, or Andrew Scull, LaCapra thinks it misplaced to worry about Foucault's gradings against orthodox historiographical standards; but he prefers to feel confident that Midelfort's gradings are not far wrong. Megill is not in the business of deciding what actually occurred in early modern Europe, but makes a point of establishing that Foucault's version is unacceptable to the specialists. The historians' verdict is at once immaterial (and hence immune from close checking) and fundamental (and hence continually repeated).

No doubt some historians are philistines, or at least conceptually hard of hearing. But another philistinism is exhibited, and moreover arbitrarily wished on Foucault as well, in the slightly contemptuous sterotype of historiographical activity as stolid fact-gathering, propagated by those who claim Foucault was up to something altogether different. In his exchanges with Jacques Leonard and the historians of the Société Robespierre (a key document on these issues), Foucault mocks both this stereotype and its obverse.

> With perhaps a touch of cruelty, [Leonard] makes him [a fictive typical historian reacting to Foucault] act the great unflattering roles in the repertoire; the virtuous knight of exactitude ('I perhaps don't have many ideas, but at least what I say is true'), the inexhaustibly knowledgable doctor ('you have not said this, or that, or again that, which I know and you certainly do not'), the great witness to the Real ('no grand systems, but life, real life with all its rich contradictions'), the desolated savant bewailing his little domain which the savages have laid to waste – as though after Attila the grass will grow no more. In short, all the clichés: the little true facts against the great vague ideas; the dust versus the cloud.
>
> (1980: 29)

One would not normally think it necessary to gloss this passage by explaining that its point is not to vindicate cloudy vagueness and belittle scrupulous exactitude, but to reject a belittling image of historical work which makes rigour the enemy of thought; the more so because in this essay Foucault proceeds to defend himself, and counterattack Leonard's fictive critic's strictures, on the terrain of attention to pertinent fact and detail. Except that Andrew Scull has written the following:

> The dangers of treating Foucault as though he were indeed a historian, in
> the conventional sense of that term, are perhaps suggested by his response

to critics who had charged him with gross historical inaccuracies: to query him on such points, he sniffed, is misleadingly to pit 'little true facts against great big ideas'.

(1989)

Leonard's essay, which has been selectively mined, notably by J. G. Merquior (1990), as though it presented a thoroughgoing demolition of Foucault's kind of history, follows its rehearsal of possible objections with an extended and generous appreciation of Foucault's contribution to the discipline:

> This much having been said, one can henceforth affirm that Michel Foucault is himself a historian, and a historian of incontestable originality, to whom it is in our interest to listen. . . . Reading Foucault, one is readily persuaded that history is still very young.
>
> (16–18)

Which is very much what Braudel and Mandrou had written in 1962, and what Paul Veyne said in 1978 in his essay *'Foucault revolutionne l'histoire'*, and what was said in the two obituary pieces on Foucault by Roger Chartier (1984a; 1984b). Chartier's commentary is noteworthy because of its particular attentiveness to Foucault's methodological writings on discourse and discontinuity, on which he writes that *'les questions de Foucault deviennent celles de toute histoire vivante'* (1984b).

This is not, of course, to say that Foucault's work was always, or indeed ever, an object of official or mass enthusiasm among French historians. Allan Megill's trawl of the citation indexes affords quantitative verification of this fact, although there is evidence for every stage in Foucault's work from 1961 of significant interest and influence among an innovative minority in the profession; while the few illustrations I have given here and in my initial paper reflect a certain significant difference between the French- and English-speaking tones of what has been perceived as normal, acceptable or profitable historical comment on Foucault's work.

'Why worry about Foucault's reception by "the historians"?' My opening question was not, *pace* Anthony Pugh (this volume, p. 131), intended rhetorically. There is ground for worry, or at least for the courtesy of careful attention – courtesy including, of course, recognition that 'the historians' have individual and differentiated contributions to the discussion.

RHETORICAL LOBOTOMY

Foucault's exact relationship to the discipline of history is not a question which has had, or perhaps needs to have, one single, clear and comprehensive answer. One can nevertheless make plenty of sense of that relationship, and its productive value, simply on condition that one allows for the possibility of a history that can think. Foucault said once that he liked to cope with Marxist critics by including passages from *Capital* in his work without quotation marks, because the quotation would regularly go unrecognized. One is inclined to suspect a similar tactic when Foucault draws, in his response to Leonard, a distinction between two kinds of historical enquiry, one focused on a *period* (e.g. a chapter in the history of punishment), the other (which is Foucault's) focused on a *problem* (e.g. why the prison?): the forms of pertinent evidence (and counterevidence) are not the same in the two cases (Foucault makes a point here of saying that the distinction is not one between the concerns of two different professions). Precisely the same distinction had been made by Lucien Febvre.

Foucault may not have found all his exchanges with history and historians easy or satisfactory, but he had many of them, throughout the course of his career. Fernand Braudel was an influential supporter of Foucault's candidature at the College de France (Eribon 1989: 210, 227), and wrote of Foucault's death as an occasion for 'national mourning' (1984). Foucault, for his part, found himself intellectually at home with the French historical school of his early career, which he characterized as the main space of interdisciplinary intellectual exchange within French culture. Very arguably, Foucault could not have become the kind of philosopher he did, had French history not been what it was. A protest needs to be entered at LaCapra's treatment of this connection in terms of a strand of 'scientific or even positivistic structuralism' in Foucault's *Histoire de la folie*, 'which may have endeared him to an earlier generation of Annalistes who recognised their official self-image here' (1990: 37). The item in the Annalistes's programme which was perceived by Braudel as having been executed in *Histoire de la folie* was, as I have previously noted, Febvre's 'history of mentalities' – a project whose structuralist and positivistic orientation does not exactly leap to the eye. Allan Megill feels that Foucault is interesting just because he is unacceptable. Dominick LaCapra seems to hold a complementary view: where Foucault is acceptable, he is uninteresting and obsolete.

I have not tried to show that Foucault is just like any conventional professional historian, but only that such historians can profitably read him, and even read him with some care. This is not a matter, as Megill suggests, of drafting Foucault into an inappropriate discipline. It is rather a matter of what needs to happen for the disciplines, including history, to live and breathe: or of what Foucault himself calls 'work in common by people who seek to "de-disciplinarise" themselves'. The experiment does not always work, of course. I do not myself think that the estimable art of rhetoric has been used to notably liberating effect in some of its cross-disciplinary applications to Foucault's writing. A book may speak in more than one voice: now cool, now passionate. It does not follow from this that the art of reading has to be structured like a lobotomy.

BOOKS HAVE THEIR FATES

Everyone seems to agree that the reception of Foucault's book is one of the odder and more chequered stories of its kind. Robert Castel and Geoff Pearson have provided accounts drawing from personal experience of its French and British episodes. Robert Castel recalls that the 1961 French edition was initially read and received as an academic work and in an academic mode (as was natural enough, for a doctoral thesis). The fact that it conjoined a philosophical and a historical component was noticed, but not perceived as a fundamental obstacle to acceptance. The same text, a few years later, was to be taken up by a political movement, linked to a militant intention unperceived in the text by its earlier readers, and subjected in the process to a number of intellectually impoverishing glosses – a process about which Foucault himself, partly for reasons set out in his 1972 preface, and partly for reasons of practical sympathy with the critical movements in question, chose not to protest.

Foucault's biographer Didier Eribon, while drawing extensively on an earlier essay on this theme by Robert Castel, adds a further perspective on the initial responses of psychiatrists to Foucault's earlier book. Eribon writes that the reaction of one important reformist group within the profession, *Evolution psychiatrique*, 'seems to have been relatively sympathetic', and quotes Foucault as saying in an interview that some Marxist and liberal psychiatrists showed a certain degree of interest in its ideas, although later on, after its adoption by the antipsychiatry movement, some of the same persons denounced the book as 'psychiatricidal' (Eribon 1989: 150).

Castel rightly infers from these French experiences that the corresponding adventures of Foucault's book in English are almost certainly not attributable to its abridged format alone. But this longer French history of the reception of a book always available in an uncut edition does also show that, in the absence (as in the early 1960s) of a context of overt politicization, that reception was not invariably difficult. Contrary to Peter Barham's supposition, the work has not always been experienced by psychiatrists as a threat to their profession (though Foucault certainly never saw it as an obligation of his work to make professionals feel good about themselves: see his comments on this point in the interview, 'Questions of method'. Barham's suggestion that a historical work unflattering to the self-image of psychiatrists must stand discredited if it fails to propose adequate solutions to the present-day problems of his profession is an unfortunate but typical evidence of that profession's intellectual insecurity and its propensity to moral blackmail). In contrast to Geoff Pearson's celebration of creative misreadings, the example of Robert Castel's work illustrates how a full and accurate grasp of Foucault's analysis can also help to make possible one of the most productively 'active' of readings.

To turn, now, to the English translation: two points need to be clarified.

In the first place, justice for Richard Howard. Andrew Scull is quite unwarranted in calling *Madness and Civilization* a 'bad translation'. 'Madness and Civilization' is actually a very good translation, in terms of style as well as accuracy: considerably superior, for example, to Alan Sheridan's subsequent handling of *Birth of the Clinic*. This is why, when signalling one significant mistake made by Howard, I also signalled its rarity. The myth of a defective translation should not be allowed to operate, alongside the myth of an impenetrable style, as an alibi for the carelessness with which many English-language critics, Scull included, have so often dealt with *Madness and Civilization*.

Second, on the question of the abridgement. I did not comment in my paper on Midelfort's hypothesis (1980) that Foucault himself may have preferred the abridged format of *Madness and Civilization*, with its sometimes abrupt transitions, because this suited his later doctrines of historical discontinuity. I suspected this might have been meant only as a joke about things Parisian. It transpires from the present discussion (41) that this is a long and seriously held theory of Midelfort's, and that the same idea has also been put forward by Andrew Scull (1989: 15). Foucault, they think, preferred to make historical changes appear as abrupt and mysterious as possible; by the cutting from his own text of passages of transition and explanation, the earlier work was brought more into line with the later discontinuist doctrine. For good measure, Dominick LaCapra has an alternative notion: Foucault perhaps kept the earlier book abridged so that his later ones would look more original.

In the face of such interpretations, one is forced to recognize that encounters with Foucault's work can produce moments of genuine disorientation in otherwise lucid minds. At times such as these the commentators seem to lose, or to relinquish, all sense of what beliefs or motives it is plausible to attribute to an author. It would take a little time to show from the text of *The Archaeology of Knowledge* and *L'Ordre du discourse* how Foucault's interest in certain forms of discontinuity differs from a bias against historical intelligibility and explanation; and that the latter concerns are in any case not exactly expunged from the text by the abridgement of *Madness and Civilization*. Let us stick here to a few simpler facts.

The first abridged version of Foucault's book was in French, a 10/18 series volume published shortly after and alongside the full Plon original. Both editions in due course went out of print. Foucault then authorized, in 1972 (two or three years after the publication of his discussions of the theme of discontinuity), an unchanged reprinting of the text of the full edition. The abridged edition was not, and has never been, reprinted; instead, Gallimard published an edition complete except for its 1972 appendices, in their cheaper 'Tel' series. *Histoire de la folie* was translated during these years into Spanish, German and Italian, in each case without significant abridgement. As far as I know, Foucault never initiated, or exercised close editorial control over any foreign-language translation of any of his books (except that, in the case of *Madness and Civilization*, he arranged for some passages omitted from the French pocket edition to be restored in the English abridgement). He objected (unsuccessfully) to the English translation of his *Maladie mentale et psychologie* (Eribon: 92); but this was an early book which he had long kept from being reprinted in French. Foucault knew that *Histoire de la folie* was not fully translated in English. My recollection from conversation with Foucault on this subject is that he regretted this and would have been happy to see the omission rectified. I know of no evidence suggesting that Foucault himself ever obstructed or discouraged any attempt to do so, or that any proposal to do so was ever put forward in his lifetime by an English-language publisher. He did not obstruct, but neither, I suppose, did he think it his business to initiate. One would think this a reasonable position for an author to take.

I am pleased to read corroboration by Anthony Pugh of these factual points. The elements of Andrew Scull's attempt, in notes added to his essay reprinted here, to salvage some credence for his peculiar allegations in this matter requires a brief comment, if only to vindicate the innocent third parties whom he maligns.

The *Association pour le Centre Michel Foucault* administers an archive of published and unpublished materials by and about Foucault, contributed by individual donors. (It does not own or control access to Foucault's own papers.) The archive is held in the Bibliothèque de Saulchoir, a theology library of the Dominican order located in Paris. This library provides access to the Foucault material for persons authorized by the *Association*, and this authorization is given to anyone having a research interest in the materials. Photocopying is allowed, subject to the usual copyright restriction, on all published materials. In short, the Saulchoir archive is administered in the same way as the holdings of any academic research library in the world. It provides a valuable scholarly resource created and maintained on the basis of voluntary initiative. Scull's allegations against those concerned are utterly groundless.

The provision of Foucault's will prohibiting posthumous editions of his unpublished work, and its interpretation by his heirs, have been subjects of natural public concern and discussion. Scull's representation of this provision as signifying a form of culpable manipulation of the author's public reputation surely shows a degree of distortion beyond the bounds of the reasonable.

EXCURSIONS: SHIPS OF FOOLS

I dealt rather briefly with the ships of fools; a defensible choice, if one goes by their place in Foucault's book. The passages which have attracted critical interest cover six pages (1972: 18–24) out of six hundred; of these six pages, controversy centres on three sentences: 'for they really existed, these boats that conveyed their insane cargo from town to town'; 'Often . . . the cities of Europe must have seen these "ships of fools" approaching their harbours'; and the sentence about 'pilgrimage boats, highly symbolic ships of madmen in search of their reason'. The tenor of Foucault's discussion has been heavily glossed in terms of one further phrase I have shown to be a mistranslation, about the 'easy wandering life' of the medieval insane. But several respondents (LaCapra, Midelfort, Scull, Megill) are unwilling to marginalize this issue. And indeed it is true that Midelfort's original strictures on Foucault's phantom, the ship of fools (amplified elsewhere by Maher and Maher), have been retailed too often and with too much coat-trailing relish for the sport to be easily spoiled now.

Foucault, of course, knew and said that the literary 'ship of fools' of Brant's poem and Bosch's picture were allegories and not transcriptions from contemporary social reality. He did not say that there existed medieval social practices resembling a literal actualization of Brant's or Bosch's image: none of the evidence he presents is taken as documenting the existence of boats entirely occupied or manned by the insane, navigating seas or rivers of Europe at will or at random. What Foucault is saying, by saying that there were actual ships of fools in the Middle Ages, is that some mad people travelled, for various reasons, in boats along European rivers in the course of the Middle Ages. Some were being got rid of by towns which had expelled them, or sent back to their own; others (very probably, to judge from Foucault's data, the most numerous category) were pilgrims journeying to shrines reputed to cure madness.

Midelfort thinks that Foucault wildly over-estimates the former categories of insane voyagers, since the three individual cases of riverborne transportations which Foucault cites apparently turn out to be the only ones ever known to have occurred. Foucault certainly seems to have thought there were more, and that his handful of known cases were samples of a more frequent practice, though (to reiterate a point) he does not say that it was a systematic or universal one, and in the case of Nuremberg he suggests it was relatively short-lived. On Foucault's own showing, it is manifestly dubious exactly how 'often' Rhineland cities 'must' have found insane passengers disembarking on their quays. This 'must' is probably one of the kind which actually (rather as with Megill's *'sans doute'*) conveys a less than apodictic certainty; there are many notes of tentativeness in the course of these few pages.

If Midelfort is right and (as every subsequent commentator appears to take for granted) his archival searches conclusive and exhaustive, then Foucault made a wong inference, and, incidentally but interestingly, the secondary nineteenth-century sources that Foucault used here would seem to have been more impressively thorough and exhaustive than Foucault himself possibly supposed.[1]

Where Foucault is far less evidently off-target is on the matter of his other category of data, the pilgrimages of the insane, the 'highly symbolic' boats of mad persons *en route* to the indubitably real and frequented pilgrimage shrines of Larchant, Gournay, Besançon and Gheel. One may indeed concede to Midelfort that they did not go alone, or unsupervised, or only by river, or only in the Middle Ages. Still, they did go, they were real, and they seem to have been quite numerous. Midelfort's 1980 paper does at one point – as LaCapra says – advert to their existence, but he unfortunately fails there to advert to any possible connection between their existence and Foucault's text.

It may reasonably be said that Foucault, writing at the extreme initial margin of his theme and period, elaborates his material with a certain degree of poetic licence, at times blurring together the possible symbolic meanings of material practices and cultural motifs. Maher and Maher show how this led to enthusiastically over-the-top retellings of his story by anti-psychiatric readers, some of which Maher and Maher proceed to read back into Foucault himself (1982: 751 ff.). Foucault's actual ships of fools are (a rhetorician would say) a slightly hyperbolic usage of the latter term. But this does not mean, as Megill contends, that Foucault's text is in some sense being radically ambiguous about the mad in the Middle Ages. Foucault was not saying something ambiguous, he was saying that something was ambiguous, or 'liminal': namely, the cultural and symbolic status of madness in late medieval society.[2]

Neither can it be said that this period is presented in Foucault's discussion, as Megill also contends, as a scene of happy, primal openness and undifferentiation. Foucault thinks that in the fifteenth century the threat or challenge of madness came to occupy a newly focal place in cultural and moral anxiety, one previously occupied by the theme of death. He also argues that the same motif of the ship of fools is implicated, in its respective literary and pictorial renderings, in two quite different structures which coexist in medieval culture: in the former case, rational moral satire; in the latter, cosmic disorientation and dread. Contrast this with Megill's gloss: 'we are told of the undifferentiated experience of madness, represented best by the images of Bosch, Brueghel, and Dürer'. Megill is saying here that Foucault represents medieval culture as the actual temporal site of what his 1961 preface called 'that degree zero in the course of madness at which madness is an undifferentiated experience, a not yet divided experience of division itself' (1961: i). But Bosch's paintings are certainly not, in Foucault's account, images of such a beginning state, where madness has yet to separate itself out from, and in the sight of, the sentience of the non-mad. They represent, on the contrary, the collapse of that separation, interpreted as the portent of apocalypse; 'it is the tide of madness, its secret invasion, that shows that the world is near its final catastrophe; it is man's insanity that invokes and makes necessary the world's end'. Foucault himself moves rather quickly to forestall Megill's conflation, by stating that the distinctively European duality of reason and unreason considerably predates Bosch (and will long survive Nietzsche and Artaud) (1961: iii; 1965: xi). It is a rather simple-minded understanding of the place of the literary and pictural materials in Foucault's study to suppose that every artist or poet cited is invoked as a witness to one identical, metahistorical essence of the mad. The material is actually rather carefully differentiated. It is a document of modified experience, not a hot-line to Being.

Midelfort takes issue with Foucault's ensuing discussion of the Renaissance, contending that Foucault over-accentuates secular and humanistic ideas about madness, at the expense of consideration of religious ones. This is not quite true. Foucault notes the apogee of prestige attained in the sixteenth century by the themes of I Corinthians, that divine folly is wiser than the wisom of men, and that the wisdom of the world is folly in God's sight (1, 25; 3, 19). He discusses these topics in the writings of Calvin, Franck and Erasmus among others (41−3). On the question of the medical status accorded to religious possessions, a topic whose neglect here Midelfort deplores, one should consult Foucault's article '*Les deviations religieuses et le savoir medical*', in J. Le Goff ed., *Heresies et Societes* (Paris-La Haye 1968). This piece provides at least a fragment of the separate discussion of this issue which Foucault had promised in *Histoire de la folie* (1972: 39). Later in his book, Foucault pays attention to the changing theological significance of both poverty and madness in the Classical Age, the latter theme being related to thought and works of Saint Vincent de Paul among others (1972: 170−3; 1965: 78−82).

ANTICRITICAL MISCELLANY

An attack of *apodioxis*

Allan Megill observes that my chapter employs a 'tactic' also favoured by Foucault, that of 'responding to a critic by claiming that the critic has inverted the work being criticised', a procedure which is a variety of the rhetorical figure of *apodioxis*, 'the indignant rejection of an argument as impertinent or absurdly false'. As a commentary I find this rather less disagreeable than a diagnosis of paranoia; as an argumentative gambit, however, it seems equally well calculated to obfuscate the facts of the matter in question.[3]

Jan Goldstein's generous essay neatly refutes an argument repeatedly employed against Foucault by Scull, which concerns the medical or non-medical character of the early moral treatments introduced by Pinel and Tuke. In a passage of his response to my chapter which is reproduced bodily from his earlier essay, 'Reflections on the historical sociology of psychiatry' (but, subsequently, heavily modified in the revised version reproduced here), Scull demolishes Foucault's quoted assertion that Tuke and Pinel 'opened up the asylum to medical knowledge'. Tuke and Pinel were, he shows (citing against Foucault work by Scull, Goldstein and Castel), in fact markedly sceptical towards medical therapeutics for the insane. Goldstein shows that Foucault's full discussion of Tuke and Pinel, if read with a modicum of attentiveness, can be seen to expound the same view as Scull's on this matter. One detail she refrains from noting is the way Scull quotes Foucault. He quotes him, as it happens, in French:

> It is, Foucault claims, '*Tuke et Pinel [qui] ont ouvert l'asile a la connaissance medicale*'.
>
> (Foucault 1972: 525; 1965: 271)

Looking up the quoted passages in the French and English, one finds the following (emphases added):

> *On croit que* Tuke ont ouvert l'asile a la connaissance medicale. *Ils n'ont pas introduit une science, mais un personnage, dont les pouvoirs n'empruntaient à ce savoir que leur deguisement, out tout au plus, leur justification.*

> *It is thought that* Tuke and Pinel opened the asylum to medical knowledge. *They did not introduce a science, but a personality, whose powers borrowed from science only their disguise, or at most their justification.*

Richard Howard's translation is fine. Scull's technique of citation is not so fine.

Few words have been so loosely or inappropriately used by contributors to the present discussion of *Histoire de la folie* as 'ambiguity'. Foucault says some complex things in this book, and often heightens the saying of them by antithesis and other rhetorical means. Several commentators of indubitably state-of-the-art theoretical accomplishment appear as readers to show a near-zero level of tolerance for complexity. Jan Goldstein shows a momentary lapse of this kind when discussing Foucault's views on medicine and the asylum. There is absolutely no chance of making sense of this discussion unless one distinguishes, with Foucault, between the respective status, content and meaning of the medical practitioner, medical knowledge, the activity of medical therapy and the medical institution. This essential distinction having once been recognized, Foucault's analysis of the birth of the asylum, although slightly complex, is, as Goldstein duly concludes, consistent and unambiguous. Scull, by persisting in ignoring these distinctions, maintains, in his revised contribution to this volume, his acrimonious confusion regarding the essential points of that analysis.

What the analysis shows is that the professional identity of the therapist acting within the new institution is (on the comparative evidence of the French and English cases) of less significance than his role as organizer of the medicalization of the internment institution; while it is the valorization of that new institution and its logic, and not the coded medical knowledge which would be the proprietary attribute of the medical profession, which rationalizes the new content given with the asylum to therapeutic activity. That is, the peculiarity of the new form of medicinal activity which in due course becomes psychiatry is partly captured in the observation that the special role and personage of the new asylum therapist is not originally linked to the possession of professional medical qualification, at least not in so far as that qualification reflects ownership of a corpus of scientific medical knowledge. To be sure, as Scull, Castel and others have shown, the professional doctor, complete with qualifications and science, in due course comes to power in nineteenth-century asylums everywhere. But Foucault's analysis (closely and explicitly followed in this regard, one may add, by that of Robert Castel) entitles one to doubt whether this latter process of itself suffices to clarify either the peculiar medical characteristics of psychiatry or the peculiar institutional characteristics of the asylum.

How great an internment? (French ideas and English facts)

Porter points out, *contra* Foucault, that many or most mad people were not shut up in public institutions in eighteenth-century England, and that those who were shut up were not generally compelled to work. Gauchet and Swain, in a fierce French debunking of *Histoire de la folie*, made a similar point about the French statistics. Porter and others note that asylum populations in the nineteenth century rose to far higher levels than the eighteenth-century ones.

These are facts which Foucault seems not to have overlooked or denied. Foucault discusses (1972: 401–3) the statistics of internment for France, noting the relatively slow eighteenth-century rise in the figures for the insane. He attributes this slowness partly to the number of persons who were still being left at liberty, and partly to the opening of new houses, private and religious, destined specifically for the custody of the mad. On the matter of work, Foucault describes its place in the regime of internment which was prescribed for the correction of the indigent, and hence by extension for that of the indigent mad; he also notes the widespread practical failure of the labour schemes actually instituted within the *hopitaux*, and the further difficulties experienced in extending these to the insane in them (1972: 79–85, 417). Foucault does not in fact lay any notably moral or medical stress on the connectedness of idleness with insanity in seventeenth- or eighteenth-century thought. What he does, however, document (though not, as Porter would have it, by way of an 'ideological' Freudo-Marxist deduction from an essence of capitalism) is a new early-modern Christian perspective on the pauper, common to Catholic and Calvinist cultures, in which an accent is shifted from charity towards culpability.

Foucault's book is still being reduced by historians (including those who will pay it any homage except that of reading) to the compass of three or four striking tableaux: the medieval insane messing around in boats; the carceral monolith of the Great Internment; unreason treated as animality; the spurious emancipation of moral treatment. But Foucault's Classical Age is very much more than the history of an internment: witness, among much else, his great, neglected chapters on medicine and therapeutics. As to the massive populations of the late nineteenth-century asylum, what else is Foucault thought to have been referring to by his often cited and censured words on the 'gigantic moral imprisonment' foreshadowed by the alienists?

I would refer here to Jan Goldstein's adroit discussion of how the Frenchness of Foucault's material has been cast by critics as a historiographical defect. The Anglo-Saxon attitude of bluff robust empiricism, refuting foreign ideology with English fact, has certain limitations here, not least because it does not discriminate too well between the un-Englishness of Foucault's data and that of his ideas. Foucault himself may not have been the complete comparative historian (no one is perfect), but this does not make his work unusable as a comparativist resource: one might also be able to learn something from French facts.

The preceding paragraph illustrates the drawbacks of polite (or timid) failure to make the names of those one disagrees with. I, in fact, had here in mind specifically the Anglo-Saxon attitudes of Roy Porter, who in his recent book *Mind-Forg'd Manacles* makes the characteristic complaint that Foucault 'seems to project French ideology onto the rest of the Continent' (p. 9). Andrew Scull, whom I have criticized elsewhere in this chapter, is mistaken in thinking himself my intended target here. I regret the misunderstanding. *Collins Dictionary* defines the adjective 'bluff' as meaning 'good-naturedly frank and hearty'.

When was there deviancy?

Midelfort has accepted some of my glosses: I would like to clarify one which he has read askew (though Nikolas Rose's essay already develops this point very lucidly). I did not make Foucault say, as Midelfort puts it, that the coming of the Great Internment marked the 'strange and sudden birth' of deviance. Foucault's hypothesis about deviance (developed in the untranslated chapter '*Le monde correctionaire*', *passim*) is that the whole period of that internment contributes towards making possible the subsequent, modern *concept* of deviancy, as a generic notion applying to a variety of distinct categories of persons and behaviours. Indeed, the Classical Age was not the first one which confined some of its mad alongside others. What Foucault thinks was new about it was (to summarize drastically) the systematicity, the breadth of scope, and the consistent, unified rationale of its internment practice.

When was there psychology?

Foucault denies that eighteenth-century mental medicine was psychological, thus puzzling Roy Porter. Porter (121) thinks Foucault must have ignored the eighteenth-century view of the madman as 'he who reasons wrongly — and who may therefore be capable of re-education and reform'. But

Foucault acknowledges, and considers at some length, the presence in eighteenth-century medicine of this perspective ('which is based on the discursive movement of reason reasoning with itself, and which addresses madness as error'), alongside others which 'consist in modifying the qualities common to body and soul' (1965: 183f; 1972: 348). He cites Sauvages's (perfectly Lockean) affirmation that 'One must be a philosopher to be able to cure the diseases of the soul' (1965: 183; 1972: 347). But Foucault thinks mental medicine only enters the realm of the psychological, in that particular modern sense of this term which he privileges (that of 'the psychological inwardness where modern man seeks both his depth and his truth'), when it seeks specifically to address and command the *moral* self-awareness of the subject, and when therapeutic rectification of ideas mutates into moral correction and subjugation. His account also recognizes the complexity and the gradualness ('little by little during the classical period . . .' (1965: 186; 1972: 350)) of this transition.

Versions of experience

Allan Megill suggests that Foucault's use of the term 'experience' in *Histoire de la folie* can be clarified by reference to his 1954 essay on Binswanger's 'Dream and existence'. This is true, but not quite in the way Megill proposes. The Binswanger essay combines a short history of western methods of dream interpretation, an argument against semiotic and linguistic styles of interpretation in favour of an ontological procedure which interprets the dream as a structure of experience, and an exposition of that structure as recapitulating the major ontological themes traversed in the preceding history of oneirocritical doctrine. In *Histoire de la folie* Foucault keeps, and vastly enriches, the historical component of the analysis, flirts at times with a Nietzschean metanarrative of the death and return of the tragic, but abandons any central ontological approach, at least so far as any description of the experience of being mad is concerned, substituting in its place a kind of secondary historical ontology of sane persons' experiences of encounter with the existence of madness.

'Experience of madness' in the *latter* sense, is the major organizing concept of Foucault's book, recurring in dozens of its focal passages.[4] Though there is from the outset an intimation that the two ontologies are anthropologically linked: ' "Pascal: Men are so necessarily mad, that not to be mad would amount to another form of madness (*un autre tour de folie*)".' Didier Eribon tells us that '*L'autre tour de folie*' was Foucault's first intended title for his book.

MORAL

My moral is: what we have is a failure to communicate. Habermas's vocabulary seems appropriate: the English-language reception of *Histoire de la folie* is a zone in which the conditions for communicative competence are endangered by unusual distortions and deformations. It would be premature in these circumstances to strain towards a serenely consensual summing up of the current discussion. The priority must be to find ways of unblocking this cramped space.

Most of the respondents to my article have agreed, albeit backhandedly, that something has gone badly wrong. To treat the properties of the text itself, complete or abridged, as a sufficient reason for its own miscomprehension seems, in the end, a too manifestly facile way of understanding what has happened. On the other hand, it has often and truly been observed that Foucault's book retains, more perhaps than any other, the perturbing power of its subject-matter. In a certain way, while not bereft of an entirely recognizable commitment to discursive rationality, it carries thinking, and hence the postulates of some existing discourses, to a point of actual challenge. The defensive element in some of the academic reactions is perfectly understandable. Normal science cannot be practised while teetering over an abyss: it has, often enough, sufficient insecurities of its own. It is legitimate to decline a challenge; where, however, this is done in ways which reveal an unusually drastic economizing of intellectual and scholarly means, this may be a sign that areas of normal science are in a state of what Canguilhem somewhere calls 'retracted life'. Foucault is difficult, perhaps immoderately difficult. Others have made it a little too easy for themselves to deal with this difficulty. The anomalous status of the text is made to license a regime of commentary under which anything goes.

Aspects of the present discussion show that these habits, once acquired, die hard. It would be tiresome and impolite to enquire whether every contributor of scholarly judgement on *Histoire de la folie* has, as a matter of fact, ever managed to find the necessary time to read it, let alone to reread it. Because there is now a prospect of a full translation finally appearing in the near future, the question has arisen of whether this will cause some revision in prevailing opinions of Foucault's book. But the particular note of meteorological tentativeness manifest in several opinion-makers' forecasts of this outcome might suggest that the content of the text awaiting reception itself remains, for the forecasters, largely a matter of judicious guesswork. In this respect, at least, my essay failed in its purpose.

NOTES

The original version of this piece was commissioned by *History of the Human Sciences* as an immediate and concise reply to their original twelve responses to my essay. That reply has, in turn, become a subject of further thought contributed for this volume by Andrew Scull and Anthony Pugh. To my regret, I have not had leisure sufficient to transmute my hurried thoughts into the more synthetic and, perhaps, serener kind of concluding reflection which might have better fitted the occasion of the present re-publication and the spirit of our editors' intent. In the event, therefore, the present piece has been given only a new title, some local stylistic repairs, and the insertion of some additional animadversions and rebuttals. I take this opportunity to convey greetings to two old friends, Robert Castel and Nikolas Rose.

1 Though the available numbers would only count drastically against Foucault if one confined the argument to cases of riverborne eviction; the total recorded numbers which Foucault cites of fifteenth-century expulsions of mad persons from a town such as Nuremberg was considerably higher. Another minor detail: Foucault considers the incoming as well as the outgoing traffic of wanderers; in the fourteenth century, in contrast to later custom, Nuremberg seems to have incarcerated rather more than its native tally of insane; Foucault postulates (though he is unable to demonstrate this) that such cities may have been used as dumping places.

2 (a) It is not quite sufficient to ascertain from a dictionary, as Allan Megill does, that a French word has two meanings, in order to establish that a French writer is being ambiguous when he uses it. The word '*alors*' in Foucault's sentence, '*Les fous alors avaient une existence facilement errante*' certainly does not mean 'therefore' as well as, or instead of, 'at that time'. '*Facilement*' might, as Megill's French-speaking informants reported, be rendered here as either 'often' or 'most often'. Foucault's adverb is (in the circumstances, very reasonably) extensionally imprecise. Imprecision is not ambiguity. (b) Correcting the mistranslation 'easy wandering life' has a bearing on much of the polemical commentary on this chapter because it eliminates the only textual basis of possible inferral from Foucault's chapter that the general material condition of the insane in the Middle Ages was more favourable than in other periods. Foucault's data on imprisonments and deportations do not exactly project a picture of medieval society as a palladium of social tolerance and dialogue. The spectacle of the contemporary decarcerated on inner city streets ought in any case tend to dissuade one from too promptly reading 'merrie' connotations into an account of a past condition of vagrancy.

Anthony Pugh, writing as the designated translator of the final completed English version of *Histoire de la folie*, finds this argument both trivial and comical (as indeed it is), but does not inspire confidence by contributing a Derridian-solipsistic mistranslation of his own, or by ignoring the utilization of the original error in the service of a highly influential critique. To suppose that the deconstructive patter of 'language that defers, rather than refers, refusing to make immediate sense', 'self-referential rhetorical artifices', 'dislocation from the literal' is a suitable means to convey insight into Foucault's thought or writing is to display a tin ear both for style and for ideas. Pugh's elaborately rehearsed difficulties in dealing with certain artificially isolated sentences in Foucault would have never arisen in the first place if the sentences had been read in the context of a sustained and coherent *argument* which they conclude and encapsulate. Occasionally, the help of a dictionary (as for the transitive form of the verb *obséder*) need not be disdained. The idea that there is something intrinsically obscure or elusive about Foucault's writing is an invention of English-speaking commentators.

The polemical literature on Foucault's chapter contains its own drastic internal contradictions. Foucault's other scholarly critics Maher and Maher, who are cited by Midelfort and Scull, and who conducted a postal search of Foucault's European archival sources, perceived in the 'Ship of Fools' chapter the precise contrary of Andrew Scull's happy Foucaldian Cockaigne, holding rather that Foucault had fabricated, for his own antipsychiatric ideological purposes, a *horrific* vision of the medieval treatment of madness: 'it is important to the scape-goat theory of mental illness that it be demonstrated dramatically. The image of the storm-tossed soul cast adrift from rational society fills the bill perfectly' (1982: 760).

3 It is entirely legitimate to interest oneself in ways of saying as distinct from the propositional truth-value of what is said. But, just as some ways of saying can be ways to evade the question of the truth of what is said, some ways of focusing on ways of saying can dispense rather too rapidly with the question of what it is that is being said. Megill writes: 'I turn aside, however, from adjudicating the particular dispute between Foucault and Stone . . . for the concern here is not to determine what was or was not the case in early modern Europe but rather to gain some insight into the rhetorical structure of Foucault's text' (page 94). The crux of the particular dispute between Foucault and Stone which Megill has just touched on here is not, as this implies, about the truth of certain historical propositions, but about whether Foucault had in fact stated the historical propositions which Stone attributed to him, or their opposite.

4 See, notably, the following places in the 1972 text: 94, 97, 106, 136 f., 139, 150, 155, 176 f., 181 f., 182–6, 188, 191, 192, 198, 200, 212, 232, 243, 261, 268 f., 273, 292, 299, 315 f., 359 f., 371, 383, 399 f., 445–6, 463 f., 479, 481, 496, 523, 529, 537, 540, 547 f.

BIBIOGRAPHY

Barham, P. (1990) 'Foucault and the psychiatric practitioner', *History of the Human Sciences* 3: 327–31.

Braudel, F. (1984) Obituary tribute to Michel Foucault, *Le nouvel observateur*, 29 juin, 63.

Castel, R. (1990) 'The two readings of *Histoire de la folie* in France', *History of the Human Sciences* 3: 27–30.

Chartier, R. (1984a) 'Les chemins *de l'histoire*', *Le nouvel observateur*, 29 juin, 44.

Chartier, R. (1984b) 'Les discourse en series', *Liberation*, 30 juin/1er juillet, 25.

Eribon, D. (1989) *Michel Foucault*, Paris: Flammarian.

Eribon, D. (1990) *Michel Foucault*, Paris: Flammarion.

Foucault, M. (1954) Preface to L. Binswanger, *Le rêve et l'éxistence*, Paris: Desclee de Brouwer, 9–128.

Foucault, M. (1961) *Folie et déraison: histoire de la folie à l'âge classique*, Paris: Plon.

Foucault, M. (1965) *Madness and Civilization*, trans. Richard Howard, New York: Random House.

Foucault, M. (1972) *Histoire de la folie à l'âge classique*, Paris: Gallimard.

Foucault, M. (1980) 'La poussiere et le nuage', in M. Perrot (ed.) *L'impossible prison*, Paris: Seuil, 29–39.

Goldstein, J. (1990) ' "The lively sensibility of the Frenchman": some reflections on the place of France in Foucault's *Histoire de la folie*', *History of the Human Sciences* 3: 333–41.

Gordon, C. (1990) '*Histoire de la folie*: an unknown book by Michel Foucault', *History of the Human Sciences* 3: 13–26.

LaCapra, D. (1990) 'Foucault, history, and madness', *History of the Human Sciences* 3: 31–8.

Leonard, J. (1980) 'L'historien et le philosophe', in M. Perrot (ed.) *L'impossible prison*, Paris: Seuil, 9–18.

Maher, W. B. and B. Maher (1982) 'The Ship of Fools: *Stultifera navis* or *Ignis fatuus*?', *American Psychologist* 37: 756–61.

Megill, Allan (1990) 'Foucault, ambiguity, and the rhetoric of historiography', *History of the Human Sciences* 3: 343−61.

Merquior, J. G. (1990) 'Back to the *Histoire de la folie*', *History of the Human Sciences* 3: 39−40.

Midelfort, H. C. E. (1990) 'Comment on Colin Gordon', *History of the Human Sciences* 3: 41−6.

Pearson, G. 'Misunderstanding Foucault', *History of the Human Sciences* 3: 361−71.

Porter, R. (1990) 'Foucauit's great confinement', *History of the Human Sciences* 3: 47−54.

Rabinow, P. (1990) 'Truth and society', *History of the Human Sciences* 3: 55−6.

Rose, N. (1990) 'Of madness itself: *Histoire de la folie* and the object of psychiatric history', *History of the Human Sciences* 3: 373−80.

Scull, A. (1989) *Social Order/Mental Disorder*, London: Routledge.

Scull, A. (1990) 'Michel Foucault's history of madness', *History of the Human Sciences* 3: 57−67.

15 Michel Foucault's *Madness and Civilization*

A selective bibliography with critical notations

Mark Erickson

The difficulty in philosophy is to say no more than we know. E.g., to see that when we have put two books together in their right order we have not thereby put them in their final places.
(Ludwig Wittgenstein *The Blue and Brown Books*, p. 45)

It could be said that Foucault's work, at many points, proposes an alternative approach to the human sciences in general, and offers particular strategies to counter the received wisdom of traditional social science.[1] As much of the material presented here will witness, Foucault has changed radically the way in which history, social science and philosophy can be practised: the breach of the boundaries between disparate disciplines has been extensive due to the impact of Foucault's writings. It would therefore seem reasonable to assume that an alternative bibliographic methodology would suggest itself from an immersion in Foucault's iconoclastic work. Alas, this is not the case, and what is presented here is a standard listing of bibliographic details, accompanied by critical notations to enable the reader to survey the English-language material relating to *Madness and Civilization* and *Histoire de la folie*, up to September 1990. The critical notations themselves offer a brief outline of the piece itself, and remarks concerning the importance of the article with respect to assessing the critical academic response to Foucault's work on madness. The bibliographic details have been compiled from the original texts themselves, most of the research for this project being carried out at the British Library and the National Library of Scotland. Initially, items for investigation were collected from the Social Sciences Citation Index[2] but, as the investigation proceeded, more items were collected from other bibliographies. In some cases, items have been included more for their significant lack of mention of Foucault's work. A great many items described in the S.S.C.I. as making reference to *Histoire de la folie* and/or *Madness and Civilization* have been excluded as the comments are too trivial or the only mention is in fact a bibliographic citation. I would refer the reader to Michael Clarke's excellent study for a full list of these.[3] Some items, possibly of great interest, must have been omitted from this bibliography as a consequence of the method employed, but it is hoped that these will be of the barest minimum.

The material contained in this bibliography is divided into sections according to the nature of the particular item as follows

- Works by Foucault: This section lists books and articles by Foucault on the history of madness, and his general work on mental illness.
- Reviews of works by Foucault: The reviews of *Histoire de la folie* and *Madness and Civilization* have been collected from a wide variety of sources – academic texts, newspapers and magazines – in an attempt to show the range of reactions to Foucault's first large work, and the variety of publications that included notices of its publication.[4]
- Books about Foucault: Many of the standard texts written about Foucault are included here, although some have been omitted due to their lack of reference to *Histoire de la folie* or *Madness and Civilization*. Most of these texts simply précis Foucault's main arguments, although some do give a sustained treatment of the critical issues in Foucault's work on madness.
- Articles on Foucault: All journal articles that are about Foucault's work and make specific reference to *Histoire de la folie* and/or *Madness and Civilization* are included in this section. Some of the key pieces in the debate about the veracity of Foucault's historiography, and the arguments over the validity of the abridgement of *Histoire de la folie* are located here.
- Books and articles on the history of insanity: The items included here give us a good idea of just how influential Foucault's work has been on subsequent historical work on madness and mental illness.
- Miscellaneous items: Includes articles and books that are not in the above categories, but which make specific mention of *Histoire de la folie* and/or *Madness and Civilization*.

The material in each section is arranged chronologically.

The eminent historian Martin Gilbert maintains that in explanation 'chronology is everything', and a chronological survey of the English-language responses to Foucault's work on madness is illuminating in a number of ways.

The themes of the book that are identified by commentators, as one would expect, remain constant, but the emphasis that these receive changes quite dramatically with time. Initial responses to *Histoire de la folie* and *Madness and Civilization* treat Foucault as a historian, and there is very little criticism of the historical data that he has used. Rather it is Foucault's style that receives most criticism. In the late 1960s, with the rise of anti-psychiatry, it is Foucault's criticism of contemporary techniques of the treatment of mental illness that becomes the focus of interest. This is compounded by some of the key figures in the antipsychiatry movement claiming Foucault as one of their own. As Foucault's work begins to reach a wider audience, in the early 1970s, it is his work on the history of ideas that receives most attention. In this phase, we see *Madness and Civilization* and *Histoire de la folie* becoming important as source texts for a number of studies on the history of madness. However, as these studies proliferate, Foucault's own historical data come under closer scrutiny, and a number of writers offer harsh attacks against Foucault's historiography. Finally, in the 1980s, and particularly after Foucault's death, we see the assimilation of all Foucault's work into one complete *oeuvre*, and this results in *Madness and Civilization* and *Histoire de la folie* being treated as theoretical treatises, at least in part, on a par with *The Order of Things* and *The Archaeology of Knowledge*. Foucault the philosopher is promoted at the expense of Foucault the historian.

The question of the abridgement and translation of *Histoire de la folie* is one that recurs throughout this bibliography, with most commentators being of the opinion that the English version is a poor imitation of the French original. It is, however, only when Foucault's historical data come under close scrutiny that the issue becomes critical, with writers highlighting the fact that they have, for example, used the French version in their article. Judging from recent articles (items 53 to 66), this issue is by no means resolved.

Also unresolved is the question of how to classify Foucault himself. He is variously described as a historian, a philosopher, a psychiatrist, a Marxist, a structuralist, a poststructuralist, and simply as French.

The range of responses to Michel Foucault's work is very wide; from highly praiseworthy to excessively dismissive, hypercritical to trivial. As the following texts show, Foucault can certainly not be described as uncontroversial at any point in his academic career.

WORKS BY MICHEL FOUCAULT

1   Foucault, M.
1954   *Maladie mentale et personalité*. Paris: P.U.F.

2   Foucault, M.
1961   *Folie et déraison. Histoire de la folie à l'âge classique*. Paris: Plon.
The first edition of this work.

3   Foucault, M.
1962   *Maladie mentale et psychologie*. Paris: Initiation Philosophique, no. 12.
This is the second edition of *Maladie mentale et personalité* and is extensively revised. A third French edition appeared in 1966.

4   Foucault, M.
1964   *Histoire de la folie*. Paris: U.G.E.
A shortened version of item 2, the abridgement being carried out by Foucault himself (see item 53 for a synopsis of the printing history of *Histoire de la folie*), upon which the English translation was based.

5   Foucault, M.
1965   *Madness and Civilization. A History of Insanity in the Age of Reason*. New York: Pantheon.
The first English-language edition of *Histoire de la folie*, translated by Richard Howard from the abridged second French edition.

6   Foucault, M.
1965   *Madness and Civilization. A History of Insanity in the Age of Reason*. London: Tavistock.
The first British edition of *Histoire de la folie*, translated by Richard Howard.

7   Foucault, M.
1972   *Histoire de la folie à l'âge classique*. Paris: Gallimard.
The second French edition of the book, with a new preface by the author (who suppressed the first preface), and two appendices.

8   Foucault, M.
1976   *Mental Illness and Psychology*. New York: Harper and Row.
Translated by Alan Sheridan. Foucault attempted, unsuccessfully, to prevent the translation of this work, the translation being based on the 1962 second (revised) edition. Foucault had already refused all reprint rights to the first (1954) edition.

9   Foucault, M.
1977   *Language, Counter-Memory, Practice*. Edited by D. F. Bouchard. Ithaca: Cornell University Press.
Included in this collection of essays and interviews is Foucault's review of J. Laplanche's *Hölderin et la question du père*, entitled *'Le "non" du père'*, *Critique* 178 (1962). Translated here as 'The Father's "No" ', Foucault discusses the themes of madness and art.

10   Foucault, M.
1978   'About the concept of the "dangerous individual" in 19th-century legal psychiatry', *International Journal of Law and Psychiatry*. 1: 1–18.
Foucault discusses the discrepancies between the legal system and the criminologists of the early nineteenth century.

11   Foucault, M.

1980   *Power/Knowledge*. Edited by Colin Gordon. Brighton: Harvester.
Although much of this book deals with themes from Foucault's later work,
the chapter entitled 'Truth and power' includes Foucault's reflections on
Madness and Civilization, and other early works.

REVIEWS

12   Anon.

1961   'The story of unreason' (Review of *Histoire de la folie*), *The
         Times Literary Supplement* No. 3110, 6 October 1961: 653–4.
According to O'Farrell (see item 44) the author of this review was Richard
Howard, who later translated *Histoire de la folie* for Tavistock.

   This article provides a long account of Michel Foucault's research to date
and an extensive précis of the main points of the book. The reviewer concludes with this appreciative passage: '[Foucault's] brilliant book, erudite,
but overloaded with antithesis and abstruse generalisations, is the most
original contribution that has been made to the wretched story of unreason
in the Age of Reason. Carried to a later period, his studies might illuminate
problems that have contemporary urgency' (654).

13   Simon, J. K.

1963   (Review of *Histoire de la folie*), *Modern Language Notes* 78 (1):
         85–8.
An excellent account of the principal themes of the book is given in this
large review. Simon picks out the principal contention of the book, namely
that Reason acts as a despiritualizing force, negating the social role of
madness in medieval society – that of replacing leprosy as the necessary
symbol of death – through the banishment of irrationality. Simon criticizes
the book for its somewhat haphazard use of figures from literary and
artistic history, and the difficulty of the task of reading the text. Simon also
points to the potential that the book may have in contemporary discussions
of our metaphysical and aesthetic preoccupations.

14   Anon.

1965   (Review of *Madness and Civilization*), *The Christian Century*
         82, 16 June 1965: 780.
A short review in this Christian Science journal. The full text runs as follows.
'In the Age of Reason men of unreason represented a new kind of problem.
Asylums were built to separate the madmen from the relatively normal and
the history of insanity entered a new phase. Spellbinding history' (780).

15   Gay, P.

1965   'Chains and couches', *Commentary* 40 (4): 93–6. (Review of
         Madness and Civilization by Michel Foucault)
A shallow, but long, review of the book, concentrating on Foucault's style
(seen as based on inflated rhetoric and existential cant) rather than on the

issues raised by the author. A brief account of a few historical points is concluded by a defence of Reason as an instrument of freedom and an appeal for Foucault to avoid nostalgia.

16   Matza, D.
1966   (Review of *Madness and Civilization* by Michel Foucault),
            American Sociological Review 31 (4): 551–2.
A glowing review which avoids any attempt to describe the book in anything but the largest generalizations. Matza describes *Madness and Civilization* as a 'major contribution to sociological thought' (551), which, although a difficult book, will be rewarding to the reader. For Matza, Foucault has grappled with the intricate process by which madness has been assembled and then obscured through different historical epochs.

17   Marcus, S.
1966   'In praise of folly', *New York Review of Books* 7 (7): 6–10.
            Reprinted with corrections in *New York Review of Books* 7 (8):
            36–9. (Review of *Madness and Civilization* by Michel Foucault)
Although a work of unquestionable originality and importance, Marcus levels strong criticism again Foucault, particularly over stylistic matters. 'It is written in a prose of an obscurity so dense as to be often impenetrable. This is not so much the result of its genuine difficulty of thought as of the author's arrogance, carelessness and imprecision. Helterskelter he employs whole sets of technical philosophical terms which are only half-assimilated to the matters he is discussing. Indeed he rarely bothers to define them, much less to use them consistently. . . . The author's scholarship is to say the least irregular; . . . and of Foucault's material on England, well, the less said the better.' It is interesting to note that many of these criticisms will feature much later in discussions of Foucault's work in the 1980s.

   Marcus notes that much of Foucault's work here can be considered to be a study of secularization. Foucault's apparent neglect of explanatory frameworks for the social processes at work is put down to his rejection of the feasibility of such frameworks, and his denial of the possibility of explaining madness or unreason. Marcus's final point is to note that the rejection of nineteenth and early twentieth century systems of thought, without having replaced them with anything of comparable magnitude, has created the intellectual conditions to allow Foucault to write such a work.

18   Anon.
1967   (Review of *Madness and Civilization*), *Publishers Weekly* 192
            (17) 23/10/67: 53–4.
A short review quoting a passage from Peter Gay's review in *Commentary* (item 15), and concluding that *Madness and Civilization* is 'a history of madness in the age of reason, the sixteenth, seventeenth and eighteenth centuries, when the madman was the outcast from society'.

19   Comfort, A.
1967   'Breakdown and repair', *The Guardian* 5/5/67: 5. Review of *By Reason of Insanity* by John Balt, *Madness and Civilization* by Michel Foucault, and *Medieval Minds* by T. F. Graham.

A fairly brief but favourable review of Foucault's book. 'For the professional and philosopher this is an important book, however, and its evidences of deep insight will increase with re-reading. . . . As a contribution to medical history alone Dr. Foucault's study is well worth the task of reading' (5).

20   Freeman, H.
1967   'Anti-psychiatry through history', *New Society* 19 (240): 665–6. (Review of *Madness and Civilization* by Michel Foucault)

Freeman gives a brief précis of the book and notes that it fits in with the current antipsychiatry movement, hence the introduction by David Cooper. He points out that there is a somewhat Gaullist emphasis in the book towards events in France and excluding, for example, the existence of the Bethlem Hospital in London. Foucault's history is on an anecdotal level, avoiding sociological issues surrounding the Great Confinement. Freeman criticizes the book for its casual treatment of witchcraft, its vague final chapter, and the lack of an index. 'On the whole this is an interesting, but very uneven contribution to the history of psychiatry' (666).

21   Gorer, G.
1967   'French method and madness', *The Observer* 23/4/67: 30. (Review of *Madness and Civilization* by Michel Foucault)

A brief review noting the narrowness of the field that Foucault has investigated although the reviewer does stress Foucault's erudition. Gorer concludes that the book will make heavy demands on the reader.

This review in *The Observer* shows us the way that Foucault was presented to a potential new audience. Gorer describes Foucault as 'an exceedingly erudite philosopher and French psychiatrist and the author of a number of highly esteemed books' (30).

22   Laing, R. D.
1967   'The invention of madness', *New Statesman* 71 (1892): 843. (Review of *Madness and Civilization* by Michel Foucault)

Madness and Civilization was published in English by Tavistock in the *Studies in Existentialism and Phenomenology* series, the editor of which was R. D. Laing. The review of *Madness and Civilization* written by Laing in the *New Statesman* is a long one, a full page, and it is fulsome in its praise for Foucault. Laing describes Foucault as 'a new voice' (843) and *Madness and Civilization* as 'a work of such distinction that it takes time to accustom oneself to its sustained intensity and verbal momentum, before one can begin to come to terms with the measure of its truth' (843). Laing gives a reasonable account of the book and the method behind its writing, which he describes as archaeological and phenomenological, although he gives heavy emphasis to the aspects of the book dealing with enforced confinement and the repression of the mentally ill (the topics that have received most criticism from historians). Noting that *Madness and Civilization* has been abridged, Laing suggests that this is entirely reasonable given that a new chapter has been contributed, which turns out to be one of the best.

Laing concludes his review with reference to the antipsychiatry movement, suggesting that David Cooper's introduction is too short and quoting Cooper's final remarks: 'The true significance of his book resides most precisely in the terror that it may produce in a significant few of us'. To which Laing adds: 'Exactly so. But there will be others, I think, who may even eke out some solace from having especially their worst fears validated' (843).

Of all the reviews, and indeed articles, written in English concerning *Madness and Civilization*, this is the strongest attempt made by the antipsychiatry movement to claim Foucault's work is akin to their own. We should also note that *Madness and Civilization* was considered to be an antipsychiatry book by a number of other reviewers and commentators, possibly for the simple reason that this was a useful way of pigeon-holing a book that does not easily fit into any category.

23   Richman, G.
1967   'Beware of false prophets', *Tribune* 31 (34): 10. (Review of
           Madness and Civilization by Michel Foucault)

A highly critical review of Foucault's work from a socialist perspective. Richman immediately locates *Madness and Civilization* in the context of Laing's antipsychiatry and existentialism, and complains that the very use of madness in the title is a cheat: one of the greatest advances in understanding mental illnesses was the differentiation of the various disorders that comprise it. Equating madness with folly is similarly a confidence trick on the reader. 'Language in the book is used to mystify and carry the reader uncritically along, sniffing the flowery phrases whilst being entangled in the roots of false logic' (10). Richman certainly favours an empirical approach to this type of subject, and he outlines a method by which to write a history of mental illness:

several themes must be explored. What is the incidence of such illness at different times and in different societies, and what are the various kinds? How do social factors enter into the origin of illness? And how do societies describe, explain, and treat the mentally ill? This book fails to base itself on these themes. In the meanwhile let us beware of false prophets. (10)

24 Leach, E.
1967 'Imprisoned by madmen', *The Listener* 77 (1993): 752–3.
(Review of *Madness and Civilization* by Michel Foucault)
Leach, in line with other reviewers at this time, locates *Madness and Civilization* in the school of antipsychiatric thought. He sees the book as a comment on the imposition of conformity on the mentally ill by psychiatrists, probation officers and policemen, the 'lackeys of a sadistic conservatism' (752). Leach sees Foucault's book as a fine proof of the unreasonableness of reason, one that would concern even the most bigoted rationalist.

No one should try to dismiss Foucault's argument simply because the Marxist–Existential world of intellectual Paris makes a habit of turning all conventional assumptions upside down, or because Foucault himself is too fond of barely meaningful aphorisms: 'Where there is a work of art there is no madness'. (753)

25 Paulson, R.
1968 (Review of *Fielding's Social Pamphlets* by Malvin R. Zirker, Jr. and *Madness and Civilization* by Michel Foucault), *Journal of English and Germanic Philology* 68 (1): 161–5.
The two books considered for review here are almost wholly unrelated, apart from considering, at points, a common historical epoch, and Paulson makes little effort to tie them together, although he does make another, somewhat bizarre connection: 'Foucault's book – like those of our own counterpart Marshall McLuhan – beckons towards the pleasures of a parlour game' (165). The reviewer gives a brief outline of *Madness and Civilization* and looks at the theme of unreason versus reason, suggesting that the chief vice visible in English literature at the time of the Classical Age was sloth, thus giving rise to the designation of the mentally ill as lacking any form of social usefulness. Paulson also relates the use of the symbol of 'the mob' in the work of Dryden, Swift and Pope, a symbol representing all that is evil, to the treatment of the mad that Foucault's work uncovers.

26 Dumont, M. P.
1968 'What is madness?' *Social Science and Medicine* 1968 2: 502–4.
(Review of *Madness and Civilization* by Michel Foucault and *Psychiatry and Anti-Psychiatry* by David Cooper)
A brief outline of *Madness and Civilization*, that Dumont describes as a 'brilliant and beautiful book [that] demonstrates how socio-economic perspectives are manifested in definitions of mental illness' (503). Although this is a joint review with Cooper's definitions of antipsychiatry, Dumont does not describe Foucault as an antipsychiatrist. Nor does he describe Cooper as an antipsychiatrist.

27   Parry-Jones, W. Ll.
1969   (Review of *Madness and Civilization* by Michel Foucault), *The British Journal of Social and Clinical Psychology* 8 (2): 191.
Parry-Jones's equation of Foucault's work with that of David Cooper once again locates *Madness and Civilization* in the antipsychiatry camp. He sees these two authors as performing essentially the same task, albeit in different historical periods. 'Not all agree with the concept of "antipsychiatry", but this should not deter anyone concerned with madness from reading this book' (191).

28   Rousseau, G. S.
1970   (Review of *Madness and Civilization* by Michel Foucault), *Eighteenth-Century Studies* 4 (1): 90–5.
Although a review of *Madness and Civilization*, Rousseau concentrates on the French version, *Histoire de la folie à l'âge classique*. Rousseau berates his contemporaries for ignoring Foucault's work, suggesting that this may be due to prejudice against Frenchmen and French scholarship.

Foucault's thesis is described as being a study of the creation of the concept of madness in the seventeenth and eighteenth centuries, and that this was ultimately an act of repression that has not yet been removed. This thesis, according to Rousseau, is original and historically supportable. 'If Foucault's book does nothing more than compel us to recognize that the epoch simply cannot be called "An Age of Reason", it has served a great purpose and has a mighty theme' (92). As to the implications of Foucault's theory, Rousseau points to two. First, the persuasive argument that scientific theory was 'perhaps never less objective than in evolving the theory of medical madness. . . . the theories of the Enlightenment "mad doctors" were hardly pure' (93). Secondly, Foucault is the first historian to account for the rise of melancholy and hysteria in this and no other epoch, as the true eighteenth-century disease.

Concluding, Rousseau sees Foucault's book as a work of invention. Foucault's thesis can be described as neither right nor wrong 'for such designations are meaningless when applied to a province of intellectual history as elusive and theoretical as this' (95).

Unlike the English reviews of this time, Rousseau makes no mention of antipsychiatry.

29   Scruton, R.
1971   'Roger Scruton on madness and method', *The Spectator* 227 (7476): 513. (Review of *Madness and Civilization* and *The Order of Things* by Michel Foucault)
A brief, but frequently highly critical, review. Scruton describes the main thesis of *Madness and Civilization* to be the discovery that each successive age finds a similar 'truth' through which the experience of madness can be transcended into sanity and that these 'truths' are now exhausted. Foucault

appeals to Goya, de Sade, Hölderlin, Nerval, Van Gogh, Artaud and Nietzsche to prove this exhaustion. Scruton points out that the language of madness is not similar to the 'hard remorseless logic of *The Twilight of the Idols*, or to the precise symbolism of *Les Chimères*. Foucault's heroes would have been unable to use this language, even in their final madness, and if we can understand them it is without its aid.'

Scruton does admit that, despite its faults, '*Madness and Civilization* is an interesting and often brilliant book' (513).

30   Peters, M.
1971   'Extended Review', *The Sociological Review* 19 (4): 634–8. (Review of *Madness and Civilization* by Michel Foucault and *Structuralism* by Jean Piaget)

Peters concentrates on the difference between Foucault's 'discursive and (ultra-literary) account of the stages in the evolution of the Western mythology about "science"' (636) and Piaget's conception of a scientific methodology of structuralism, and for the most part sides with Foucault. *Madness and Civilization* is described as a difficult book to read: 'it should not be undertaken at all unless one is prepared for the labour of unwrapping the ideas from the language' (636). Foucault's demolition of the pretensions of psychiatry is associated with the antipsychiatrists Laing, Cooper and Szasz.

> There is no greater damnation possible of the pseudo-scientific psychiatries of the present than to grant a tolerant hearing to these psychiatries of the past. Their absurdities seem so comprehensive, yet the confidence they inspired is so uncanny that one's dismay inevitably spills over in the form of grave doubts about their descendants. (637)

31   Hacking, I.
1981   'The archeology of Foucault', *New York Review of Books* 14 May 1981: 32–7. (Review of *Power/Knowledge* by Michel Foucault)

Hacking proposes, in a brief excursus on *Madness and Civilization*, that Foucault is hinting at a Kantian story, where our experience of the mad is a conditioned phenomenon created out of thought and history, and that there is also a thing-in-itself which we call madness. Foucault's somewhat romantic account suggests that this thing-in-itself is a pure thing, and possibly even good in itself. It is in *Madness and Civilization* that the roots of Foucault's later work on power/knowledge lie: the book is hinting at something else. Foucault himself noted in a 1977 interview that he was really talking about power in *Madness and Civilization* and *The Birth of the Clinic*, although he did not realize it at the time. Hacking depicts the events described in *Madness and Civilization* in terms of a formula to be repeated in a number of later works: 'He presents a reordering of events that we had not perceived before. The effect is heightened by brilliant before-and-after snapshots taken on either side of the great divide during which one tradition is transformed into another' (32).

32   Stone, L.
1987   *The Past and the Present Revisited*, London: Routledge.
One chapter in this book of essays collected mainly from *The New York Review of Books* is devoted to *Madness and Civilization*: a review of the book from the *NYRB* of 16/12/82 is reprinted along with an exchange of letters between Stone and Foucault. Stone's principal contention with Foucault's thesis is whether there is any firm basis for the application of a term such as 'the age of confinement' to what was a very small-scale trend in the late eighteenth century. It is not so much the broad generalizations that Foucault makes that disturb Stone, but the discrepancies from historical fact in Foucault's account. Stone offers a number of examples of this: madhouses did not start in disused leprosaria, but grew out of medieval hospitals, based on Arab models. Very few mad people were incarcerated in France or England before 1830. Stone concludes the review of *Madness and Civilization* by praising the book for drawing attention to the growth of confinement, and for its wealth of detail concerning the treatment of insanity. 'It is he who has set the agenda for the last fifteen years of research' (282).

Part II of this chapter contains a letter from Michel Foucault written in reply to Stone's review of *Madness and Civilization*, and Stone's reply to Foucault's letter. Foucault's letter (amounting to some 1,700 words) is very detailed in its refutation of Stone's criticisms, and at times quite scathing. Stone's very detailed reply (some 2,500 words) is equally scathing at times and, although Stone admits the possibility of one or two errors of judgement, particularly over the discrepancy between the work of Foucault and the actions of Foucauldians in the psychiatric world, he refutes Foucault's comments point by point. The question of the link between Foucault's work on madness and contemporary policies for the mentally ill is discussed by Stone:

> Can Foucault's pessimistic evaluation of lunatic asylums be held to have been a factor in the recent discharge of thousands of helpless psychiatric patients onto the pitiless streets of New York? Dr Gerald Weissman of the New York University School of Medicine believes that these tragic cases are indeed a remote by-product of Foucault's negative evaluation of the philanthropic dream of Pinel, coupled with the fashionable claims by the English [sic] revisionist psychiatrist R. D. Laing that schizophrenia is not a disease. (289)

This point remains unproven either way, and seems to be outside the purview of most other discussions of Foucault's work.

BOOKS ABOUT MICHEL FOUCAULT

33 Sheridan, A.
1980   *Michel Foucault. The Will to Truth*, London: Tavistock.
The first English-language introduction to Foucault's writings, Sheridan's book acts as a useful primer to all Foucault's main texts.

    Madness and Civilization is discussed in the first chapter, although Sheridan for the most part confines himself to providing a précis of the book, with a few appropriate expansions and elucidations. Sheridan does point out that the translator's task is particularly difficult in the case of *Histoire de la folie*, as the French word *folie* covers both the English words 'folly' and 'madness', used in quite different ways before the mid-seventeenth century.

34 Cooper, B.
1981   *Michel Foucault. An introduction to the study of his thought*,
        New York: The Edwin Mellen Press.
Includes a short, but comprehensive account of *Madness and Civilization*, although little commentary on the text is made. Cooper does mention antipsychiatry 'with which Foucault was in great sympathy' (25), and also offers a reading of the themes of *Madness and Civilization* in the light of Foucault's later work on power/knowledge.

35 Dreyfus, H. L. and Rabinow, P.
1981   *Michel Foucault: Beyond Structuralism and Hermeneutics*,
        Chicago: University of Chicago Press.
A short account of *Madness and Civilization* is given, although the book is not given any sustained analysis. Dreyfus and Rabinow point to the differences between this phase of Foucault's thought, based on a hermeneutical approach, and his later work, where the search for depth is abandoned.

36 Major-Poetzl, P.
1983   *Michel Foucault's Archaeology of Western Culture*, Brighton:
        Harvester.
Major-Poetzl and Gutting (see item 45) are the only two English-language commentaries to include a detailed comparison of the ideas presented in *Mental Illness and Psychology*, and those in *Madness and Civilization*. These two books display similar perspectives on madness, although Major-Poetzl points out the important distinction that must be made: madness is no longer seen as an object in *Madness and Civilization*, whereas it is treated as a continuous, if changing phenomenon in *Mental Illness and Psychology*. Both *Madness and Civilization* and *Mental Illness and Psychology* are looked at in depth here, and Major-Poetzl concentrates on the metaphysical aspects of *Madness and Civilization*, particularly the relation between reason and unreason, which she describes as having been largely ignored or

satirized by Anglo-American reviewers, who frequently attempt to look at Foucault's analysis of either reason or unreason, failing to notice that the two concepts define each other, and are thus inseparable.

Major-Poetzl's account of *Madness and Civilization* is a broad but essentially uncritical one. No reference is made to the veracity of the historical material presented in the book, although the lack of any reference to modern medical theories in *Madness and Civilization* is criticized.

37   Racevskis, K.
1983   *Michel Foucault and the Subversion of Intellect*, Ithaca: Cornell University Press.
In the chapter dealing with *Madness and Civilization* and *The Birth of the Clinic*, Racevskis is concerned with the consequences of Foucault's archaeological approach than with the details of plot in either text. A short outline of *Madness and Civilization* is given: Foucault is, according to Racevskis, highlighting the discursive strategies of a culture seeking to justify its procedures of banishment and social exclusion.

The archaeological method relies on Foucault's creating metonymical associations of the themes of intellectual activities. Through this device he shows how the Real, the reality of the subject, is created through the interplay of the Imaginary and the Symbolic.

38   Wuthnow, R., Hunter, J. D., Bergensen, A., Kurzweil, E.
1984   *Cultural Analysis. The works of Peter L. Berger, Mary Douglas, Michel Foucault and Jürgen Habermas*, London: Routledge & Kegan Paul.
Gives a brief mention to *Madness and Civilization*, including a short précis of the book and the comment that this was the base for all of Foucault's later historical analyses. Foucault's comment that *Madness and Civilization* is about power, although not explicitly, is also mentioned.

39   Cousins, M. and Hussain, A.
1984   *Michel Foucault*, London: Macmillan.
Part II, entitled *The Asylum, the Clinic, the Prison*, offers a very detailed account of *Madness and Civilization* but, in line with many of these books written specifically about Foucault, very little in the way of commentary is given. Cousins and Hussain see the constant theme of the book to be the creation of mental illness as a distinct entity (as opposed to physical illness) and that this was achieved through the placement of the madman in a morally ordered world. 'However, it needs to be said that the precise argument at issue in this claim is extremely difficult to unravel, not least because it is enveloped in phenomenology, which permeates the whole of *Histoire de la folie*' (138).

40   Merquior, J. G.
1985   *Foucault*, London: Fontana (Modern Masters Series).
Chapter 2 of this brief book deals with *Histoire de la folie* and *Madness and Civilization*. Merquior immediately points out the problem of the abridgement of the original French text, but bases his critique of Foucault's work on madness on the English-language version.

Merquior, after a very brief précis of the book, challenges Foucault's historiography in general, but focuses on three specific points: Foucault's stress on the medieval dialogue with madness; Foucault's treatment of the great confinement as unprecedented; Foucault's treatment of Tuke and Pinel's therapies as entirely new. Foucault is inaccurate on all three occasions, but Merquior's evidence for this comes from Sedgwick (item 79), Midelfort (item 51), Rothman (item 68), and Stone (item 32), rather than his own investigations. In the same chapter Merquior discusses *The Birth of the Clinic* which he sees as well written and free of the outbursts that characterize *Madness and Civilization*. He concludes that Dörner (item 70) is 'a natural corrective to Foucault's Manichaean picture' (30).

It is probably fair to describe this critique as unwise given the constraints of space facing Merquior. Ultimately, neither *Madness and Civilization* nor the specific criticisms of it receive the attention they both deserve.

41   Blanchot, M. and Foucault, M.
1987   *Foucault Blanchot*, New York: Zone Books.
Blanchot's section of this book is entitled 'Michel Foucault as I imagine him', and, although dealing specifically with the themes of literature and criticism, Blanchot gives a good treatment of *Histoire de la folie*, Foucault's first book '(or let us say it was his first one)' (64). Foucault is only indirectly investigating madness: 'he examined above all that power of exclusion which, one fine or awful day, was implemented in a simple administrative decree, a decision that divided society not into the good and the evil, but the reasonable and the unreasonable' (65). The investigation of this process leads to a disclosure of the impurities of reason. Blanchot sees the theoretical approach towards this subject as being particularly subtle, in that Foucault highlights a certain discontinuity (the exclusion of the mad), without making that discontinuity a break (as before the mad there were lepers).

On at least two occasions, Foucault reproached himself for having been seduced by the idea that there is a depth to madness, that it constitutes a fundamental experience situated outside history and to which poets (artists) can serve as witnesses, victims, or heroes. (67)

It was through this error that Foucault was able to realize how distasteful he found the notion of depth.

42   Logan, M.-R.
1988   'The Renaissance: Foucault's lost chance?', in *After Foucault.*
Humanistic Knowledge, Postmodern Challenges, 97–109. Arac,
J. (ed.) London: Rutgers University Press.
Foucault's concern for the Classical Age, rather than the Renaissance, was
one of the reasons for the hostility of certain American reviews of *Madness
and Civilization* and *The Order of Things*. Midelfort's criticisms of
Foucault (item 51) are a result of a misunderstanding of Foucault's methods
and perspective, resulting in a view of Foucault as a fashionable Left Bank
thinker whose criteria for research are at best questionable. Logan points
out the somewhat unfair advantage available to Midelfort, and other 1980s
commentators on *Madness and Civilization*: namely, that they have at their
disposal a wealth of cross-disciplinary information, collected in the twenty
years since the publication of *Histoire de la folie*.

43   Harootunian, H. D.
1988   'Foucault, genealogy, history. The pursuit of otherness', in
*After Foucault. Humanistic Knowledge, Postmodern Chal-
lenges*, 110–37. Arac, J. (ed.) London: Rutgers University
Press.
Foucault's pursuit of Otherness began with *Madness and Civilization*; he
found that madmen appeared once reason and history had established their
dynasty: this was the form of otherness. It is the creation of opposites, and
oppositions in his work, that characterizes Foucault's project. Harootunian
goes on to look further at these opposites in the construction of the identity
of the Other.

44   O'Farrell, C.
1989   *Foucault. Historian or Philosopher?* London: Macmillan.
O'Farrell focuses on two works, *Histoire de la folie* and *What is Enlightenment?*, from a philosophical and historical standpoint – an investigation of
the 'limits' of history, society and culture. In this very detailed analysis of
Foucault's investigation of madness, three things stand out. Foucault's
historical analyses are not constant, they employ shifting periodizations
depending on the subject of investigation. What is a historical object for
Foucault? Critics charge Foucault with failing to see madness existing
outside of discourse or world-view: it is rather that Foucault sees madness
as an object constructed in history, not as a thing at all.

The role of madness in society is to reveal the limit between the Same and
the Other, and through this to reveal the truth in both of them. Foucault, in
an earlier work (*Maladie mentale et psychologie*), argued that this was true
for all societies. In *Histoire de la folie*, Foucault is more cautious, and
excludes all mention of non-western and primitive societies.

In *Histoire de la folie*, Foucault suggests that the most extreme limit of
our culture is madness. However, this was to have a rather shortlived career.

'In an article written in 1962, Foucault had already shifted his position and appeared to have some difficulty in deciding which limit was more important: death, madness or language?' (79).

All three limits are present in *Histoire de la folie*, as indeed they are in *Raymond Roussel* and *Naissance de la clinique*, although in these two later works it is death that wins out.

This text is a very comprehensive commentary on the philosophical aspects of, and historical methodology in, Foucault's work.

45   Gutting, G.
1989   *Michel Foucault's Archaeology of Scientific Reason*, Cambridge: Cambridge University Press.

Gutting covers all the main works of Foucault to place them in the context of recent French history and philosophy of science, particularly with reference to George Canguilhem and Gustave Bachelard.

A full chapter is devoted to Foucault's work on madness and mental illness. Unlike most other commentators, Gutting places *Histoire de la folie* in the context of Foucault's two previous works on mental illness: *Maladie mentale et personnalité* (1954) and *Maladie mentale et psychologie* (1962), a significantly revised edition of the 1954 work, that shows Foucault's move away from Marxist principles and categories, and towards a historical analysis of the disciplines of psychology and psychiatry. Gutting notes that the existential anthropology of this second edition is the precursor of *Histoire de la folie* in that the aim of the project is to 'explain the contingent historical origin of modern psychology and psychiatry (along with their concept of mental illness) through a historical understanding of past ages' experiences of madness' (69). It is, however, only in *Histoire de la folie* that Foucault carries out this project.

Gutting provides a very detailed outline of the main points of the book, splitting the subject into the three areas of (a) the classical age, (b) the age of confinement and (c) the modern approach to mental illness. Gutting stresses that it is only through Foucault's use of an archaeological approach that our current conception of madness can be examined and questioned.

Gutting offers a 'value-free' account of *Histoire de la folie*, but subsequently looks at some of the shortcomings of the work. The archaeological method used by Foucault is never properly elucidated and the references made to 'experience', as in 'experience of madness', become confused – it is left unclear who, or what, is the experiencing consciousness in question. 'Consequently, the archaeology of *Folie et déraison* remains a technique of reading historical texts and practices for which Foucault is able to offer no satisfactory reflective account' (103). Foucault himself tacitly acknowledges this in later work by moving away from any form of analysis based upon 'experience'. There are also historical inaccuracies in the text: Gutting highlights the criticisms made by Klaus Dörner (item 70) and Roy Porter (item 73), who both point out that the Great Confinement was not, as claimed by

Foucault, Europe-wide, but was probably confined to France. David Rothman's analysis of early nineteenth-century American mental treatment (item 68) is cited by Gutting as a refutation for Foucault's claim for the hegemony of Tuke and Pinel's medical model of mental illness, and H. C. Erik Midelfort's criticism of Foucault's use of medieval material (item 51) is also cited. However, Gutting, although no apologist for Foucault's historical methodology, does offer a defence to these critics:

> Foucault is not concerned with formulating exceptionless empirical generalisations from the historical data but with giving an overall characterisation of a society's fundamental attitudes towards madness. Such attitudes may well not be manifest in all texts and practices, and their existence can even be compatible with a variety of contrary tendencies. Thus, when Foucault presents the seventeenth and eighteenth centuries as 'the age of confinement', he should not be taken as maintaining that there were no instances of confinement prior to that period. His point is rather that in the Classical Age confinement takes on a new and particularly central role in the treatment of the mad. Such a thesis is not an empirical generalisation that can be refuted by a few contrary instances. . . . This is an important – and I think decisive – response to the claim of some critics that Foucault's account is a blatant misrepresentation, easily dismissed by a few quick factual references. (105)

Gutting does go on to point out that Foucault's account is seriously defective in other ways. The fundamental failure is Foucault's assumption that there is some simple unifying conception of madness in each major historical period. There are, indeed, trends, but these do not amount to the unified experiences that Foucault identifies. A further failing of *Histoire de la folie* is its assault on the contemporary institutions of psychiatry and psychology. No detailed analysis of modern psychiatric methods is offered, and the extrapolation to the present day from the work of Tuke and Pinel is inappropriate. Foucault's historical accounts, even if wholly accurate, are not sufficient to undermine contemporary psychiatry and psychology, as many of Foucault's followers claim.

Gutting's criticisms point to a positive role for *Histoire de la folie*. Gutting sees the book as an important heuristic preliminary to a critique of contemporary psychology and psychiatry, and this role reduces both the burden of historical accuracy and the intention of offering a critique of the mental sciences.

Gutting offers this conclusion to his analysis of *Histoire de la folie*:

> Overall, then, *Histoire de la folie* must be recognized as the foundation of the entire body of Foucault's work. Although there are many significant revisions and innovations, it lays down the basic methods, problems, and values that inform everything else he wrote. (110)

46 Boyne, R.

1990 *Foucault and Derrida. The other side of reason*, London: Unwin Hyman.

Boyne's detailed book looks at the debate between Foucault and Derrida concerning the nature of 'otherness'. He shows, through an analysis of Foucault's work that Foucault did in fact take up Derrida's critique, and displays how Foucault's conception of otherness changes significantly through the course of his work.

Histoire de la folie is discussed in some detail, both as a major part of Foucault's *oeuvre*, and as a significant contribution to the conceptualization of 'otherness'. It is, in particular, Foucault's positing of pre-Enlightenment madness as the example of difference which can be regarded as 'pure' that receives the heaviest attack from Derrida, who suggests that knowledge of such otherness is not possible. Boyne sees *Histoire de la folie* as being composed of three major narratives: the political economy of madness, the representation of madness in art and literature, and the relation between madness and science. All three are examined in some detail.

Boyne addresses the question of Foucault's historiography. He notes that *Madness and Civilization* is, as Cousins and Hussain described it (item 39), 'a pale version of the original' (34), although, in the chapter of his book specifically relating to Foucault's work on madness, citations from *Madness and Civilization* outnumber citations from *Histoire de la folie* roughly two to one. As for specific attacks made against Foucault's historical research (particularly by Midelfort (item 51) and Merquior (item 40)), Boyne is unequivocal in stressing that the value of Foucault's work is to be found not in its historical facts, which are actually well grounded, but in its cultural and philosophical material.

ARTICLES ON FOUCAULT

47 Cranston, M.

1968 'Michel Foucault', *Encounter* 30 (6): 34–42.

A general discussion of Foucault's work to date, with some specific discussion of *Madness and Civilization*. Foucault is described as a brilliant writer who has managed to be a hit despite his high seriousness and melancholy themes.

On *Madness and Civilization*: 'Foucault holds that madness is not a disease at all. . . . Madness, he says, is a fusion of reason and unreason; and he denies that reason has any objective privilege over unreason' (37). Of the method behind Foucault's investigation, Cranston suggests that 'it is arguable that the Marxist notion of "infra-structure" plays a crucial role in his theory' (38).

Cranston is strongly opposed to Foucault's use of the word 'archaeology': it has a perfectly good meaning so why give it another one? It is also unfair to treat Foucault as a historian as none of his boldest statements about the past are backed up with any evidence. 'Foucault can, I think, be best understood as attempting to explain the cultural history of Europe in the light of this theory which he has derived from Lévi-Strauss' (41).

Foucault, like Lévi-Strauss, is tied to a binary principle that life is composed of opposites in tension that can be resolved symbolically. This principle does not lend itself to the service to which Foucault puts it. 'Something employed to explain everything, ends up explaining nothing; and what happened to the dialectic in the heavy hands of Karl Marx happens to it again in the delicate fingers of Michel Foucault' (42).

48   White, H.
1973   'Foucault decoded: notes from underground', *History and Theory* 12 (1). Reprinted in *Tropics of Discourse. Essays in Cultural Criticism*, 1978. Baltimore: Johns Hopkins University Press.

This is mainly a consideration of *Les Mots et les choses* and *L'Archéologie du savoir*, but reference is made to *Folie et déraison*, which White sees as 'a rambling discourse on the madness lying at the very heart of reason itself' (245). White is critical of Foucault's use of a very limited body of data, but does credit Foucault with providing an original contribution to the history of ideas in showing that the true content of the concept of rationality could only be discovered by looking at the ways in which the insane were regarded. In addition, Foucault's analysis of the history of medicine shows that medicine is not a science at all, and that its development is tied to 'the ongoing praxis of society rather than to a deepening understanding of the human animal' (248). Predictably, historians of medicine were critical in their responses to *Histoire de la folie*, missing the point that Foucault had intended to highlight the contradictory nature of theories of madness and the irrational nature of treatment of the insane.

White's detailed analysis of Foucault's main texts is illuminating and the précis he offers of *Histoire de la folie*, although concise, is broad.

49   Hayman, R.
1976   'Cartography of discourse? On Foucault', *Encounter* 47 (6): 72–5.

A general and shallow discussion of Foucault's work, which does include reference to *Madness and Civilization*, apparently Foucault's first book. '*Madness and Civilization* already showed him to be an ingenious cartographer of discourse: his spiral progress has made him into a better teacher of cartography' (74).

50   Gordon, C.
1977   'Birth of the subject', *Radical Philosophy* 17: 15–25.

A survey of Foucault's post-1970 writings (at this point untranslated): *L'Ordre du discours; Surveiller et punir; La Volonté du savoir*.

Later developments in Foucault's theories did not amount to an overall rejection of his earlier work, but were rather an explication of its implicit orientations – no doubt with a little help from the May events.

> When I think back now, I say to myself, what could I have been speaking about in *Madness and Civilization* and *Birth of the Clinic*, if not power? Now, I'm perfectly conscious of not having used the word then and of not having had this field of analysis at my disposal.
>
> (Foucault quoted from *Politique Hebdo* 247: 30–1)

51   Midelfort, H. C. E.
1980   'Madness and civilization in early modern Europe: a reappraisal of Michel Foucault'. In *After the Reformation. Essays in honour of J. H. Hexter*. Malament, B. C. (ed.) Manchester: Manchester University Press, pp. 247–65.

Midelfort's analysis of *Histoire de la folie* concentrates on the impact that the book has made since its publication, and on the radical change in style of historiography that it represents. The initial success of Foucault's book was due in part to its strong opposition to the Whig history of psychiatry: Foucault wrote an antiheroic and antiprogressive history that stood the medical tradition on its head. It was Foucault's work on madness that provided the historical justification for the work of the British anti-psychiatrists and for Goffman and Szasz, as well as significantly influencing philosophy.

Midelfort identifies four key arguments in *Histoire de la folie*: the parallel between the medieval isolation of leprosy and the modern isolation of madness; the view of the mad in medieval times leading an 'easy wandering life'; the destruction of this way of life in the 'Age of the Great Confinement'; and the 'invention' of 'mental illness' by Tuke and Pinel. These four arguments have been undeniably influential: 'Authors who would not dream of accepting Foucault's philosophy or all four of the arguments here described have not hesitated to call his book "brilliant" ' (251). However, Midelfort goes on to look in some detail at these four key points. Foucault is criticized for his overly romantic conception of madness in medieval Europe, exaggerating the Renaissance dialogue with madness; specifically, Midelfort refutes Foucault's notion of the 'Ship of Fools', suggesting that there is no historical evidence for this whatsoever. Midelfort agrees with Foucault that the concept of mental illness was invented by the reforms of the late eighteenth and early nineteenth centuries, and overall his criticisms of *Histoire de la folie* seem to be an attempt to dilute the force of argument in Foucault's work rather than to refute it completely:

> What we have discovered in looking at *Madness and Civilization* is that many of its arguments fly in the face of empirical evidence, and that many of its broadest generalisations are oversimplifications. Indeed, in

his quest for the essence of an age, its *episteme*, Foucault seems simply to indulge a whim for arbitrary and witty assertion so often that one wonders why so much attention and praise continue to fall his way (259).

52   White, H.
1987   'Foucault's discourse: the historiography of anti-humanism', in
            *The Content of Form. Narrative Discourse and Historical
            Representation*, Baltimore: Johns Hopkins University Press.
White uses the theory of rhetorical tropes to categorize Foucault's style of discourse. Foucault's account of the history of madness is in four stages, corresponding to four tropes: resemblance (metaphor), adjacency (metonymy), essentiality (synecdoche), and doubling (irony). Foucault's style of writing is catachresis, in that 'no two things are similar to one another in their particularity. All language therefore constitutes an abuse insofar as it gives a single name to things different in their "internal natures", their locations in space, or their external attributes' (116). The discourse on madness that Foucault identifies is a form of doubling or duplicity, in that madness is identified with normality and genius at the same time as it is identified with the alienated individual and patient. Madness is measured as sickness and deviation from the norm at the same time as being the standard against which normality will be measured.

53   Gordon, C.
1990   '*Histoire de la folie*: an unknown book by Michel Foucault',
            History of the Human Sciences 3 (1): 3–26.
Madness and Civilization omits well over half the original French edition (*Histoire de la folie*), and this has led to a disparity in responses to the text between French-speaking and English-speaking historians. Gordon asserts that this disparity has been little noted. Critics aiming to measure Foucault's achievement as a historian have 'dispensed with the preliminary task of reading the unabridged text of his book' (5). *Histoire de la folie* was well received by French academic historians, but not by English-speaking ones, a result of the English translation being linked to the antipsychiatry movement and due to it predating many of Foucault's theoretical advances. This treatment by English speakers has coloured the way in which much of Foucault's later work has been appraised: Foucault's work on madness 'has been often praised but seldom grasped' (6).

Gordon moves from a discussion of the general uptake of *Madness and Civilization* to a defence of specific criticisms made against it. He first looks at Midelfort's critique of *Madness and Civilization* (item 51). Midelfort's four main critical points are each in turn refuted. The final issue, of whether or not the mad led 'an easy wandering life' in medieval Europe, and whether or not the ship of fools actually existed, is put down to being 'the product of a rare lapse by [Foucault's] translator' (17). Gordon stresses Midelfort's inaccurate attacks on Foucault, and goes on to show the reliance placed on Midelfort's remarks by other authors, notably Sedgwick (item 79), Merquior (item 40), and Stone (item 32).

Gordon moves on to the critique of *Histoire de la folie* by Derrida (1967 *L'écriture et la différence*, Paris: Seuil). In this, Derrida latches on to the phrase in the original introduction to *Histoire de la folie* in which Foucault appears to claim that he is attempting a 'history of madness itself', and shows that Foucault has not achieved this. Gordon points out that Foucault in fact went on to doubt the possibility of such a project, and that the subsequent uptake of this line of critique shows a failure of basic critical understanding.

Gordon's final main point of defence rests on Foucault's use of the notion of 'experience' (see Gutting, item 45). The omission of certain key sections of *Histoire de la folie* concerning experiences of madness has led to a general misunderstanding of the concept, as effectively only half the story is told.

Gordon offers a plea for the full translation of *Histoire de la folie* to be made available, and suggests that subsequent re-readings of the text will afford Foucault the rightful place of both historian and philosopher with respect to *Madness and Civilization*.

This article is the basis for a wide-ranging discussion of *Histoire de la folie/Madness and Civilization* in *History of the Human Sciences*, items 54 to 66 below.

54   Castel, R.
1990   'The two readings of *Histoire de la folie* in France', *History of the Human Sciences* 3 (1): 27–30.
Although in total agreement with Gordon concerning the truncated version of *Histoire de la folie* published in English, Castel suggests that the intellectual gap between the early 1960s, when Foucault's book was treated as a purely academic text, and the early 1970s, when *Histoire de la folie* was used as a cover for institutional struggles, is an equally compelling reason for its misinterpretation.

55   LaCapra, D.
1990   'Foucault, history, and madness', *History of the Human Sciences* 3 (1): 31–8.
As it is Foucault's most impressive book, *Histoire de la folie* deserves to be more widely read, and to be translated in full. LaCapra agrees with Gordon that the key to appreciating *Histoire de la folie* is to see it as an attempt to find a common audience for the philosopher and the historian, but disagrees with Gordon on a number of points. LaCapra suggests that Midelfort's and Derrida's critiques of Foucault cannot be lightly dismissed, nor entirely refuted. LaCapra further suggests that the abridgement of *Histoire de la folie* into *Madness and Civilization* may have been a deliberate ploy by Foucault to make his later work appear more original.

56   Merquior, J. G.
1990   'Back to the *Histoire de la folie*', *History of the Human Sciences* 3 (1): 39–40.

A reassessment of Foucault's work on madness based on the full text of *Histoire de la folie* is welcomed by Merquior. However, the misinterpretations of Foucault that Gordon describes are chiefly Foucault's own fault. Merquior suggests that it was Foucault himself who approved the abridgement of *Histoire de la folie*, and this, coupled to Foucault's style, supports the resulting sweeping generalizations. Above all, there are plenty of criticisms of Foucault's historiography that cannot be refuted by a return to the original text: Merquior cites Rothman (item 68) and Dörner (item 70) as examples.

At a more personal level, Merquior rejects Gordon's allegation that he is 'broadly hostile' to Foucault, and claims that Gordon has misrepresented his summary of *Madness and Civilization* (item 40). Finally, Merquior points out that Gordon's call for a return to the original edition of *Histoire de la folie* would be stronger 'if he were able to quote its title correctly. His paper says *Déraison et folie*. It should be *Folie et déraison*' (40).

The personal bitterness that seems to be present in this brief article may stem from an earlier altercation between Gordon and Merquior. Gordon's scathing review of *Foucault* by Merquior (item 40) led to an exchange of letters in the *Times Literary Supplement*.[5]

57   Midelfort, H. C. E.
1990   'Comment on Colin Gordon', *History of the Human Sciences* 3 (1): 41–6.

Replying to the specific points made about his critique of Foucault, Midelfort concedes the point about the mistranslation of Foucault's remark concerning the wandering life of the mad. However, he insists that Foucault 'grossly exaggerates the numbers of mad on the roads or in the ships of fools, ships fabricated by Foucault's symbol-seeking imagination' (41). Further, Foucault's footnotes do not substantiate the existence of a ship of fools. As to the possibility of Foucault being accepted as a historian, given an unabridged translation of *Histoire de la folie*, Midelfort remains sceptical, but sees the possibility of understanding Foucault better if such a text was available in English.

58   Porter, R.
1990   'Foucault's great confinement', *History of the Human Sciences* 3 (1): 47–54.

Porter replies to Gordon with a mass of reference sources concerning the treatment of the insane in Britain. Foucault's great confinement thesis does not apply to England, much less to Scotland or Ireland. Foucault is mistaken in seeing confinement as a Europe-wide attempt to lump together all antisocial elements, and to see Tuke as a major discontinuity in the treatment of madness is to accept uncritically Tuke's own propaganda, based on his blackening the reputations of his predecessors.

This is a fairly brief résumé of Porter's extensive discussion of *Madness and Civilization* given in items 71, 72 and 73.

59   Rabinow, P.
1990   'Truth and society', *History of the Human Sciences* 3 (1): 55–6.
Commending Gordon for furthering the public availability of Foucault's material, Rabinow reminds the reader that 'Foucault gave us tools to use not an agenda to follow' (55).

Rabinow sees Gordon's stance in his article as being similar to that taken by Foucault in his writing, i.e. both an ethic and a strategy. Both Gordon and Foucault avoid the use of polemic and Gordon is able to describe the polemics of others without resorting to it himself.[6]

60   Scull, A.
1990   'Michel Foucault's history of madness', *History of the Human Sciences* 3 (1): 57–67.
Scull acknowledges the debt owed to Foucault by all those who have worked on the history of psychiatry over the past two decades, but suggests that the complaints concerning Foucault's work on madness made by English-speaking scholars are not solely due to having to use an abridged edition of *Histoire de la folie*. Access to the complete text would 'strengthen conventional historians' doubts, and . . . remove the most effective defence mounted by members of the Foucauldian cult. . . . The problem is the very genuine deficiencies and vulnerabilities of Foucault's historical scholarship' (58).

61   Barham, P.
1990   'Foucault and the psychiatric practitioner', *History of the Human Sciences* 3 (3): 327–31.
Putting forward the opinion of a practitioner in the field of mental illness, Barham suggests that Foucault's exclusion of the mad individual from the pages of *Histoire de la folie* is not a result of his concern to retain the purity and integrity of madness, but is more a product of Foucault's preoccupation with the institutional system: 'it is less apparent that there was for Foucault behind the authoritative pronouncements of the asylum regime an agent to be recovered or an individual to be understood' (330).

Although disapproving of Stone's intemperate remarks concerning the release from state institutions of mental patients (see item 32), Barham does comment that 'Foucault has not been much help to us in the task of thinking through the contemporary project of closing the asylum' (330).

62   Goldstein, J.
1990   ' "The lively sensibility of the Frenchman": some reflections on
            the place of France in Foucault's *Histoire de la folie*', *History
            of the Human Sciences* 3 (3): 333–41.

In the same way that Pinel uses France in his writings to signify civilized and
enlightened culture, Foucault leaves the reader of *Histoire de la folie*
confused as to whether he is referring to the place or to western civilization
when he uses the word 'France'. Goldstein argues that this is a deliberate
rhetorical strategy on Foucault's part, to allow 'France' to occupy both
literal and synecdochic positions in the text. The result of this is to allow
Histoire de la folie to offer a global reinterpretation – and defamiliarization
of – the Enlightenment.

A full understanding of the full text of *Histoire de la folie* would allow
us to comprehend Foucault's project more deeply and 'to construe its
"errors" as strategies' (340).

63   Megill, A.
1990   'Foucault, ambiguity, and the rhetoric of historiography',
            History of the Human Sciences 3 (3): 343–61.

Megill claims that *Histoire de la folie* has been misread by English speakers,
but points out that the book cannot be read in the same way as a history
book. As a study in the rhetoric of historiography, the controversy
generated by *Histoire de la folie* is illuminating, as it brings to light the
different rhetorical conventions held by particular groups of academics.

Megill concludes by repeating that Foucault's work is not acceptable
from the point of view of 'normal' scholarly standards, and yet this is the
whole point of its impact on audiences.

64   Pearson, G.
1990   'Misunderstanding Foucault', *History of the Human Sciences* 3
            (3): 363–71.

Regardless of problems of abridgement and translation, Foucault's work
has remained elusive and controversial in a general sense. Pearson welcomes
the prospect of a full text of *Histoire de la folie*, but 'it does not follow that
the most useful response is (as Gordon does) to set about rescuing Foucault
from his critics' (363). For Gordon to suggest that the whole controversy
surrounding Foucault's work on madness is one based upon misunderstanding implies an extraordinary passivity on the part of both text and reader.

It is, moreover, perfectly appropriate that work of the stature of
Foucault's should generate such a ferment of controversy and provocation. The attempt to squeeze this ferment back into its original textual
confines, to put the lid back on as it were, is a doomed pursuit. (370)

65   Rose, N.
1990   'Of madness itself: *Histoire de la folie* and the object of psychiatric history', *History of the Human Sciences* 3 (3): 373–80.
Rose suggests that the power of *Histoire de la folie* arises from its concern
with what is specific to madness itself. Looking at *Histoire de la folie* from
this perspective will distinguish it from those two bodies it has frequently
been subsumed by: the social history of psychiatry, and the sociology of
deviance.

Histoire de la folie charts the history of madness as a network of relays, a
history that disturbs and fragments the territory from which control of the
mad has arisen. It is this philosophical and ethical aspect that distinguishes
Histoire de la folie from standard historiography.

66   Gordon, C.
1990   'History, madness and other errors: a response', *History of the
Human Sciences* 3 (3): 381–96.
Gordon replies to his critics, usually quite scathingly. This piece covers
much the same ground as item 53.

BOOKS AND ARTICLES ON THE HISTORY OF INSANITY

67   Szasz, T.
1971   *The Manufacture of Madness. A comparative study of the
Inquisition and the mental health movement.* London: Routledge & Kegan Paul.
Szasz is a principal voice in the antipsychiatric movement, and this book is a
strong attack on the aims, methods and history of modern psychiatry.
Despite taking a historical perspective in discussing certain issues, Szasz
makes scant reference to the work of Michel Foucault (there are two quotes
in the entire text), and offers no commentary on Foucault's work.

68   Rothman, J.
1971   *The Discovery of the Asylum. Social Order and Disorder in the
New Republic.* Boston: Little, Brown and Company.
An investigation of the methods and motivations behind American construction of institutions for mad and deviant members of society in the
Jacksonian era. There is an obvious crossover of interests between Foucault
and Rothman, although Rothman does not find *Madness and Civilization* a
particularly useful source for historical examples. In the introduction to
The Discovery of the Asylum, he agrees with Foucault's thesis, that the
insane asylum was created to master unreason rather than to liberate it, and
that this institution can be seen as the 'monument to a new ethic' (xvii).
However, Rothman sees the categories used in *Madness and Civilization* as
too rigid, and few other considerations are given to explaining the rise of the
asylum apart from declaring the rise of the asylum to be a triumph of a

bourgeois ethic. 'Ultimately in *Madness and Civilization* the goals of the asylum are purely intellectual; the combat is between perceptions and visions, not classes. Foucault's institutions bear only a slight relation to the society that built and supported them' (xviii).

The main aim of Rothman's book is to study the communities that created asylums, and the inmate world that resulted from this. Apart from the brief discussion in the introduction, no further reference is made to *Madness and Civilization*.

69   Doob, P. B. R.
1974   *Nebuchadnezaar's Children. Conventions of madness in Middle English literature*. New Haven: Yale University Press.
Makes two very brief references to *Madness and Civilization* in footnotes and in one (note 57, p. 37) expresses slight scepticism about the actual existence of the 'Ship of Fools'.

70   Dörner, K.
1981   *Madmen and the Bourgeoisie. A Social History of Insanity and Psychiatry*. London: Basil Blackwell.
This translation of *Bürger und Irre* follows T. S. Kuhn's thesis of scientific revolutions to look at the genesis of a new science of psychiatry and its changes through recent history. Dörner addresses the questions of why psychiatry grew so prominent in Europe from the mid-seventeenth century, and why there are such larger regional differences in types of psychiatry and mental disorder. Dörner proposes that this was due first to the pressure that a bourgeois work ethic put upon people, and that such regional differences that are visible are due to the unequal growth of the bourgeoisie in Europe.

Despite Dörner's work being obviously predated by *Madness and Civilization*, Foucault receives only eight brief mentions in the text. Dörner is respectful, but critical of Foucault's work:

> Foucault was the first to point out the significance of the movement towards the sequestration of irrationality. It figures in his book under the title of 'The Great Confinement'. However, his structuralist approach makes him lose sight of the historical differences between the various European countries, which results in frequent distortions and false generalisations. . . . Like its predecessors, it proves that only a few efforts in psychiatric historiography have gone beyond recording the 'national standpoint', and are able to see the development of psychiatry within the framework of bourgeois society and thus perceive the historical differences between the developmental stages of individual countries.
>
> (note 39, p. 303)

Roy Porter's review of Dörner's book (*Social Studies of Science* 12, 1982 (item 71 below)) is a useful introduction to this wide-ranging work.

71 Porter, R.
1982 'Shutting people up' (essay review), *Social Studies of Science* 12: 467–76.

A review of Dörner's *Madness and the Bourgeoisie*, and other books on the history of psychiatry. Porter introduces the topics under consideration by reference to Foucault:

> There is nothing new in translating the epistemological couplet, lunacy/ mental science, into the social couplet, madman/psychiatrist. Michel Foucault, George Rosen and Thomas Szasz are just three of the scholars who, from back in the 1960s, were arguing that both insanity and psychiatry are cultural artefacts. Showing just *how* that process of the social construction of the science its object operated, however, is a more daunting task – one which, arguably, Foucault at least shirked. (468)

72 Bynum, W. F., Porter, R., Shepherd, M. (eds)
1985 *The Anatomy of Madness. Essays in the history of psychiatry*. London: Tavistock (3 volumes).

The editors' introduction to Volume I of this work contains the only main reference to Foucault's work on madness. They point out that, although *Madness and Civilization* is a 'truly magisterial work' (4), it would be a mistake to assume that its historical evidence can be considered sound. 'Hence, for our generation to bandy around slogans like "the ship of fools", "the great confinement", "the medicalisation of madness", or "the discovery of the asylum" would be no advance on chanting the ancient war-cries of the march of scientific psychiatry' (4).

Many of the articles in these three volumes mention *Madness and Civilization* in footnotes, or bibliographies, but no further discussion of Foucault's work is given.

73 Porter, R.
1987 *Mind-Forg'd Manacles. A history of madness in England from the Restoration to the Regency*. London: The Athlone Press.

In his introduction to this book, Porter offers a strong refutation of Foucault's concept of 'the great confinement', and also Dörner's thesis of psychiatry being a creation to police the poor. Although Foucault may be correct in suggesting a framework of sequestration of the mad in France, the actual number of lunatics locked up remained small, and tiny in England, where public asylums did not become statutory until 1845. Both Foucault and Dörner suggest that the bourgeoisie were affronted by the idleness of the mad, and the lunatics of western Europe were set to work to remedy this, as a moral duty. On the contrary, Porter notes that eye-witness accounts of lunatic asylums at this time state that life in the madhouse was characterized not by work, but by idleness. The brutality meted out to inmates of asylums, cited by Foucault, is a contradiction of the Enlightenment writers on insanity, whom Foucault is trying to explain.

Overall, Foucault's characterization of a 'great confinement' proves dubious for interpreting English developments during the 'long eighteenth century'. Indeed, his notion of reason chaining 'unreason' in new custodial institutions hardly applies anywhere (it seems to project French ideology onto the rest of the Continent). Throughout peasant Europe . . . little confinement of lunatics occurred. (8)

Foucault's thesis, echoed and expanded on by Dörner, that the 'great confinement' was started by the bourgeoisie to police the poor, at first appears to be tenable because of the numerical imbalance of confined lunatics when analysed by social class. However, Porter sees it as a mistake to 'underestimate the numbers of the bourgeoisie, gentry, and nobility who were also being confined. Without their well-heeled clientele, the "trade in lunacy" would have floundered. Psychiatry was not just – probably not even primarily – a discipline for controlling the rabble' (9).

Porter's reassessment of Foucault's historiography of madness here is the most coherent refutation of the historical data included in *Madness and Civilization*. Foucault is seen as misinterpreting social discipline, as making wild generalizations that are untenable for most, if not all, of Europe, and misconstruing the motives of the Enlightenment 'psychiatrists' and their immediate followers. However, Porter does agree with Foucault on a number of points: a history of rationality is a necessary condition for a history of irrationality. And despite their disagreements over the historical facts, Porter and Foucault agree that the mad were silenced during the eighteenth century.

74   Porter, R.
1987   *A Social History of Madness. Stories of the Insane.* London: Weidenfeld & Nicolson.
This book reconstructs a history of madness through accounts of madness recorded by the mentally ill, with commentaries on these texts by Porter. Foucault is mentioned briefly, and Porter restates his ideas on *Madness and Civilization* first proposed in *Mind Forg'd Manacles* (item 73).

75   Scull, A.
1988   'Keepers', *London Review of Books* 29/9/88: 21–3.
In this review of six recent books on the history of madness and medicine, Foucault's *Madness and Civilization* is used as the reference point by which to judge the debates and the form of historical analysis.

MISCELLANEOUS ARTICLES AND BOOKS

76   White, H.
1969   'The tasks of intellectual history', *The Monist* 53: 606–30.
In a wide-ranging survey of recent trends in Continental thought, White briefly considers the way in which Foucault, through his utilization of a

variety of theoretical perspectives, unearths the structures that make specific styles of thought possible.

> In his *Histoire de la folie*, Foucault examines attitudes towards sanity and the insane as a way of determining what the 'age of reason' *really meant* when it characterized itself as such. . . . But Foucault is not writing institutional history either; he contributes nothing new to our knowledge of how the insane, the indigent, and the criminally deviant were incarcerated. His interest is in the 'structure' of 'confinement' in all its manifestations; and he finds a common structure perduring in the history of Western man from the late seventeenth through early twentieth century. This structure was marked by a kind of 'communication' between the confined and the confiners throughout all the changes that took place in the definitions of what or who was insane during that time, and which has disappeared, in his view, in the totalitarian atmosphere of the twentieth century. (622)

Although White gives no further consideration to Foucault's work in this article, it should be noted that this is the first English-language article (as opposed to a review) to include a sustained analysis of *Histoire de la folie* or *Madness and Civilization*.

77   Hillier, S.
1975   'Review article: Anyman goes mad', *Sociology* 9 (2): 323–8.
            Review of *Approaches to Insanity* by Jeff Coulter.
A long review of Coulter's work and ethnomethodology in general. Hillier points out that Coulter makes no mention of Foucault's *Madness and Civilization*, although it represents a similar approach to the subject, even though Foucault 'is not concerned to destroy the concepts used in psychiatry to evidence psychopathology' (327).

78   Lasch, C.
1980   'Life in the therapeutic state', *The New York Review of Books*
            12/6/80: 24–32. Review of *At Odds* by C. N. Degler, *The History of Sexuality, Volume 1* by M. Foucualt, *The Policing of Families* by J. Donzelot.
Foucault's earlier works (*Madness and Civilization, The Birth of the Clinic,* and *Discipline and Punish*) display the growth of disciplinary apparatus, and this theme is extended in the study of medical jurisdiction over sex in *The History of Sexuality*. 'Nineteenth-century philanthropists, whatever their intentions, created a more effective and pervasive system of social control based on systematic observation and surveillance. Similarly the exposure of sexual life to scientific scrutiny contributed to the rationalisation, not the liberation, of emotional life' (27).

79   Sedgwick, P.
1982   *Psycho Politics*, London: Pluto Press.
A survey of the antipsychiatry movement, focusing on the work of Goffman, Laing, Foucault and Szasz.

In the section on Foucault, Sedgwick begins by criticizing the historical method that Foucault uses: 'As a researcher on historical themes, Foucault can be quite careless and even licentious in the handling of evidence' (9). Foucault's denouncement of Reason in *Madness and Civilization* is seen by Sedgwick as being paradoxical; Foucault's account becomes contained in the very rationalism that he is denouncing due to his neglect of the current social pressures that produced medical and scientific ideas.

A further criticism of Foucault's historical method comes from Sedgwick's view that the overwhelming display of concern in *Madness and Civilization* for the logic of 'classical' diagnosis, 'overlooks some of the older, subterranean traditions of psychiatry, which always functioned as a minority option for some of the mentally ill during the darkest days of exclusion for the great bulk of the insane. . . . We must try to remember that the evolution of the medical model of intervention against insanity and the development of the total psychiatric institution have somewhat separate histories' (140).

Finally, Sedgwick takes issue with Foucault over the latter's call for a dialogue to be established between Reason and Unreason. 'Unlike Foucault, however, we propose that it actually be implemented' (145).

Sedgwick suggests that *Madness and Civilization* will be measured 'to the extent to which it can aid in the formation of an informed political practice, the key which can both open and destroy the locks, bars and fetters of psychiatric and social confinement' (148).

These strong criticisms of Foucault's work are countered, to a certain extent, by Colin Gordon in his review of *Psycho Politics* (item 80).

80   Gordon, C.
1982   'The deviancy of disease', *The Times Literary Supplement*
            16/7/82: 773. Review of *Psycho Politics* by P. Sedgwick.
Over half of this short review is devoted to pointing out errors in Sedgwick's criticism of Foucault and defending the charges made. Sedgwick notes that he was working from the shortened English translation of *Histoire de la folie*, and that the full text has many important passages omitted from the translation, although these are not crucial to Foucault's argument. Gordon's reply to this is: 'Coming from a commentator avowedly preoccupied with scholarly exactitude, this is perhaps not an entirely candid way of conveying the fact that *Madness and Civilization* omits more than half the main text of *Histoire de la folie à l'âge classique*, as well as the bibliography and over 900 of its notes. One must indeed suppose that Sedgwick has not read the full text of the book he is writing about, since the untranslated parts of the *Histoire*, whether or not "crucial to Foucault's

argument'', are highly germane to much of Sedgwick's' (773). Gordon points specifically to Sedgwick's charge that Foucault neglects the late medieval institutions for the care of the mentally ill. '*Histoire de la folie* in fact contains quite detailed discussions of all these matters, in passages not included in the English abridgement. Sedgwick compensates elsewhere for this subtractive brand of interpretation by mounting a spirited attack on the nineteenth century evolution of the asylum. I can find nothing on this topic in either edition of Foucault's book' (773).

Gordon is continuing a theme familiar in most of his writing on *Histoire de la folie* and *Madness and Civilization* (see item 53, for example), namely that the abridgement of the former has caused the latter to be widely misinterpreted.

NOTES

1 I am grateful to my comrades at Durham Community Co-operative fruit and vegetable shop for providing me with the time and support necessary to complete this project. Also to John Erickson who provided me with useful suggestions and comments on earlier drafts of this chapter. The staff of both the National Library of Scotland and the British Library were extremely helpful in finding obscure journals and books. All or any errors contained in this paper are mine alone.

2 *The Social Sciences Citation Index. An International Multidisciplinary Index to the Literature of the Social, Behavioural and Related Sciences.* Philadelphia: Institute for Scientific Information. Annual publication.

3 Clarke, M. (1983) *Michel Foucault. An Annotated Bibliography. Tool Kit for a New Age.* New York: Garland. This is an exhaustive survey of all the material relating to Foucault's work.

4 Foucault did respond to some of his reviewers in a quite savage way. For example, George Steiner's review of *The Order of Things* is treated as ignorant nonsense written by a second-rate journalist by Foucault in 'Monstrosities in Criticism', *Diacritics* 1 (1): 57−60. Steiner's quite reasonable reply to Foucault's diatribe (*Diacritics* 1 (2): 59) receives the rudest reply possible from Foucault (*Diacritics* 1 (2): 60), where Steiner is again vilified. An interesting footnote to this exchange between the two is that Foucault refutes quite categorically that he borrowed his conception of historical periodization from Kuhn: 'When I read Kuhn's book during the winter of 1963−4 (I believe it was a year after its publication), I had just finished writing *The Order of Things*' (*Diacritics* 1 (2): 60).

5 See: Gordon, C. (1986): 'Attacks on Singularity' (Review of *Foucault* by J. G. Merquior, and *Michel Foucault* by Barry Smart), *Times Literary Supplement* 6/5/86: 626. Merquior replies to Gordon's stinging attack on his book in *TLS* 13/6/86, and receives a very forceful reply from Gordon in *TLS* 4/7/86.

6 Concerning the lack of polemic in Michel Foucault's writing, I refer the reader to the items mentioned in note 4 above.

Name index

Adorno, T. 111
Alexander, F. G. 3
Allderidge, P. H. 123n
Alpers, S. 5
Althusser, L. 4, 37
Andrews, J. 123n
Arac, J. 63n
Arnold, T. 122
Artaud, A. 46, 66, 90, 98, 112, 175, 195
Auerbach, E. 63n
Azouvi, F. 108n

Bachelard, G. 4, 65, 201
Bade, J. 89
Bakhtin, M. 62
Barchillon, J. 14n
Barham, P. 4, 49n, 171, 209
Barthes, R. 126, 130, 140n
Battie, W. 40n, 122
Baudrillard, J. 130
Becker, E. 114
Beddoes, T. 123n
Benedict, R. 23
Benjamin, A. 36
Benjamin, W. 128
Bentham, J. 71
Bergensen, A. 198
Bernstein, R. J. 5
Beroul 139
Bershady, H. J. 11
Bessière, J. 127
Binswanger, L. 99, 180
Blanchot, M. 199
Bleuler, M. 49
Bonnafous-Sérieux, H. 23
Bosch, H. 32, 89, 90, 98, 174–5
Bouchard, D. F. 188
Bové, P. 1, 62n, 63n

Boyne, R. 203
Brant, S. 32, 88, 89, 90, 174
Branthomme, H. 106
Braudel, F. 19, 30, 100, 116, 169, 170
Brisset, A. 140n
Brissot de Warville, J. P. 40n
Bromberg, W. 3
Brueghel, P. 32, 98, 175
Brunschwicz, M. 65
Burke, H. 130, 131
Butterfield, H. 3
Bynum, W. F. 2, 3, 5, 154, 213

Calvin, J. 176
Canguilhem, G. 4, 39n, 54, 63n, 65, 181, 201
Castel, R. 129, 171, 176, 178; Foucault on 46; 'Les aventures de la pratique' 39n; *The Psychiatric Order* 23, 113, 155; *The Regulation of Madness* 155; 'The two readings of *Histoire de la folie* in France' 47, 65–8, 207
Cavaillès, J. 65
Cézanne, P. 75
Champier, S. 89
Char, R. 35, 39, 40n, 81
Chartier, R. 169
Chatelain, P. 23
Chélini, J. 106
Clarke, M. 185
Cohen, S. 115
Comfort, A. 191
Connolly, J. 122
Cooper, B. 197
Cooper, D. 6, 21, 194, 195; introduction to *Madness and Civilization* 4, 14n, 112, 191, 192

Subject index